1926
general
strike
workers taste power

1926
general
strike

workers taste power
by peter taaffe

published by Socialist Publications

May 2006

1926 General Strike
Workers Taste Power
by Peter Taaffe
© Socialist Publications 2006

First Edition May 2006

Classification: Peter Taaffe
History/Politics/Economics/Sociology

ISBN 1-870958 330 pbk

A catalogue record for this book is available from the British Library
Published by Socialist Publications for the Socialist Party
Typeset in Utopia 9 pt
Printed by Russell Press (Nottingham)

**Distribution by Socialist Books,
PO Box 24697, London, E11 1YD
Telephone +44 (0)20 8988 8789
e-mail: bookshop@socialistparty.org.uk
www.socialistbooks.co.uk**

typesetting & design: dennis@kavitagraphics.co.uk

1926 general strike

workers taste power
by peter taaffe

Acknowledgements

I wish to thank the following for their efforts in helping to ensure the publication of this book:

Kevin Parslow for his Herculean efforts in researching important documents, typing and checking the facts. He has made a big contribution to the publication of this book.

Hugh Caffrey for valuable research in Manchester. Tony Saunois, Clare Doyle, Bob Labi, Lynn Walsh, Hannah Sell and Ken Smith for reading the manuscript and making valuable suggestions. Ken also assisted with proofreading. Per-Åke Westerlund provided the information on the Swedish General Strike. Manny Thain also helped with the typing, Alison Hill searched for photographs and Dennis Rudd laid out the book.

Peter Taaffe

Introduction

The 1926 General Strike is undoubtedly the most important event in the history of the British working class. Not since the days of Chartism in the first half of the nineteenth century had the British ruling class been so shaken. Only the colossal miners' strike of 1984-85 comes near to the 1926 strike in its effects. It had many features of that strike, particularly that element of civil war in society and the coalfields.[1] But even the 1984-85 strike involved mainly the miners, whereas in the titanic nine days of 3-12 May 1926 the organised working class came out in their millions in a generalised stoppage which posed all the fundamental issues of power before the British working class.

Out of five-and-a-half million workers organised in trade unions, an estimated four million took strike action in waves or 'stages' and a million miners locked out at any one time. They were confronting the Tory government of Stanley Baldwin which included in its ranks figures like Winston Churchill and Lord Birkenhead. They were determined to crush the strikers in the hope that this would defeat the working class

Aberaman Carnival during the 1926 Strike

as a whole. At the head of the million-fold 'workers' army' stood the General Council of the Trades Union Congress (TUC). The rightwing of this body, which today would be described as 'moderate', was represented by trade union leaders like J.H. Thomas of the rail workers' union (NUR), Walter Citrine, general secretary of the TUC, and the transport workers' union leader, Ernest Bevin. These figures in general stood for a policy of 'class compromise', which they believed could be achieved through negotiation with the employers and the government. Strike action was considered as a very last resort.

In 1926, however, their approach was totally ineffective. The gulf between the classes – in reality, a yawning chasm – was too great. The mine owners – with the Tory government at their back – were determined to inflict savage reductions in wages and conditions. The systematic attacks on workers in the whole preceding period prior to the General Strike had radicalised significant sections of the working class which, in turn, was reflected in a shift to the left in the unions. This led to the emergence of left-wing trade union leaders like A.J. (Arthur) Cook of the mineworkers, Alf Purcell of the furniture trades union and A.B. Swales of the Engineers union (AEU). The right-wing trade union leaders were dragged reluctantly into the General Strike but were forced to do so because of the monumental pressure from below.

The working class on the one hand placed great faith and confidence in the left union leaders to energetically fight for them in the coming battle. When the strike began, the response of the working class was immediate and massive. The wheels of industry ground to a halt. The arteries of Britain – its roads and railways – were choked and silent. All the carefully laid plans of the government to defeat the strike lay in ruins as the working class, kept in the dirt by capitalism, rose as in Shelley's poem – "rise like lions" – in a magnificent display of working-class power. They created a network of 'Councils of Action' or 'Strike Committees'. In significant parts of the country, these bodies began to assume the role of a rival workers' 'government' to Baldwin and his local representatives – cars and lorries carried notices "with the permission of the TUC". This terrified the ruling class and the right-wing trade union leaders, particularly as with each day the enthusiasm of the strikers, the numbers coming out on strike and those clamouring to do so grew with an irresistible force.

The capitalists, through the Baldwin Tory government, were determined to unload all the burdens of the crisis which afflicted British capitalism onto the shoulders of the working class, beginning with the miners. Baldwin had spelt this out in 1925 in an interview with union leaders when he stated: "I mean all the workers of this country have got to take reduction of wages to help put industry on its feet."[2] This met with furious opposition from the working class and a determination to back the miners to the hilt. However, faced with a powerful and embattled working class and unprepared for a showdown in 1925, the Tory government bought time by proposing a nine-month subsidy to the coal industry. Like the retreat of Thatcher in 1981, who then took on the miners in 1984-85 when the Tory government was prepared, so the ruling class also then temporarily backtracked while they organised to crush the miners and thereby the working class.

The role of the young Communist Party of Great Britain (CPGB) in these events is also an important aspect of this book. The Communist Party was a small but important party in 1926. As the British section of the Communist International (Comintern), its membership drew most of its support from workers who defended the Russian workers' state and who considered themselves as revolutionaries. However, the CPGB became defenders of the Stalinist regime in the Soviet Union and, with the collapse of that regime and its satellites in Eastern Europe in the 1980s and 1990s, the Communist Party itself disintegrated. Only fragments now remain, with little influence inside the British labour movement.

Why go over once more perhaps the most discussed subject in the history of the British working class? One reason is in order to acquaint the new generation with these events, which are in danger of fading from the memory, given that it is 80 years in 2006 since the General Strike. In addition to this, while on the surface British society may appear to be decisively separated from the events of the General Strike, the underlying difficulties of British capitalism in this neo-liberal, globalised era point towards a mighty collision between the classes at some stage in the foreseeable future. Also, the issue of the 'general strike' – in the first instance, for one day – has come back onto the agenda of the workers' movement today.

When local government workers went on strike on 28 March 2006, union leaders warned that it "would be the biggest since the General Strike", indicating that 1926 is still an important reference point for the British labour movement.

Relevance today

Throughout the 1990s, a 'boom' period, there was stubborn resistance on the part of the working class to the neo-liberal agenda – privatisation, 'flexibility', downsizing, etc. – which was relentlessly pursued by the bosses. In the early part of that decade there was significant workers' resistance to the neo-liberal agenda of the capitalists, particularly the attacks on the public sector: the mass movement of the miners in Britain in 1992; the Belgian public sector strikes; the anti-Juppé public sector strikes in France in 1995, which laid the basis for the downfall of that country's then right-wing government. Similarly, in 1994, the four-hour strike of the Italian workers led to the collapse of the first Berlusconi government.

This resistance appeared to subside in the latter part of the decade because of the grip exercised by the right-wing trade union leaders and the political disenchantment which followed in the wake of the decisive shift towards the right of the leaders of the ex-workers' parties in Europe. Now, however, the continued and more brutal capitalist offensive, particularly in the public sector, has provoked fury in the ranks of the working class. From the poorest countries in Europe – Greece and Portugal – to the twin props of 'Old Europe' – Germany and France – as well as the 'intermediate' countries of Spain and Italy, reaction to these attacks is to take to the streets and strike. Britain has joined in with the threat of a five million worker public-sector strike in answer to the Blair New Labour government's offensive on pensions.

The mere threat of a one-day public-sector strike compelled the government to retreat, partly because this came just before the 2005 general election. They returned to the offensive after the election but yet again they partially retreated in the teeth of public sector workers' and their trade unions' resistance to the plans of the government. This was not a complete victory because the unions conceded the raising of the retirement age for 'new starters', which was a retreat from the previous arrangements. The reason for this is to be found in the right-wing character of the majority of trade union leaders in Britain today.

With the exception of the Public and Commercial Services Union (PCS), which has a Left majority on its National Executive Committee – in which Socialist Party members play a decisive role – as well as unions like the Rail and Maritime union (RMT) and the Fire Brigades Union (FBU), the majority of trade union leaders' initial reaction to any attack by the bosses or the government is to seek 'compromise', which in plain language is a tacit acceptance of the need for 'concessions' to the employers. If the whole of the trade union movement was of the same character as the PCS then it would have been possible to maintain the status quo on pensions through the threat and, if needs be, the actual implementation of a 24-hour public sector strike.

However, given the prevarication, in reality acquiescence, of right-wing trade union leaders, to even force the government to maintain the same pension arrangements for existing staff was an achievement in the circumstances. The task now remains for the trade unions to fight for the same conditions for 'new starters', as well as a determination to maintain the present pension arrangements for existing staff. (At the time of writing it is not certain that local government workers will enjoy the same pension rights as others in the public sector, which has resulted in strike action.) This could be repeated if the employers and the government do not relent.

In the partial retreat of the Blair government on public sector pensions, there is the fear on the part of the capitalists – of which he is the representative *par excellence* – of anything which smacks of strike action of a generalised character. In this it seems that the British ruling class are "different". Their counterparts in parts of Europe at least view one-day strikes if not with equanimity but as 'inevitable', as a means of ventilating the anger of the masses at the attacks of big business. Italy, Greece, Spain, France, Austria and other countries have all experienced either a one-day general strike, a partial strike or a public sector strike. Even in Germany, with its rotten right-wing trade union leadership, such was the opposition to Schröder, the Social Democratic Chancellor before the present government, moving down the same neo-liberal path as Blair that the issue of a one-day general strike came onto the agenda of the workers' movement.

In Britain, however, almost alone in Western Europe, there has been no experience of a complete one-day general strike. It has come close to the edge on many occasions, such as following the jailing of the Pentonville Five dockers in 1972, which unleashed a wave of solidarity action by other workers with the dockers. On that occasion the then general secretary of the TUC, the late Vic Feather, threatened a general strike but only because he was assured that he would never be forced to act on his threat because the 'Official Solicitor', a government-appointed lawyer, was already in the process of freeing the dockers from jail! In this incident is revealed the tendency of the British ruling class and right-wing union leaders on many occasions to go to the brink of an all-out conflict only to withdraw at the last moment.

They have been allowed to do this partly because British capitalism in the past had sufficient stored-up fat that it has been able to make economic concessions whenever it was faced with a decisive challenge from the working class. But an additional factor has undoubtedly been the shadow cast over the present by the events of 80 years ago. This shook to their foundations the British ruling class and its echoes within the labour movement, the right-wing trade union leadership. "Never again" was their duet in the aftermath of the General Strike and it has remained so until the present. They have succeeded in avoiding the kind of set-piece confrontation which unfolded in May 1926. This is no guarantee that they will be able to maintain this stance in the stormy economic and social period which is about to open up in Britain, Europe and worldwide.

Baldwin in 1925-26 proclaimed his devotion to 'industrial peace'. Right-wing trade union leaders like Jimmy Thomas of the National Union of Railwaymen or Walter Citrine, general secretary of the TUC, desperately sought to avoid the confrontation of 1926. They failed and their counterparts of today will be unable to conjure away the colossal social collisions which are coming. Of course, British society has also changed since 1926, as has the labour movement with, for instance, the decisive transformation of the Labour Party into a capitalist party along the lines of the Democratic Party in the USA. The trade unions, and particularly the weight of different sectors such as the industrial unions, have changed. The social and political outlook of the British people has changed, in some ways in quite a dramatic fashion. Deference by those at the bottom to those at the top has gone. Nevertheless, the fundamental character of capitalism as a system of crises and the conflict between the classes which this engenders remains the same. So does the preparedness of the ruling class to seek a way out by attacking the past gains of the working class. Moreover, the fear of the tops of the labour movement, particularly in the trade unions, for the battles that loom, are the same – more intense, if anything – as they were in the period up to 1926.

Why did the general strike take place when it did? How effective was it and did the government defeat it through its strikebreaking organisation? What was the political outlook of the majority of the working class in the strike? If it had gone on for longer than the nine days, would it have succeeded? Why did the trade union leaders call it off when the strike was growing? These and many other questions we hope to answer in the following pages.

We hope to trace out, if only in outline, the fundamental features of this period, the outlook of the contending classes. The actions of the leaders of the trade unions, both of the Right but particularly the Left, are examined. So is the potential that existed for the young and weak Communist Party to transform itself into a much more powerful force, which in turn could have shaped the development of subsequent events. History is important, not in itself but in order that socialists and workers today can learn from and absorb the lessons of both victories and defeats, and in this way prepare for the battles to come. We do not live in the past but we seek to learn from it.

1 British Capitalism's Post-war Crisis

So explosive were class relations in the post-First World War period that Britain appeared, on a number of occasions, to be on the verge of a general strike before 1926; in 1919, 1921 and 1925 in the run-up to 'Red Friday' to name but three. The roots of this heightened class polarisation were to be found in the changed relationship of forces between the main competing capitalist-imperialist powers issuing from this great conflict. First born amongst the major industrial nations, British capitalism came under intense challenge from the new rising star, Germany, and, in the first decades of the twentieth century, from the United States. British capitalism, more than others, desired and planned for war against Germany and its allies. In this way, it could deliver a crushing blow to the 'upstart', thereby enhancing its dominant position in the capitalist firmament.

However, it had reckoned without the tremendous development of US capitalism, which stayed out of the First World War just so long as it took the European powers to exhaust themselves and only then did it intervene. This established a superior

Striking miners

position for US imperialism to the detriment of British capitalism, which was reflected economically, militarily and diplomatically in the post-1918 situation. This was not immediately evident as British capitalism was still able to rely on the super-exploitation of its 'empire'. On the other hand, a revolutionary wave swept over Europe in the wake of the Russian Revolution, exercising a huge impact in Britain. The revolutionary upheaval – for that is what it was – of the period from 1911 to 1914 re-emerged, expressing itself in the inrush of workers into the trade unions, which filled out from four million members in 1914 to more than eight million by 1920.

The year 1919 was a period of revolution throughout Europe and even in the US. In Britain this was expressed that year in the actions of the engineering, shipyard and other workers, united under the leadership of the Clyde Workers Committee and the shop stewards in the struggle to shorten the working week "which everyone sensed was no ordinary strike".[1] The British ruling class feared an uprising and troops were rushed to Glasgow after the 'Battle of George Square'. Clydeside workers were asking for a 40-hour week and the Belfast workers, who also joined the movement, were asking for a 44-hour week! In January 1919 the miners were also prepared for battle, demanding a 30 per cent wage increase, a six-hour working day and nationalisation of the mines with a measure of workers' control. This in turn led to a revival of the Triple Alliance, formed during the First World War in 1915 but which had been largely dormant since. The combination of miners, railwaymen and transport workers was a new departure for the British working class. However, inter-union rivalries and the fact that the crisis did not develop at the same time in all industries meant that the alliance did not really work at that stage. But David Lloyd George, the Liberal Prime Minister, who led a coalition government of Conservatives, coalition Liberals and even 15 'Coalition Labour', took fright particularly at the threat of a miners' strike, supported by the railwaymen and transport workers.

Mining Industry

The one million British miners constituted fully ten per cent of the labour force at this stage and the coal industry was the 'root and trunk' of British capitalism. The state of this industry and the conditions of the workers in it reflected the parlous state of British capitalism as a whole. The mines were under effective government control during the war but were returned to the owners, a group of 'hard-faced' brutal employers. The miners, however, had the sympathy of the majority of the population who supported the raising of the minimum wage from 50 shillings (£2.50) to 60 shillings (£3) a week. Lloyd George was an adroit representative of the British ruling class and well schooled in the tradition of British capitalist rulers of bending when faced with hostile social winds. It has to be remembered that these developments were taking place against the background of a stormy industrial situation which

infected even the police who went on strike in London and Liverpool, with unfortunately, the victimisation of the strike leaders later in the year. Every day in 1919 saw an
average of 100,000 workers out on strike. Moreover, Lloyd George had witnessed
himself the revolutionary upheaval which had infected even British troops, some of
whom marched on Whitehall in 1918. Therefore, faced with the threat of a miners'
strike, the government set up a 'Coal Commission' under the chairmanship of Sir John
Sankey.

This was to be the first of many 'coal inquiries'. This has a topical ring because
whenever governments, particularly Blair's New Labour government in Britain, are
faced with a difficult question the tendency is invariably to set up a 'commission' to
bide time and dissipate whatever anger has been generated on the issue. However, the
miners were in no mood for a long drawn-out inquiry and pressed for the commission
to report quickly. Sankey decided to take the report in two halves with recommendations on wages and hours coming first. It suggested increases to miners' wages,
instead of an eight-hour day, a seven-hour one, with a six-hour day to come. By
dividing the recommendations, by postponing the second part of the report on the
organisation of the mining industry and ownership, they presented the miners with a
dilemma. The miners' leaders, in good faith, called off their proposed strike action to
await the second part of the report. When it came, a bare majority of its members was
in favour of nationalisation of the mines, although there was unanimous approval for
public ownership of coal.

The 'Labour' representatives such as Sidney Webb and R.H. Tawney proposed joint
control on a co-ordinating committee, while Sankey – a judge in the King's Bench
Division of the law courts but distinctly sympathetic to the miner's aspirations –
recommended management by district councils with only a minority of members
appointed by the workers. The three miners' representatives on the commission
opposed giving any compensation to the owners of the land on which the collieries
stood, while approving it in the case of colliery concerns themselves, whereas the
three Labour representatives were in favour of compensation for all property taken
over by the state! Marxists are not in principle opposed to compensation for the
takeover of industries by the state but only on the basis of 'proven need'. Full compensation to the ex-owners of industries that they have invariably ruined only cripples the
industries when coming into the state sector. This was the experience of industries
nationalised by the Labour government of 1945 to 1951, where lavish over-compen-
sation was paid to the ex-owners and the boards of management were invariably
made up of those, in the main, hostile to public ownership. This was, however, the
music of the future in 1919. Lloyd George used the divisions over the ownership of the
mines to kick the second part of the Sankey Commission report into the long grass.

Capitalism, in general, is not prepared, unless forced to by active mass pressure, to take over even bankrupt inefficient industries as the example of the railways in Britain under the Blair government demonstrates. Today, there is an overwhelming majority of the population in favour of renationalisation of the railways, given its catastrophic safety record, the massive hike in fares and the plundering of its assets by the privateers. Blair has instructed his transport ministers that they can take whatever measures of state aid that are required for the railways "as long as you don't call it renationalisation".[2] And there are sound reasons from a capitalist point of view why he adopts this position. Once one industry is taken over the planning that would follow this, even of a partial 'state capitalist' character, would provide a platform, a springboard, for workers in other industries, particularly those which were in danger of collapsing, to demand similar steps be applied in their industries.

This was particularly the case in 1919 and later. The coal industry only expressed in the most acute form the crisis afflicting British capitalism as a whole. It is true that the post-war boom of British industry provided jobs, with relatively low unemployment until perhaps the middle of 1920. Then deflation set in with a drop in prices, industrial retrenchment and the rise in unemployment. At the same time the miners were demanding higher wages to compensate for the rise in the cost of living during the war with the ratio of wages to output and the cost of living lower than they were in 1914. In 1920, the highs of industrial militancy intersected with a powerful demonstration of the raised political consciousness of the British working class with revolutionary implications. This was reflected in the setting up of Councils of Action to prevent British imperialism's intervention in support of the Polish capitalists in the conflict against the Russian workers' state. Such was the pressure that, incredible as it sounds today, the Parliamentary Committee of the TUC, the National Executive Committee of the Labour Party and the Parliamentary Labour Party joined together and warned the Lloyd George government that "the whole industrial power of the organised workers will be used to defeat this war".[3]

Black Friday

The Trades Union Congress together with the Labour Party held a special conference on 9 August 1920 which called for its whole industrial power to be used in the event of war against Russia. It called for the formation of councils of action. The National Council of Action held a meeting on 13 August attended by 1,044 delegates from trades unions, local Labour parties and trades councils. This was backed up by the actions of the immortal London dockers who blacked a ship, the 'Jolly George', which was intended to be used to ship weapons to Poland. This generated a tremendous fever within the working class, which frightened the right-wing summits of the Labour and trade union movement in Britain more than it did the capitalists. And this was not the last time that we would see such a reaction once a movement began to develop from below. The government retreated and the Councils of Action were put into cold storage. Nevertheless, a powerful example had been imprinted into the minds of the British working class, particularly of its leading and guiding layers, that would come into play both before and during the 1926 General Strike.

But, taken aback at the determination and audacity of the working class, and no doubt encouraged by the contrasting conservatism of the trade union and labour leaders, the government went on the offensive and introduced the Emergency Powers Act (EPA), which for the first time in British peacetime history gave the government sweeping powers over industrial disputes in order to maintain 'essential services'. They were encouraged in this by the prevarication within the Triple Alliance. J.H. Thomas, 'Jimmy' to his bourgeois friends, General Secretary of the National Union of Railwaymen, played a perfidious role as a brake on the workers' movement. This was a role he was to play again and again up to and during the 1926 General Strike. He had demanded that the Triple Alliance be vested with final authority to settle the miners' dispute, when the time for negotiations arrived. With sure class instinct the miners refused – if only they had maintained this position during the General Strike when they wrongly ceded control to the General Council of the TUC – and came out on strike themselves. A few days later the railwaymen, notwithstanding Thomas's dithering, also came out on strike.

But by early 1921 the industrial slump had firmly set in which severely affected the coal industry. The government chose this time to hand control of the mines back to the mineowners. With the one million unemployed used as a whip against the miners, this was the moment that the owners decided to introduce savage wage reductions. The resistance of the miners led to a huge lock-out, which was answered with the miners once more calling for the Triple Alliance to act. The TUC and Labour Party condemned the government and the owners' actions and were compelled to support the miners. The approach of the government this time, however, was entirely different to 1919 as they in effect prepared for civil war against the working class.

When Trotsky warned later, in 1925, particularly in his marvellous book *Where is Britain Going?* of civil war and the possibility of a general strike, this was dismissed as "Moscow phantasmagoria". Yet, according to a well-known historian: "In 1921 the military preparations to combat the strike were plain for all to see. A State of Emergency was declared, reservists were called to the colours, machine guns were posted at pitheads, and troops in battle order were sent to many working class areas." He compares the government's reaction to the 1921 display of militancy to its attitude in 1926 which he maintains was "positively pacific".[4] This was not true, as we will see; if there is any difference between 1921 and 1926 it did not lie in military preparations which were evident in both situations, but in the expectation, if not the certainty, that by 1926 they could rely on right-wing trade union leaders to betray and the quiescence of the trade union and Labour Left.

Any doubts on the role of the trade union leaders were washed away by their action or lack of it in 1921. The leaders of the Triple Alliance sat in continuous session at the railwaymen's headquarters. The key position of Miners' Federation of Great Britain secretary was held by Frank Hodges. Formerly a militant, he moved to the right until at the time of his death in 1947 he left an 'estate' worth more than £100,000, which would make him a millionaire in today's terms. The night before the strike was to begin, he suggested that a temporary settlement could be established on the basis of wages settled on a district basis. This was totally at variance to the miners' executive's insistence that there must be a national agreement. The executive immediately disowned him but that was used as an excuse by the other union leaders, particularly Thomas, to call off any action in support of the miners. This event marked the end of what workers bitterly called the 'Cripple Alliance'. This became fixed in the consciousness of the British working class, as the infamous 'Black Friday', which saw the miners betrayed. They struggled on for about three months until they were forced back to work by starvation and exhaustion with wages slashed and agreements torn up.

What followed was a mild 'festival of reaction' in industry. Wage reductions were enforced on whole groups of workers: shipyard workers, builders, seamen. Cotton operatives were locked out. By the end of the year six million workers had imposed on them average wage cuts of six shillings a week. Also engineering workers were locked out. This was aimed at crushing the newly-formed Amalgamated Engineering Union (AEU). Membership of the unions dropped by nearly three million. At the same time unemployment began to rise and social services were slashed so that the unemployed in particular were plunged into misery.

The causes of the collapse of the Triple Alliance and the defeat of the working class at this stage were political: the unwillingness of the trade union leaders to mobilise the full power of the organised working class in particular in support of the miners. In turn, this was ultimately founded in a lack of understanding of the gravity of the underlying crisis of capitalism as well as the craven pro-capitalist position of some like Jimmy Thomas, described as "one of the best waltzers in London" in a capital-ist paper. He lived on the Astor estate and often "shared Lord Derby's box on Grand National Day".[5] But the collapse of the Triple Alliance was perceived in some quarters, even amongst the Left, and particularly the young Communist Party, as demonstrating a weakness, organisational in character in the main, at the top. This was to lead to the adoption of the mistaken slogans of firstly "More power" and later "All power" to the General Council of the TUC. This was to take on flesh through the campaign of the Communist Party for the replacement of the Triple Alliance with a more authoritative General Council of the TUC.

"All Power to the General Council"

The General Council was perceived as the general staff of the labour movement for the coming war against the bosses and their government. It was summed up in the slogan "All Power to the General Council", which in 1926 meant vesting authority in the hands of right-wing trade union leaders and Left leaders who are here shown to be politically unreliable. This was to prove disastrous during the General Strike itself. While it is necessary sometimes for socialists and Marxists to fight for a strengthening of the official organisations of the trade unions, to seek to centralise struggles (national negotiations, etc.), at the same time this must always be counterbalanced by democratic control and the building of structures such as the shop stewards movement, which can more accurately reflect the ordinary members. This can act as a check on the leaders at the top, no matter how radical their credentials may be. For socialists and Marxists, whether or not the official structures should be strengthened is dependent on the concrete circumstances at each stage.

That is particularly the case in the heightened class polarisation evident in the period leading up to and during the General Strike itself, as it is today. The capitalists and their government have an array of weapons to ensnare, corrupt and, if necessary, to use to crush the working class and destroy its basic class organisations, the trade unions. To counter this, a militant, accountable and politically aware leadership must be built. This is why the Socialist Party and class conscious workers fight today for trade union officials to live on no more than the average wage of skilled workers and to be subject to regular election and recall. This should be combined with the building of powerful workplace representation and a shop stewards' movement.

The workers' councils (soviets) – witnessed in the Russian and other revolutions – are undoubtedly the most representative form of organisation of working class people seen in history. They first appeared in Russia in the 1905 revolution in St Petersburg and were inspired by the example of the committees established by the Paris Commune of 1871. It was the means of immediately gathering together a scattered mass of hundreds of thousands of people, previously having no organisational means of expression which had been denied to them under the tsarist autocracy. The left and working-class parties which existed at the time had a few hundred members with thousands who supported their ideas. These parties fought and argued against each others' ideas. This made the need for a "non-party organisation absolutely essential... [which] had to be based on the broadest representation".[6]

Since only industry linked the working class together, who organisationally were inexperienced, the representation to the soviet was adapted to the factories and plants. One delegate was elected for every 500 workers and was subject to recall, to be held accountable, by those electing them. Small industrial undertakings combined into groups for election purposes. The new trade unions which had been created sent delegates as well. However, the rules were not strictly kept to and in some cases delegates represented less than 500. This was a kind of 'parliament' of the workers, but much more democratic and representative than the tsarist duma (parliament) which met alongside it and competed for power with it.

Yet no organisational form in and of itself, separated from politics, can accurately express the views of the working class, particularly in a rapidly changing situation which characterises general strikes and revolutions. There were soviets in Russia controlled by those who were not prepared to break landlordism and capitalism, the Mensheviks and Social Revolutionaries.

This did not prevent the Bolsheviks under Lenin and Trotsky from raising the slogan "All Power to the Soviets". This practically meant putting the class conciliators into power – the Social Revolutionaries and Mensheviks initially had a majority in the soviets – in order to show to the workers and peasants of Russia in action the limitations of their programme and their unwillingness to struggle to overthrow capitalism and landlordism. However, if they had left it there, the mere repetition of this agitational slogan would have been completely inadequate, would not have prepared the working class and poor peasants for the 1917 October revolution. They combined this call with criticism of the other parties – Mensheviks and Social Revolutionaries – at each stage and posed what the alternatives were. Moreover, the Bolsheviks worked to build up their support by going below, into the factories and workers' districts to convince workers of their ideas.

In 1926, the model of Russia, the example of the revolution and 'soviet power', was a powerful factor amongst the working class and CP members. Therefore, superficial comparison between the General Council of the TUC and 'soviet power' could exist. Workers wanted to strengthen their organisations against the bosses. But when the right-wing trade union leaders were the ultimate defence of the bosses' system, the slogan "All Power to the TUC" could become a trap for the working class. Even the mistaken slogan of 'All Power' would not have been so harmful in 1926 if the leaders, both left-wing as well as right-wing, were subject to searching criticism by the CP. This, unfortunately, was not the case, as we shall see.

The slogan "All Power to the General Council", advanced by the young and politically immature Communist Party, particularly leading up to the General Strike, could in no way be compared to the slogan of "All Power to the Soviets". The trade unions, by their very nature, were much narrower and sectionalised, as the events since 1918 had demonstrated, than would be the case in developed Councils of Action or soviets. While objectively the situation began to acquire many of the features of a revolutionary or pre-revolutionary situation in the lead-up to the General Strike, it had not yet matured into the kind of situation seen in Russia between February and October 1917. Then the floodgates of revolution, mass participation of the working class took place and soviets were created. Nevertheless, the tendency to form Councils of Action, evinced in 1920 in particular, and the formation of factory committees would have been a better starting point for the agitation, propaganda and approach of the CP rather than the misconceived "All Power to the General Council" slogan.

This is in no way a concession to the misconceived crude sectarian 'rank-and-filism' favoured by some Left organisations in the recent past in Britain. This took the form of counterposing rank-and-file organisations to the official union structures, boycotting elections to official positions, which if Left trade unionists had accepted, would have amounted to political abstentionism in the trade unions, thereby ceding control to the right wing. This is in a trade union movement where the official apparatus and leadership retains considerable authority amongst the membership! The trade union movement in Britain, the oldest in the world, traces its origins back to before the French revolution. These organisations acted as a mighty lever to raise the working class in Britain out of the muck and filth of capitalism to provide, at least, adequate if still deficient living standards for working class people.

Moscow and the Communist Party

The essence of a correct trade union policy for socialists and Marxists is to struggle at the base, particularly through the branches, in the workplaces and shop stewards organisations of the trade unions, and also to strive to win influence in the official structures of the trade unions. This was the case in the early 1920s and subsequently as it is today. But the mistake that was made by the young CP was to place too much faith in the Left union leaders. They did not sufficiently criticise and organise against not just the right but also the left-wing leaders of the trade unions in preparation for the mighty movement that loomed. This was not generally the case when the Communist Party had just been formed. It criticised, for instance, in a somewhat crude fashion, the Triple Alliance in 1920 because it was "in the main run by reformist leaders. A Triple Alliance strike means a general strike, and a general strike means probably a revolution... *Remember that reformists will shrink back at the last moment.*"[7] This was superior to the position which the CP adopted later between 1924 and 1927, but it was not a fully worked-out analysis or programme for the stormy events to come.

However, they were not entirely to blame for this. As we shall see, by the time of the General Strike the young militants of the Communist Party, who represented in the main the flower of the British working class at that stage, were misled by the mistaken policies of the Communist International (Comintern), then under the direction of Stalin, Bukharin and, earlier, even Zinoviev (before he joined Trotsky in the Left Opposition). Impatient at the slow development of the young CP, they exerted pressure which led to the formation of the Anglo-Russian Trade Union Committee. This was a bloc between the Russian trade unions and the General Council of the TUC, and particularly with its left wing. Only mild criticism was made of the leading Lefts, which did not adequately prepare the working class for the inevitable retreats that these lefts made during and after the General Strike. For Marxists, impatience, an attempt to skip over and artificially develop a small force into a larger one, can be a source of opportunism. In place of a friendly but firm and systematic criticism of the inadequacies of the Left, the Communist Party leaders were pressurised into an unprincipled bloc. This led to muted criticism of the Left, even when they gave more than adequate warnings in the run-up to the General Strike of their opportunism and adaptation to the Right within the General Council and the Labour Party.

The political rationale for this, both from Moscow and from the leaders of the CP was the need for a united front between the genuine revolutionary Marxist forces gathered around the Communist Party and other political trends, particularly of the Left. The united front was then a vital weapon in the hands of Marxists as it is today, in seeking to maximise the strength of, and unify the working class in the struggle against the bosses and their system. But it is not a panacea, a substitute for correct policies. It requires from its practitioners skill, an understanding of how and when to form such a bloc, and crucially, how to break it if the leaders at the top fail to prosecute the struggle to the end. A failure to adhere to this approach by the leaders of the Comintern and the young CP was to have fatal consequences in the great battle to come.

2 Red Friday

After Black Friday, the employers put the boot into the working class. The miners were defeated by June and six million workers suffered savage wage cuts. The working class fought a series of rearguard actions but against the background of a recession wage cuts were carried through. The unions were severely weakened as their funds were drained away in a series of defensive struggles. However, one of the consequences of Black Friday was a deepening of the hatred, particularly by the miners, of the 'traitor Thomas' and increased support for the Left. In 1924 Frank Hodges was forced to resign as the secretary of the Miners' Federation following his appointment as Civil Lord of the Admiralty in Ramsay MacDonald's minority Labour government. He was replaced by A.J. Cook, miners' agent for Central Rhondda in a national ballot. Cook was a giant in championing the workers' cause, especially in comparison to the right-wing trade union leaders then and now. Fred Bramley, right-wing general secretary of the TUC until his death in September 1925, was so demented by Cook's election that he rushed into the office of his assistant and successor, Walter Citrine, shrieking: "Have you seen who has

Boot co-op during the Strike

been elected secretary to the Miners' Federation? Cook, a raving, tearing Communist. Now the miners are in for a bad time."[1]

In fact, A.J. Cook was a former member of the Communist Party. He resigned in 1921 when he was criticised for backing the disastrous agreement forced on the miners by the collapse of the Triple Alliance. He was a sincere militant and working-class fighter but although he professed to be a follower of Lenin, he did not have a rounded-out perspective or programme. His cloudy ideas on the general strike, formed by involvement in industrial struggle and the influence of syndicalism – the idea that trade union militancy and struggle was sufficient by itself to overthrow capitalism – meant that even this great class fighter was not adequately prepared for the General Strike. The hatred and fear of him by the capitalists and their shadows in the labour movement – Fabian guru Beatrice Webb described him as "an inspired idiot"[2] – was more than matched by the love and veneration of the miners and leftward moving workers for his tireless devotion and work for their cause. If he was to rise to the occasion of the General Strike and lead the miners and left in particular to a more successful outcome then this would only have been possible on the basis of positive criticism of his political inadequacies. Unfortunately, under the influence of the Communist International, the CP leaders went in for friendly diplomacy instead of politically intransigent and systematic criticism of the political shortcomings of not just Cook but of Purcell and Hicks as well who played disastrous roles in the General Strike and its aftermath. George Hicks was the leader of the Bricklayers Union while Alf Purcell, another ex-member of the Communist Party, led the Furnishing Trades Association.

French imperialism's occupation of the Ruhr in Germany in 1923 led to protest strikes from the German miners. This in turn gave an unexpected fillip to the British coal trade, with exports increasing. Wage concessions were made by the employers and a steady drop in unemployment was manifested throughout 1923. At the same time, the working class, checked on the industrial plane, which is what Black Friday represented, swung towards the political terrain, which resulted in the coming to office of the first Labour government led by MacDonald in 1924. This was a short-lived political episode with the government evicted at the end of the year through the use during the election campaign of a red scare over the so-called 'Zinoviev letter'. This was probably the greatest example of electoral fraud in British history. In the subsequent general election, the Baldwin-led Tory party was returned, dubbed from the outset by the trade union and labour movement as the "forgers' government".

MacDonald, who had unbelievably been perceived in 1922 as the standard bearer of the unions and Labour, became the complete tool of the capitalists when in power.

His government confronted workers who went on strike, with one union leader, Ben Tillett, proclaiming that he had never heard from Tory or Liberal ministers "the same menacing tones or the same expressions of fear".[3] Labour historian Allen Hutt commented that MacDonald's announcements that "major services must be maintained" and that the government "must give protection to those engaged in legal occupations" had a "clear strikebreaking ring".[4] The government even invoked at one stage the hated Emergency Powers Act, introduced by Lloyd George and later to be used in the General Strike. MacDonald had a "taste for gracious living", which isolated him from the draughty Labour halls and trade union committee rooms; the patrician pose, which excited coy speculation amongst society *grandes dames* about the mysterious "nobleman". This led to his discrediting amongst all wings of the labour movement even then. Trotsky, writing in the 1930s, comments on a newspaper photograph of MacDonald, when he no longer held power, which indicated "something of the flunky running all through him, even in his posture in talking to Mussolini".[5]

This thumbnail sketch could equally apply to Blair today as he kneels before George Bush and the rich who are now the main backers of New Labour, as it would to Kinnock who preceded him. There is a striking similarity between the political position of MacDonald at that time and Blair today. The first minority Labour government counted amongst its crimes against the working class the charging of J.R. Campbell – acting editor of the Communist Party's journal *Workers' Weekly* – under the Incitement to Mutiny Act 1795. This was for an "insolent article in *Workers' Weekly*… [which]… had urged members of the armed forces to help the workers smash capitalism".[6] The Attorney General was forced to withdraw the prosecution, which was a signal for the Tories, supported by the Liberals to pass a motion in the House of Commons that brought down MacDonald.

At the end of this inglorious 'experiment' MacDonald was opposed by all wings of the labour movement, including trade union leaders like Ernest Bevin of the transport workers, who could by no means be counted as standing on the Left. He survived, much like Blair today, because of the lack of a viable alternative on either the Right or the Left. Arthur Henderson, the Gordon Brown of this period, was urged to stand against MacDonald but had already been wheeled out once, during the First World War, when MacDonald had been replaced by the Parliamentary Labour Party for his pacifist views.

The consequence was a turn once more to the industrial plane by the working class and its organisations. This coincided with a new offensive by the coal owners against the miners. This in turn arose from the changed economic situation confronting British capitalism. Terrified by the possibility of revolution in Germany in 1923, US capitalism, with the support of Britain's Labour leaders MacDonald and Henderson, introduced the Dawes Plan, the aim of which was to stabilise German capitalism and lay the basis for an economic recovery. After the revolutionary opportunity was let slip by the German Communist Party in the autumn of 1923, the plan did succeed in rejuvenating German capitalism but at a considerable cost to British capitalism and particularly its coal industry. The British bosses in turn, in classical fashion, attempted to impose the burden of this onto the shoulders of the working class. This was summed up in the decision of the Baldwin government through the aegis of Winston Churchill, who then represented the most extreme, rabid and bitterly anti-working class wing of the government and the capitalist class, to go back to the Gold Standard in 1925. Churchill, it was, as Home Secretary, who had drafted troops into the South Wales coalfields in 1910 and it was he who, as Secretary for War, had pressed for intervention against workers' Russia in 1920. It was this, as we have seen, which led to the setting up of the Council of Action and the threat of a general strike that was not carried through then because of the retreat of Lloyd George on this issue.

The return to the Gold Standard was an attempt on the part of British imperialism to recapture its lost position, particularly vis-à-vis American imperialism. The first aim was to enable the pound to "look the dollar in the face" and re-establish the supremacy of Sterling at a pre-war parity. It had some of the features of the present European Monetary Union, the Euro, with a rigid setting of the currency rate, irrespective of the economic circumstances in each country. The Euro has yet to break down but the lack of 'flexibility' – the ability to lower the value of the currency *vis-à-vis* others when economic circumstances dictate – means a loss of competitiveness and a worsening of the economic situation in some countries. Undoubtedly, the breakdown of the Euro, the unilateral exit from the union of countries such as Italy or Germany, could be posed in the foreseeable future. The decision of the Baldwin government to accept Churchill's proposal to fix the pound at a level overvalued, in effect, by ten per cent and rigidly adhere to the Gold Standard had immediate consequences. Foreign buyers of British goods had to pay out ten per cent more in their own currency while British exporters were forced to accept ten per cent less in Sterling.

Red Friday

Already, British industry was under severe strain and the bosses naturally resorted to the traditional method of solving this problem by attacking the working class. Even at Sterling's rate of 1924, British capitalism found difficulty in selling its goods in competitive overseas markets. The famous capitalist economist John

Maynard Keynes attacked Churchill, saying that the working class and the miners in particular were "victims of the economic Juggernaut... They [the miners] and others to follow are the moderate sacrifice still necessary to ensure the stability of the Gold Standard. The plight of the coalminers is the first but not – unless we are very lucky – the last of the economic consequences of Mr Churchill... Mr Churchill's policy of improving the exchange by ten per cent was sooner or later a policy of reducing everyone's wages by two shillings in the pound."[7]

The coal owners suggested a joint inquiry with the miners into the "extremely serious condition of the coal industry". As the Ruhr mines resumed production, a consequence as we have seen of the Dawes Plan, a renewed flood of German coal poured into European markets. Coal exports from Britain plunged and unemployment in the mining industry consequently rose. The coal owners began to whine about a plunge in profits after a net profit of £59 million in 1923-24. They then declared that the agreement with the unions would end on 31 July 1925. Immediate wage reductions of between 10 and 25 per cent were proposed, combined with the abolition of the national minimum wage, which established the ratio of wages to profits. This had only been achieved in 1921 and yet the bosses now proposed to snatch it back. Some miners, under these new proposals, such as those in the Forest of Dean, would receive just four shillings and fourpence a day (22p), less than they would get on the dole!

The miners rejected the coal owners' proposals, refusing even an "interchange of views" until the notices terminating the current agreement were withdrawn. The Miners' Federation set in motion steps to revive a new industrial alliance. The membership of the Miners' Federation (the forerunner of the later National Union of Mineworkers) stood at over 800,000 immediately after the war and still represented a colossal, potentially the most important, class force pitted against the government. The Triple Alliance was composed of railway workers, transport workers as well as the miners, but also including the engineers who had developed rapidly since the formation of the AEU in 1920. The Baldwin government and the mine owners were in league with each other in demanding cuts in wages not just for the miners but for all workers as Baldwin had indicated (see introduction). Later, Lord Londonderry summed up the determination of the ruling class when he declared, after the short-lived workers' victory on Red Friday, that "Whatever it may cost in blood and treasure, we shall find that the trade unions will be smashed from top to bottom."[8]

To begin with, however, the government attempted to bring the mine owners and the miners together but the latter refused to appear before the court of inquiry which was set up on 13 July 1925. The economic situation, the stance of the government and of the employers, not just the mine owners, convinced the trade union movement as a whole that the British capitalists had decided on a generalised attack on all workers in Britain, as Baldwin had indicated. The working class, for its part, also prepared for the coming battle. This was to take two forms: pressure on the official trade union leaders to back up and support the miners to the hilt and, at the same time, the creation of the National Minority Movement (NMM) in 1924. This had been preceded by the steps to organise the militants in the South Wales coalfield into a Miners' Minority Movement. This was conceived as a counterweight to the 'moderate' right-wing union leaders and comprised of the most militant fighting elements in the British trade union movement.

The National Minority Movement's first conference in August 1924 was attended by 271 delegates representing 200,000 trade unionists. At its height, however, it had between one million to one-and-a-quarter million formally behind its banner, one quarter of organised trade unionists in Britain. The first conference was presided over by Tom Mann, who had known Friedrich Engels – founder with Karl Marx of the ideas of scientific socialism – and Harry Pollitt, leading member of the Communist Party and general secretary of the NMM. The aim of the Minority Movement, correctly, was not to supplant or skip over the existing trade unions and their structures but to act as a rallying point for the Left and revolutionary elements in the trade union movement. This would naturally involve organising from below as well as using the NMM to prosecute the Left and revolutionary case, particularly in support of the miners and mass mobilisation to defeat the government and employers' offensive. It defined its aims as "not to organise independent revolutionary trade unions, or to split revolutionary elements away from existing organisations affiliated to the TUC... but to convert the revolutionary minority within each industry into a revolutionary majority".[9] One of its weaknesses, and that of the Communist Party, which was largely indistinguishable from the Left trade union leaders, was not to propagandise and organise sufficient workers' actively from below for the idea of factory committees linked to future councils of action. The working class was therefore politically disarmed in the face of the retreat of the trade union leaders during the General Strike. They had also not been prepared sufficiently to create their own independent organisations as counterweights to the TUC.

The NMM did manage to build support within all trades – engineers, transport workers, railwaymen, building workers – but it was amongst the miners that it achieved its greatest success. The Minority Movement amongst the Welsh miners was responsible for the election of A.J. Cook. He was to declare to the Minority Movement conference in 1925: "We are in danger. The united enemy is knocking at the gate... My slogan is be prepared."[10] On the other hand, there were lefts like

George Hicks and Alf Purcell who associated themselves with the Minority Movement. The NMM was undoubtedly a potentially powerful force for organising and preparing the British working class for the most important struggle in its history. But this weapon was not effectively used in the critical period opening up in the run-up to the General Strike, during the General Strike and in its aftermath. However, in 1925 the working class, led by the miners, had learned from the defeat of Black Friday and prepared more seriously than the coal owners or the government, for that matter, for the coming struggle.

The Court of Inquiry on the coal industry, which reported on 28 July 1925, was largely sympathetic to the miners' case, although the miners had boycotted its hearings. It stated that the difficulties in the mining industry could be entirely explained by "the immediate and necessary effects of the return to gold".[11] This was a criticism of Churchill and the government's adoption of the Gold Standard, which put them on the back foot. Previously, Baldwin had tried to mediate between the owners and the miners. When he asked Herbert Smith, "What have you to give?" the reply from the blunt Yorkshire ex-prize fighter was, "Nowt, we have nowt to give."[12] The efforts to induce the miners to compromise still continued, with Cook receiving an invitation to see the King at Buckingham Palace. Cook's response was: "Why the hell should I go to see the King?... I am going to fight these people. I believe a fight is certain. There is only one way of doing it. That is to fight." When the right-wing Assistant General Secretary of the TUC, Citrine, urged caution, Cook replied: "Don't forget I have something to pay back. It is just six years since they not only handcuffed me but led me in chains from one end of the train, in Swansea Station, to the other, in full view of the public. The same at Cardiff Station."[13]

It gradually dawned on the government that the unions were not bluffing and therefore Baldwin turned to the employers for concessions. They were not forthcoming and Baldwin then consulted his Cabinet and urged a policy of caution and retreat, recommending a subsidy to the industry for nine months. A report to the King by Maurice Hankey, Permanent Secretary to the Cabinet, summed up the attitude of the government: "Many members of the Cabinet think that the struggle is inevitable and must come sooner or later: the PM does not share this view. The majority of the Cabinet regard the present moment as badly chosen for the fight, though the conditions would be more favourable nine months hence. Public opinion is to a considerable extent on the miners' side... There is a strong feeling amongst some of the House of Commons Unionist [Tory] members in favour of the miners, though those same members thoroughly dislike the idea of a subsidy. Finally, a majority of the Cabinet decided on the subsidy proposal – every reasonable man would accept it and a letter from the miners to this effect was received during the Cabinet. It is true the owners will not favour a subsidy. The PM will be negotiating it through the night." The King's reaction was: "So, thank God! There will be no strike now. I am much relieved."[14]

This incident became enshrined in the memory of the working class as the famous 'Red Friday', the revenge of the working class for 'Black Friday'. The mine owners, nevertheless, were thirsting for confrontation, with the chairman of the Mine-owners' Association, Evan Williams, actually accusing Baldwin of paying 'Danegeld' to the unions. (Danegeld was an English tribute raised in the ninth to eleventh centuries to pay off Viking raiders, usually led by the Danish king, to save the land from being ravaged.) Initially, the mine owners refused to withdraw the lockout notices of the miners. But with the government's and the mine owners' eventual retreat there was, as expected, an air of victory in the working class. However, this was tempered by the understanding on the part of the more developed layers that this was a truce, an armistice, a temporary retreat by a still powerful enemy that was going to use every day of the nine months of subsidy to prepare its forces for a "stand up, knock 'em down, drag 'em out" conclusion to this battle. The capitalist press was full of denunciations of the agreement. The charge of Danegeld levelled by the mine owners against the government was also echoed by the capitalist press during the battle in Liverpool City Council when the Thatcher government was compelled to step back and grant concessions after the mass struggles of 1983-84.

Sir William Joynson-Hicks, the Home Secretary – 'Jix' was his nickname – declared shortly after the agreement: "I say to you, coming straight from the Cabinet councils, the thing is not finished. The danger is not over. Sooner or later this question has to be fought out by the people of the land. Is England to be governed by Parliament and the Cabinet or by a handful of trade union leaders?"[15] Churchill pitched in: "In the event of a struggle, whatever its character might be, however ugly the episodes which would mark it, I have no doubt that the State, the national State, would emerge victorious in spite of all the rough and awkward corners it might have to turn. But if you are going to embark on a struggle of this kind, be quite sure that decisive public opinion is behind you..."[16]

Government prepares revenge

However, not everybody, even those nominally in the Labour camp, shared the enthusiasm of the Daily Herald for what it called 'Red Friday'. Ramsay MacDonald spoke at an Independent Labour Party (ILP) summer school as though Baldwin had personally "betrayed him". He declared: "The government has simply handed over – the appearance, at any rate – of victory to the very forces that sane, well-considered socialism fears to be its greatest enemy. If the government had fought their policy out, we should have respected it. It just suddenly doubled up. The consequence has been to increase the power and prestige of those who do not believe in political action."[17] In other words, Red Friday had given an enormous boost to what MacDonald and his ilk described as the 'extreme Left', militants, combative trade unionism and socialism. Has this not been the constant theme of all Labour leaders since him? Was it not a worry for Neil Kinnock, Labour leader at the time of the miners' strike of 1984-85, who hated the miners' leader Arthur Scargill and feared the victory of militant trade unionism in this strike as did the majority of the right-wing General Council of the TUC? The same kind of bile was on display by Kinnock in his infamous and treacherous attack on Liverpool City Council and Militant in 1985. A fighting, militant struggle and particularly its leaders were hounded and driven from office. The capitalists, the right-wing trade union leaders and the Labour leadership were at one in seeking to achieve this.

Meanwhile, Red Friday had given a further fillip to the Left, reflected in the growth of support and enthusiasm for Russia, the first workers' state in history. To the horror of MacDonald, the General Council of the TUC pressed for the Russian application for affiliation to the Amsterdam based International Federation of Trade Unions (IFTU). In April, an Anglo-Soviet Trade Union Conference met in London to set up a joint advisory council to further the Russian application. The tensions were so great between MacDonald and his entourage and the majority of the trade unions that the Fabian leader Beatrice Webb speculated that it was only a matter of time before the unions severed their connection to the Labour Party entirely. She wrote: "The simple truth is that, owing to MacDonald's loss of prestige, the universal distrust and disillusion of the active workers, the inner circles of the labour movement are more at cross purposes than I have ever known them."[18]

This again is an echo of the situation which exists with New Labour in Britain today. There is, however, a profound difference between then and now. The Labour Party in 1925, even under MacDonald, was still what Lenin called a 'bourgeois workers' party'. It had a leadership pro-bourgeois in outlook and in the final analysis always with a foot in the capitalists' camp, but with a working class base and still organically connected to the trade unions. That link with the working class no longer exists although the trade union link has not yet been formally broken. This difference between then and now is summed up by the fact that MacDonald ultimately was compelled to break from the Labour Party in 1931 to form a coalition with the Tory and Liberal enemies. This was necessary because he could not get his anti-working class, anti-trade union policies through in a party which ultimately still rested on the trade unions. That is not the case any more with New Labour. On every issue – from the war in Iraq to privatisation, to the dismantling of the last parts of the

'Welfare State' – New Labour coalesces in the so-called 'middle ground' with the Liberal Democrats and Tories. We have, in effect, an unofficial National Government with Blair reliant on the votes of the Tories rather than his own MPs to get his neo-liberal measures through parliament. In fact, the main capitalist parties in Britain are, to all intents and purposes, three different wings of the same party, the capitalist neo-liberal party. 'Choice' is one of the themes of Blair and New Labour. In the interests of furthering his laudable aim, would it not be better for the capitalist parties to merge, to allow the British people a real choice? The creation of a new mass workers' party, which is what the Labour Party was envisaged to be by its pioneers but has now been buried under a neo-liberal heap by Blair, would offer the "diversity" which all crave.

3 The Nine Months

ollowing the victory of Red Friday, all sides took stock. The miners met in August 1925 but the mood, although confident, was not triumphalist. Herbert Smith said the miners and the working class "had achieved one of the finest things ever done by an organisation". However, he added: "We have no need to glorify about a victory. It is only an armistice."[1] Delegates insisted on drawing up a balance sheet of what had actually been gained. They asked what the practical outcome of the struggle had been. Had A.J. Cook, for instance, asked for an increase in wages to meet the increased cost of living, to which Cook replied that he did. Yet the struggle had been mainly about preventing big reductions in what was for the miners "not a living wage". One delegate then stated plainly: "You did ask for the cost of living; then for God's sake give over talking about a glorious victory." One historian of the strike remarks in relation to this incident: "So differently can things look to those with opposed interests that these men were actually dissatisfied with the agreement, so fiercely fought for and with such difficulty obtained, by which the

Striking miners outside Miner's Union Welfare

wages remained for nine months untouched"![2] The truth is even a standstill in wages for the miners at this stage, although a defensive battle, was a kind of 'victory' or an achievement. The essence of the whole situation in Britain was that even the semi-starvation wages and bestial conditions of the working class were under attack from the pressure of the diseased capitalist system.

Many years after the General Strike, Baldwin was asked by his biographer why he gave the subsidy which led to 'Red Friday'. His simple reply was, "We were not ready."[3] They were surprised and taken aback at the unity and determination of the working class to resist the demands of the employers and the government. This made them even more determined to be prepared for the conflict when, nine months later, the subsidy was due to run out. In 1925, there were no serious preparations by the government on the use of state measures against strikers, the organisation of a blackleg army to counter the effects of a strike. What counter-measures would be necessary if a coal strike should take place, if for instance an embargo on the movement of coal was implemented by the working class as a whole in support of the miners? While in the 1926 General Strike the government did not appear to be as abrasive on the military front in confronting the strike, in the nine months' grace that was given it did use the opportunity to set in place military measures to be used, if necessary, and, as an auxiliary, a paramilitary force to confront the miners and the working class.

Repressive apparatus

An emergency supply and transport committee was already in existence when Baldwin first came to power in 1923. This had been originally set up by Lloyd George during the 'dangerous months' of 1919 and had been ready to go into action on the eve of Black Friday in 1921. In the event, it was not needed but rather than being completely disbanded it was put into cold storage. This was despite the fact that, officially, the government had not sanctioned this, but a state official, John Davidson, maintained the plans for an organisation and a skeleton machinery, and these were dusted down to be used by the Baldwin government in preparation for the strike. Davidson was appointed Chancellor of the Duchy of Lancaster and assumed the newly created title and functions of Chief Civil Commissioner. His salary was paid not from the state but direct from Tory party funds! Ten Regional Commissioners were appointed in England and Wales and arrangements were made to take over the British Broadcasting Company, with the possibility of producing a government news sheet if the newspapers ceased publication. Thus, even in a period of alleged 'social peace' the ruling class in Britain were preparing for 'extra-parliamentary' measures, in other words the methods of civil war, in order to defeat the working class.

Their plans, however, were slightly disrupted earlier by the election of the MacDonald government of 1924. Would these 'contingency plans' be maintained or disbanded? Their fears were soon assuaged when a Labour minister, Josiah Wedgwood, turned a blind eye to this secret strike-breaking organisation. Even when the public formation of the Organisation of Maintenance and Supply (OMS) was announced in September 1925, the right-wing trade union leaders were dismissive and attacked those on the Left, such as A.J. Cook, who called for counter-measures from the side of labour such as a workers' defence force. Cramp, Industrial Secretary of the NUR, dismissed the OMS: "Personally, I have not the slightest fear of these jokers. They are people who have never worked in their lives. If they started to do it in a strike they would make a very poor job of it."[4]

In a sense, this is what happened, as we will see, in the first stages of the General Strike. But if the strike had gone on for any length of time, the OMS could have become a serious strike-breaking force alongside the official forces of the state. Its official aims were not to oppose "legitimate trade unionism" but specifically measures such as the looming General Strike! The British Fascists, who were not then a political party but a quasi-military group headed by a retired Brigadier-General and a Rear Admiral, went over *en masse* to the OMS. This 'volunteer' army was, in effect blessed by the government. Joynson-Hicks, the Home Secretary, publicly ratified its formation in replying to an anonymous and mysterious 'correspondent' in *The Times* of 1 October 1925: "There is no reason why you should object to the OMS... [or] any other citizen who would desire the maintenance of peace, order and good government..."[5]

The country was divided and controlled by government-appointed commissioners with the aim of controlling "road transport, food and fuel supplies". Each commissioner was deputed to maintain law and order in his own area and to recruit "able-bodied citizens of good character to serve as special constables". One of the commissioners, Lord Winterton, stated, "We were given further instructions in the event of a complete breakdown, to take drastic action of a comprehensive character."[6] What constituted a "complete breakdown" and the resulting "drastic action" remained unspecified but it does not take a leap of the imagination to believe that this was code for military or quasi-military measures to be used in the event of a general strike appearing to be successful and challenging capitalism.

All of this indicates that behind the professions of "peace" by Baldwin and his like, the British ruling class were preparing the most ruthless means to suppress the working class if necessary. In 1919 they relied on an open display of military force with troops at the pitheads. In the run-up to the 1926 General Strike, they were more cautious, hoping that they could rely on the right-wing trade union leaders to draw back, but at the same time making serious preparations to use whatever means 'necessary' in order to realise their goals. Capitalist historians may picture the formation of the OMS as a kind of 'Dad's Army' or as harmless 'gilded youth'[7] of the time or the organisation of bourgeois and petty-bourgeois youth eager for a spot of 'mild hooliganism'. This, however, involved attacking workers and trying to break a strike. It was not pranksters who were involved in the kidnapping of Harry Pollitt, or the hijack and crashing of a Daily Herald delivery van.[8] Imagine the headline about 'left-wing terrorism' in the rabid capitalist press if such measures had been taken by the Left.

But this was all part of the preparations of the ruling class for a serious confrontation. They were acting according to their class interests. As Marx pointed out, the government in any capitalist state is the executive committee of the ruling class. When their interests are threatened, or are perceived to be, they can consider using the most draconian measures to protect them.

Only now, in 2006, has it been confirmed that Labour Prime Minister Harold Wilson was threatened by a military coup in the 1970s. The plot had been hatched by the secret service, MI5, who intended to replace Wilson with a member of the Royal Family, Lord Mountbatten. To this end, military manoeuvres, with the deployment of tanks, had taken place at Heathrow Airport. Yet this was in a situation less polarised from a class point of view than in 1926 itself.

The British capitalist class, one of the most "treacherous in the world" in their dealings with the working class, concentrated in their leading figures and politicians the whole experience of their class. Baldwin was to put this to good use with his combination of subtlety, cultivation of right-wing trade union leaders but at the same time the most ruthless preparations in defence of his class. The same could not be said of the leaders of the other side. One historian described the approach of the TUC General Council as "studied unpreparedness". This was, if anything, an understatement.

But it was not just the Right but also the Left, including the official Left leaders and, unfortunately, the Communist Party, who were unprepared for this struggle. Those like A.J. Cook and the leadership and militants of the young Communist Party sincerely wanted the victory of the General Strike. Even the 'pragmatic' wing of the TUC like Ernest Bevin believed in the possibility of victory for the miners and the working class. As in 1925, Bevin thought he and the other trade union leaders could either bluff Baldwin to retreat by threatening a strike or, failing this, a general strike would achieve the same objective.

Theory and history of the general strike

In order to understand how things could have turned out differently in 1926, it is necessary to explore briefly the idea of a general strike, the different perceptions and misconceptions of what is involved in the use of this weapon as well as a consistent Marxist approach towards this. The idea of a general strike has a long pedigree going back even before the first independent movements of the working class, both in Britain and the world, the Chartists. It became a practical issue during the Chartist period after William Benbow in 1831 put this forward and it was accepted by the Chartist Convention. In his scheme for a "grand holiday and congress of the productive classes", he argued that if all workers simply stayed at home or took a "grand national holiday", the government and the ruling classes would be forced to submit to their demands. The Chartists attempted this in the historic failed General Strike of 1842.

In the 160 years since, there are numerous examples of different kinds of general strike. Even the bourgeois leant on the weapon of the general strike, carried out by the workers of course, in its struggle against feudalism in the 1848 European-wide revolutions. The twentieth century witnessed the great General Strike of 1905 in Russia and the Swedish General Strike of 1909. This was followed by general strikes in Limerick, Ireland and Winnipeg, Canada in 1919 and the great strike of 1920 in Germany against the failed Kapp putsch. The Belgian General Strike of 1960-61 and the famous events in France in 1968 stand out in the twentieth century. We have also seen the great Indian hartals – strikes in the countryside as well as in the urban areas – in 1921, emulated by the Sri Lankan working class in 1953 and 1980, in the Rand strike of 1922, the Ruhr General Strike of 1923, etc. In Nigeria, the labour movement has launched general strikes against rising petrol prices, while in Bolivia, there have been many general strikes but perhaps not as many as the estimated 200 military coups since independence! Highly significant as well are the state- and city-wide 'general strikes' of immigrant Latino workers in the United States, the citadel of world capitalism, in 2006.

Marxists have always understood – particularly in the era of capitalist crisis, marked by the outbreak of the First World War – that an unlimited general strike poses the question of power: which class runs society. So do the serious representatives of the capitalists. Lloyd George had declared to trade union leaders in 1919: "If you carry out your threat and strike, then you will defeat us. But if you do so... have you weighed the consequences? The strike will be in defiance of the government of the country and by its very success will precipitate a constitutional crisis of the first importance. For, if a force arises in the state which is stronger than the state itself, then it must be ready to take on the functions of the state, or withdraw and accept the authority of the state. Gentlemen... have you considered, and if you have, are you ready?" The reaction of miners' leader Robert Smillie was: "From that moment on we were beaten and we knew we were."[9] In other words, the trade union leaders of the time were not prepared to mobilise the working class to take power.

An interesting example from the history of the international workers' movement is provided in the General Strike of 1909 in Sweden. This strike is important, as are other explosive movements in the history of the Swedish labour movement, if for no other reason than that it counters the current myth of that country as the quintessence of 'social peace', as a model of class compromise. It was not always so. In 1909, the LO (the Swedish TUC) with 190,000 members, came into a head-on collision with the employers and the government. From the beginning of the twentieth century, workers had discussed the idea of a general strike and in 1908 the Minister of the Interior declared that it is "a familiar and saddening fact, that our country in recent years more than any other has become the country of strikes, boycotts and lock-outs. We have beaten the world record in this regard..."

Swedish General Strike

The tops of the trade unions, as with the 1926 General Strike in Britain, of course, were quaking at the pressure of the workers for a general strike. The LO chairperson described such a strike as a "suicide attempt", an echo of right-wing leader Jimmy Thomas's declarations in 1925 and 1926. The employers threatened a lock-out, unless their conditions were met. The answer was a general stoppage of work because what was at stake was "the existence of the entire Swedish trade union movement". The unions were not prepared but nevertheless there was massive support, described by the French socialist paper *L'Humanité* as "the greatest proletarian mobilisation we have seen in our days". Lenin, in the newspaper *Sotsial-Democrat*, regarded it as "one of the biggest general strikes in our time". There was massive support, including from England and the international working class. Moreover, many unorganised workers began to be drawn in.

At the same time , the LO and Social Democrat leaders, like their English counterparts 17 years later, made no real attempt to organise for victory. The Social Democrat leader Branting, for example, left for Germany in the most hectic period of preparations! The social democracy's paper wrote: "Workers. Use beautiful summer days and the free time to make outdoor visits. Bring good literature to the forest hills and use all opportunities to increase your knowledge... Use your freedom well, which the strike has given you." This refrain of moderate trade unionism was repeated in the 1926 General Strike. However, pioneer of the labour movement, Axel Danielsson, had predicted: "Without struggle the general strike is impossible. If it goes so far that a peaceful development is impossible, the proletariat has to prepare itself to step out onto the streets and with violence conquer the stored goods and the means of production... the workers [must not] wait with their arms crossed until the social capitulation of the bourgeoisie." In other words, unless the question of power is posed a general strike is in the end a display of "folded arms".

Most illuminating about this struggle was that the ordinary soldiers sided with the working class and if there had been a decisive struggle for power they could not have been used effectively against the workers' movement. As in the 1926 General Strike, strike committees sprung up – 549 throughout Sweden. The failure to carry through this struggle to a successful conclusion led inevitably to attacks by the employers, wage cuts and subsequent disillusionment. Membership of the trade unions dropped. This example indicates that a general strike, the most serious struggle – one step removed from taking full power – puts the question of "either-or" on the agenda for the workers' movement.[10]

Trotsky on the General Strike

This was true even in the period prior to the First World War as the example of Sweden shows. But because capitalism, in general, had not exhausted its progressive mission in developing the productive forces, science, labour and the organisation of technique, the general strike could be posed in a cloudy, imprecise fashion without being seriously put to the test. It could even in some circumstances get some short-term results. Even the great Polish-German revolutionary, Rosa Luxemburg, the 'mountain eagle', overestimated the independent importance of the general strike when it was not linked to the working class taking power and establishing its own state. She 'bent the stick' in the direction of emphasising the spontaneous activity of the masses in the first Russian Revolution of 1905 and elsewhere. This was done in order to counter the dead hand of the trade union bureaucracy in Germany, the dangers of which she was the first to identify and warn against. Also, the social-democratic parties, like those in France and Germany under Jean Jaurès and August Bebel, promised that they would resort to a general strike in the event of a war, summed up in the decisions of the famous Basle congress of the Second International in 1912. But, as Trotsky commented subsequently, this call "assumed... the nature of theoretical thunder".

Summing up the historical experience of the working class in the 1930s, Trotsky made the point: "A general strike, particularly in the old capitalist countries, requires a painstaking Marxist accounting of all the concrete circumstances."[11] Capitalism had reached a blind alley, signified by the First World War, when the productive forces had visibly outgrown the narrow limits of private capitalist ownership and the nation state. The system was in a cul-de-sac in which the struggle between the classes intensified. The interests of the ruling class faced a continual threat from the working class and the labour movement. But when fundamental and unpostponable issues are at stake, only a general strike linked to the overthrow of capitalism can fully succeed. This in turn can only be prepared by the whole preceding period of the workers' movement and particularly by the more politically developed layers.

The general strike is an important weapon of struggle but it is not universal. There are conditions when a general strike may weaken the workers more than their immediate enemy. The strike must be an important element in the calculation of strategy and not a panacea in which it submerges all other strategies. The general strike is, in the main, a weapon of the weak against the strong, an entrenched state power that has at its disposal railways, telecommunications, police and army, etc. Trotsky comments: "By paralysing the government apparatus a general strike, either 'scared' a government or created the postulates of a revolutionary solution of the question of power." It could be a means, in some instances, for workers under a dictatorship to fuse themselves together, beginning with sectional strikes leading to a general strike and the acquisition of strength by the workers to overthrow a regime.

But in other circumstances this weapon is inappropriate. For instance, at the time of Kornilov's march against Petrograd in 1917, neither the Bolsheviks nor the soviets (workers' councils) thought of declaring a strike. On the contrary, the railway workers continued to work so they could transport the opponents of Kornilov and derail his forces. The workers in the factories continued to work except for those who left to fight Kornilov's forces. At the time of the October Revolution in 1917, there was again no talk of a general strike. The Bolsheviks enjoyed mass support and under these conditions to call for a general strike would actually weaken themselves and not the capitalist enemy. On the railways, in the factories and offices, the workers assisted the uprising to overthrow capitalism and establish a democratic workers' state.

In the pre-1914 period, an era characterised by a general upswing of capitalism, it was possible under certain circumstances, for partial 'general strikes' to take place. There are instances where the government takes fright at the general strike and at the very outset, without taking matters to an open clash, makes concessions. Such was the situation in the Belgian General Strike of 1893 and in a much bigger scale in Russia in October 1905. Under the pressure of the strike the Tsarist regime in 1905 made "constitutional concessions". In Belgium, the strike was called by the Belgian

Labour Party with 300,000 workers participating, including left-wing Catholic groups. There were a number of clashes between demonstrators, police and troops. However, the strike was called off when the government granted male suffrage at 25 years of age. (The voting age had been raised to 30 in 1885. The strike victory cleared the way for the Belgian Labour Party's election victories; it won 27 seats in 1894.)

The Left – no clear ideas on the General Strike

For some of the trade union leaders at least, the coming struggle in Britain was to have the features of the pre-1914 struggles, a mass mobilisation, where the mere flexing of muscles by the proletariat would be sufficient to compel the ruling class to step back. This was probably the attitude of Ernest Bevin, leader of the Transport and General Workers' Union and others. After all, it had worked on Red Friday in compelling the Baldwin government into its humiliating retreat. For others on the Right, such as J.R. Thomas, they could not avoid the coming confrontation. There was enormous pressure from below, including from the majority of members of Thomas's union on the railways, who were as eager as all other workers to inflict defeat on their hated bosses. These right-wing trade union leaders consciously went along with the General Strike, moved to centralise power into their own hands, with the purpose of betraying it.

Thomas was to declare in August 1925 that he was "very far from happy" over the "magnificent victory" of the miners on Red Friday. He considered "nothing more dangerous for the future of the country than that employers and government were compelled to concede through force, what they had refused to concede through reason".[12] A.J. Cook, on the other hand, declared at the same time, that the victory showed that "labour could only get what it was strong enough to take".[13] But unfortunately, the full implications of precisely what "strength" meant in order to ensure victory for the working class was not fully understood by him. Later that month he declared: "Next May we shall be faced with the greatest crisis and the greatest struggle we have ever known, and we are preparing for it. We shall prepare a Commissariat department. I am going to get a fund, if I can, that will buy grub so that when the struggle comes we shall have grub [food] distributed in the homes of our people. I don't care a hang for any government, or army, or navy. They can come along with their bayonets. Bayonets don't cut coal. We have already beaten not only the employers, but the strongest government in modern times."[14] A month later he declared that Black Friday had gone for ever. The workers now possessed the power as could be seen by the actions of the prime minister in climbing down and granting the coal subsidy: "That action on the part of Mr Baldwin represented the revolution." He added: "Take it from me, there would have otherwise been a revolution. I fear there will be trouble next May."[15]

What a heroic figure A.J. Cook presents – particularly when set against the belly-crawling pro-capitalist lickspittles MacDonald, Thomas and Co. – in his absolute devotion to the cause of the miners. He showed admirable determination in demanding full support for the miners, even supporting the idea of a workers' defence force against the plans of the government and army of blacklegs, which earned him the vilification and scorn of right-wing trade union leaders. But in these above remarks is also shown the weakness of Cook, a political naïveté. He shows elements of a syndicalist approach, probably carried over from his youth, with the idea of a prolonged 'great strike'. Workers well stocked up with food could defeat the employers. Later on, before the outbreak of the General Strike, Cook declared that working class families knew that a strike was inevitable and should be laying in secret supplies of food. He unsuccessfully tried to win the Co-operative Movement to commit to providing workers with credit and food in the event of a strike. Disgracefully, the tops of the co-ops refused and, with some notable exceptions, most co-op outlets did not come to the assistance of workers or the miners. In a discussion, the dyed-in-the-wool cynic Thomas expressed scepticism about a strike. Cook replied to him: "I mean it… my own mother-in-law has been taking in an extra tin of salmon for weeks past." The meeting at which this comment was made, the Industrial Committee of the TUC, sank into an astonished silence until Thomas commented: "By God! A British revolution on a tin of salmon"![16]

The sarcastic remark of Thomas received the usual guffaws from the Right and has been commented on by sceptical capitalist historians since. But it does betray the political deficiencies of A.J. Cook, which was a huge weakness in a general strike situation. He was a sincere militant who remained true to the cause to the end. But his lack of a worked-out alternative policy to the Right, together with the other Left union leaders as a whole – Purcell, Swales and Hicks – proved to be fatal in the maelstrom of the events of May 1926 and after. A general strike poses the question of power but does not by itself solve it. For that, a programme for the working class to take power is necessary. This in turn requires a worked out revolutionary policy, a mass party and a tested leadership. This the sincere Left A.J. Cook did not have. The other Lefts had even less; during the strike they would go to the abyss, look over and draw back. Even before this, however, they had given notice of their future role by their capitulation to the Right in the Labour Party (to be dealt with later).

United Front

And the Communist Party was unable to take political advantage of the inadequacies of these individuals – who held great sway in the minds of the masses – not so much because of their own political limitations and inexperience but because of the approach which had been dictated by Moscow, which had led to the Anglo-Russian Trade Union Committee. This was established following a joint declaration between the British and Soviet trade unions in April 1925. To understand the role that this committee played and the effects that it had on the Communist Party's approach it is necessary to examine some of the background to developments in Russia at this stage. The isolation of the Russian Revolution had led to the beginning of the rise of a conservative bureaucracy, reflected within the Russian Communist Party and personified by Stalin in his struggle with Trotsky and the Left Opposition. The original internationalist aim of the Russian Revolution, that its salvation lay in the international victory of the working class, was replaced gradually by the policy of 'Socialism in One Country' and the diplomatic manoeuvres which arose from this. An attempt was made to seek influence not through a systematic growth of national sections of the Communist International – such as the Communist Party of Great Britain – but by a policy of courting the Left of the labour movement. This coalesced with an undoubted mood of support for the gains of the Russian Revolution and the workers' state, particularly when contrasted with the failures of capitalism in Britain, Germany, France, Italy and elsewhere.

Instead of basing themselves upon this rising pro-Soviet and revolutionary mood and linking it to the development of a firm independent class-struggle policy and organisation, the Comintern leadership of Stalin, Bukharin and Zinoviev (before he broke with Stalin in 1925) proposed a bloc with the trade unions in Britain and particularly its left wing. This was all done under the signboard of the 'united front' policy, as mentioned earlier. There was pressure for trade union unity in Britain and throughout Europe which the Communist Party and the Communist International were correct to take cognisance of. But Trotsky and the Left Opposition objected to the downgrading of the role of the Red International of Labour Unions (RILU), which attempted to group together all the militant fighting organisations worldwide against capitalism. Without full discussion and behind the backs of the working class of Russia and of the Communist Party, Stalin and Co. in effect were linking up with the reformist International Federation of Trade Unions (IFTU), known as the Amsterdam International., at the cost of building a revolutionary international trade union centre.

A 'united front' policy of this kind, which reformists or centrists invariably seek to use to screen themselves from the criticism of the masses, played a baleful role in its effects on the young CPGB and in the General Strike itself. One aspect of this policy was trade union unity, the other was centred on international issues and particularly the "struggle for peace", as it applied to the defence of Russia against imperialist attack and to China. Trotsky had consistently warned of the middle-class British Left leadership's preference for the "love of the distant". Radical in phrases on international issues, even revolutions far from the shores of Britain, these Lefts could pursue an entirely different policy at home. Yet foreign policy is the continuation of home policy. The Comintern under Stalin and Co. ignored this basic but vital revolutionary maxim.

These features were in full display in the Anglo-Russian Trade Union Committee. The Communist Party was pulled in different directions. On the one side, its instinct was to criticise the Lefts, while on the other it feared to do this so as not to upset the Anglo-Russian applecart. J.R. Campbell, for instance, could write in *Communist Review*, the CP's theoretical journal in October 1924, criticising the Left trade union leaders: "It would be a suicidal policy, however, for the CP and the Minority Movement to place too much reliance on what we have called the official left wing... It is the duty of the party and the Minority Movement to criticise its weakness relentlessly and endeavour to change the muddled and incomplete left-wing viewpoint of the more progressive leaders into a real revolutionary viewpoint. But the revolutionary workers must never forget that the main activity must be devoted to capturing the masses."[17] The CP, however, never consistently pursued this course. The emphasis in the run-up to the General Strike should have been on a united front from below – without, of course, making the ultra-left mistake of not putting pressure and making demands on the Left leaders. Willie Gallacher declared: "The leadership [of the TUC] has passed into the hands of good proletarians like Swales, Hicks, Cook, and Purcell. And this proletarian leadership and the proletarian solidarity it was capable of organising and demonstrating was the real big thing that came out of the struggle."[18]

CP unprepared

This uncritical stance was reflected in J.T. Murphy's comments following the Trades Union Congress of September 1925: "When Swales delivered his opening speech the real temper of the Congress began to manifest itself. The more militant he became the more delegates responded to his fighting challenge."[19] This approach was not at all automatically accepted or to the satisfaction of all members of the party. At the party congress in May 1925 a delegate from Sheffield had drawn attention to the fact that the miners' leader Arthur Cook had begun to drift away from some of the policies he had fought for in his election campaign. This Sheffield delegate pointed out: "After we have praised and said nice things about these left-wing leaders, what will the masses say about the Communist Party when these leaders fail them? We must give the necessary qualifications to our support of these left wingers."[20]

This is precisely the gist of the criticism that Trotsky and the Left Opposition were making at this stage. The policies of the Right were clear. MacDonald, Henderson and Co. were the bridle on the working class and the buckle through which the strap was passed would be played by the likes of trade union leaders such as arch right-winger Thomas. *Workers' Weekly*, in the run up to the General Strike, was full of warnings, it is true – although all the political implications had not been drawn out – about the role of the Right. But as far as the Lefts were concerned, the CP's comments amounted mainly to mutterings about their role. Even in James Klugmann's official history of the Communist Party, written later, Fred Bramley, then General Secretary of the TUC, who had denounced Cook as a "raving Communist", is described as an "ardent protagonist of unity" between the trade unions of Britain and the USSR.[21]

This linking up of the British TUC and their Russian counterparts did provoke fury in the capitalist press. They warned the trade union leaders: "The General Council in fact have sold the pass."[22] But this sound and fury from the side of the capitalists disguised the fact that the right-wing General Council was using the screen of the Anglo-Russian Trade Union Committee to justify a policy of inaction. The Communist Party, for its part, did issue warnings but of the most imprecise kind. On 28 August, 1925, *Workers' Weekly* stated: "Thirty-four weeks to go to what? To the termination of the mining agreement and the opening of the greatest struggle in the history of the British working class... WE MUST PREPARE FOR THE STRUGGLE."[23] What form was that struggle to take? It is true that the Communist Party and the National Minority Movement called for councils of action, made criticisms against the Right, but still persisted in calling for "full power to the General Council". They continued to do this even after the expulsion of the Communist Party from the Labour Party in 1925. Retrospectively, through the writings of its historian Klugmann, the Communist Party did later criticise this stand: "It can still be questioned whether this was a correct demand, whether it was correct to insist on full powers for the General Council to 'direct the whole activities of the unions', without even greater insistence that such powers would *only* be justified if it was certain they would be used for and not against the militant working class."[24]

It would be impossible to "guarantee" that such powers would not be used by conservative bureaucratic officialdom at the top of the trade unions. This is why preparation from below should have been the most important aspect of even a small party's approach in this situation. This does not preclude placing sharp demands on the TUC or demanding a concrete lead from the Left union leaders. The Communist Party did support the "idea" of councils of action, attempted to strengthen the trades councils, even when they were outlawed by the TUC and issued propaganda in favour of a workers' defence force, which was all necessary in the situation of 1925-26. But what was missing above all was the political preparation which involved an understanding of the character of the conflict that was coming and the role of the leading political trends and figures in this. If a revolution takes place and the subjective factor is small and uninfluential, lacks support amongst the broad masses of the working class, then that revolution can go down to defeat. But a force which is small but nevertheless has a correct strategy and tactics, puts forward appropriate slogans and makes the clear criticism of vacillating Lefts at the right time can come through even a defeat with its position strengthened and with an enhanced position from which to fight in the next period.

1905 or 1923?

Trotsky posed the question before the General Strike that in the test which was to come, would the Communist Party face a 1905 or a 1923-type situation? In 1905 the Russian Marxists, particularly the Bolsheviks, came through the test of revolution with a growth in their authority particularly amongst the advanced sections of the working class, although the revolution was defeated. Nevertheless, this 'dress rehearsal' was vital in preparing the Russian working class with the Bolsheviks at their head for carrying through the Russian Revolution of 1917. In 1923, on the other hand, a revolutionary situation was let slip by the German Communist Party under the misguided directions of the Comintern leadership of Stalin and co. Would it be a 1905 for the CPGB or a disastrous 1923? This could only be determined by a struggle of living forces and correct policies and organisation.

Even when a correct slogan was put forward by the CP, such as the need for councils of action and mobilisation from below of the working class, this was hedged around with caution. For instance, on the eve of the General Strike the acting secretary of the Minority Movement, George Hardy (Harry Pollitt had been jailed), proposed that work for the establishment of councils of action should be undertaken in every area but that "councils of action were to see that all the decisions of the General Council and the union executives were carried out".[25] The CP did not fully follow this course. The British working-class movement is burdened by a trade union officialdom which had developed and taken shape over a long historical period. This conservative, encrusted layer looked on any independent initiative of workers from below, any spontaneous action, with suspicion if not with outright hostility. While recognising the tendency of workers in Britain to move through the official union structures, the task of Marxists is to combine this with encouragement of movements from below and genuine organisations which reflect this.

J.T. Murphy, one of the leaders of the Communist Party, in his book *'The Political Meaning of the General Strike'*, says that the most that the CP expected from the General Council of the TUC was a repetition of the decision that led to the government retreat on Red Friday – the refusal to handle coal by the transport unions. This is despite the fact that in February 1926 Trotsky predicted that the withdrawal of subsidies would provoke "beginning with the next 1st May, a grandiose economic conflict. It is not hard to imagine what would be implied by a strike embracing not less than a million miners, backed, according to all indications by approximately a million railwaymen and transport workers."[26]

This approach has to be contrasted to the balm dispensed by the theoreticians of the Communist Party. This was summed up most clearly in the semi-official Communist Party journal, *Labour Monthly* in 1925 and 1926. The building up of the Left is quite clear in articles such as that by M.N. Roy. Buttressing the Left credentials of Purcell, he wrote: "Speaking at Baku...Mr A.A. Purcell, the head of the British Trades Union delegation, declared that on returning home the delegation would organise a 'Hands Off Egypt' movement, to prevent British imperialism from throttling weak and defenceless Egypt. This attitude taken on behalf of the militant proletariat contrasts remarkably with the official view of the Labour Party on this grave question."[27]

Labour Monthly also quoted approvingly Purcell's speech at the Soviet Trades Union Congress, November 11-18 1924: "...I congratulate you upon the colossal success of your work on behalf of the working classes of the world... you are the directors of the Soviet Republic... You have carried through this work in the interests of the workers of the world... The unity must be a real, and not merely a formal one. It must be based upon the principles of opposition to capitalism... To leave the Russian Trades Unions outside any international organisation would be like playing Hamlet without the chief character... Our duty, our obligation, is to unite all our forces for the destruction of capitalism."[28] Yet how little Purcell was prepared to destroy capitalism was on view even before May 1926 but was absolutely clear in the strike itself. Nevertheless, *Labour Monthly* commented: "The tenor of Purcell's speech was such as to seriously alarm the Right Wing clique in the International Federation of Trade Unions."[29]

R. Palme Dutt was the editor of *Labour Monthly* and had shown a certain theoretical understanding in analysing the situation in Britain. He praised Trotsky's *Where is Britain Going?* In a survey *after* the General Strike in September 1926, he wrote: "In a recent article Trotsky has pointed out that the more revolutionary in principle a resolution was at Scarborough [the TUC Conference of September 1925], the more easily it was carried; but the closer it came to an even elementary task of action, the stronger was the opposition. International Unity with the Communist-led Trades Unions of Russia was carried unanimously by the same delegates who a few weeks later were voting the expulsion of Communist trade unionists at home from the Labour Movement... Thus the move to the Left was in practice a show move to the

Left, reflecting the undoubted movement of working class opinion, but sterilised and neutralised by the skilful opportunist leadership who allowed no real change in actual policy. In consequence, the sequel of Scarborough by Liverpool, with its victory of extreme reaction and conspicuous collapse of the Left Wing, was not a contradiction of Scarborough but its completion."[30]

But such warnings against the future role of the Left were not evident from the pen of Palme Dutt or others writing in *Labour Monthly* before the General Strike. Karl Radek (a member of the Left Opposition) had written in March 1925: "The members of the Left Wing of the Labour Party are not Communists; we know this very well. We know that they will develop towards a really revolutionary position with great hesitation. The British Communists, in criticising them, must show patience and self control, and must act by means of calm explanation."[31]

It would have been completely wrong then and now, for that matter, to criticise the inconsistent reformist Left in the shrill tones of the sectarian and ultra-left groups. Militant and the Socialist Party have never indulged in such methods. In Britain, for instance, in the recent period, in 2006 a small ultra-left grouping in the Public and Commercial Services Union (PCS) denounced the union's agreement on pensions with the government.[32] This agreement was supported by the overwhelming majority of the left-wing National Executive Committee of the union. They nevertheless attacked this as a "shabby" deal and some of them accused the general secretary of the PCS, Mark Serwotka, of "betrayal". Such an approach is completely counter-productive and does not raise the level of understanding of the militants of the working class; it substitutes abuse for argument and explanation.

Criticism of the deficiencies of the Left leaders, when it is required, is an absolutely essential task for a party claiming to be Marxist. Militant, for instance, supported all the steps towards the Left of those like Tony Benn, but we never hesitated to criticise in a positive way any deficiencies in his programme, as well as his tactics and organisation. This did not mean we that we always received his benediction and praise. In point of fact, when we were part of the Left inside the Labour Party, its Marxist revolutionary wing, our members and supporters worked closely with him and others on the Left. But our refusal to be corralled into an uncritical 'broad left' in support of Tony Benn naturally raised his ire. He is not a Marxist and is not prepared to go outside the framework of left reformist ideas. The best way, as the experience of the General Strike and its run-up demonstrates in a negative fashion, is to help the Left find a correct orientation by subjecting it to criticism, to help it develop a more coherent, definitive position. By its very character, left reformism and centrism, which can develop at a later stage, are diffuse. When put to the test, invariably most reformists capitulate to the Right. The latter does have a coherent policy, resting as it does ultimately on bourgeois society, and the pressures which result from this on the trade union and labour leaders. They are pressured to conform to the needs of the capitalists and not those they were elected to represent. Before the left can gather together as a coherent, organised force, they must gather together their thoughts. There is no other way this can be done except through consistent Marxist explanation and criticism of the inadequacies of reformism, and of left reformism in particular.

The use of terms like 'reformism', 'Left reformism', and particularly 'centrism' may strike some of the younger, new generation just entering the labour movement as somewhat antiquated today. The dominance of neo-liberalism following the collapse of Stalinism and with it the idea of a "planned economy" has resulted in the corruption and political degeneration of most of the leaders of the labour movement. Left-wing ideas, including reformism which dominated the workers' movement in the 1970s and 1980s, were on the retreat in the 1990s and the first part of this decade. But support for these ideas and those leaders who advocate them is reappearing – and for socialist and Marxist ideas as well – as class polarisation and the resulting strikes and conflicts in France, Germany, Britain, etc., demonstrate. It is therefore necessary for workers to discuss these ideas and the task of Marxists is to criticise them in a positive fashion.

The absence of such an approach is clear from the Communist Party's journals and actions in the run-up to the General Strike. In June 1925 *Labour Monthly* carried the following comments on the Left in the General Council of the TUC and its support for "international trade union unity": "Our friend Purcell very frequently, and very appropriately, speaks of the 'mosaic' of our movement." There were 1,100 trade unions at the time! It goes on: "Everyone must agree with Swales [in the May Day *Sunday Worker*] that the most important achievement during the last twelve months has been the establishment of an agreement and contract with the Soviet trades union movement... MacDonald puts forward Amsterdam against the Anglo-Russian agreement. Purcell gave the fitting reply to MacDonald in the May Day issue of the *Sunday Worker* when he said that the real meaning of MacDonald's proposal was 'that we are to break off friendships with those who stand for world-wide trades union unity, and the world-wide fight for the eight-hour day, and accept the point of view of those whose attitude on these questions has been diametrically opposed to our own at numerous discussions in the past'. And this we have no intention of doing..." The author then adds: "It is most characteristic that he [MacDonald] borrowed practically all his arguments against the Anglo-Russian Trades Union Agreement out of *The Times!* It is obvious that things cannot go on in this way. The

Trades Unions must acquire an influence on the policy of the Labour Party... But this revolution will only be possible if the Left elements in the Trades Unions conclude a bloc with the Left elements of the Labour Party. The MacDonald-Thomas Alliance must be replaced by a Purcell-Maxton alliance. Such a Left bloc must be wide enough to include Swales and Cook, Hicks and Pollitt, Kirkwood and Gallacher, Maxton and Saklatvala, Lansbury and Campbell."[33]

Scarborough TUC

One month later we read in the same journal the following: "Against this die-hard resolution [of the General Council of the International Federation of Trade Unions] Mr Bramley, in the name of the General Council of the Trades Union Congress, delivered [his] speech. In the circumstances it was a clever speech and a strong speech too. Bramley termed 'an act of folly' the attempt to settle the differences between Amsterdam and Moscow by correspondence rather than direct negotiations... Bramley said: 'But when you begin to discuss Russia, you begin to suffer from some malignant disease which I am not able to say much about because I do not understand it... Why do you not follow the example of the British section, and look closely at the Russian problems, and deal with Russia as you are dealing with other countries? Get rid of the panicky fear that seems to invade and dominate your minds in dealing with Russia'..." *Labour Monthly* goes on to praise "this remarkable speech" but is then forced to add: "It is true that Mr Bramley, right through his speech, assiduously and explicitly repudiated Communism [and] the Minority Movement, that he openly declared himself to be a member of the extreme Right Wing of the trades' union movement... Bramley's speech is not simply a clever speech delivered by an astute trade union leader... It is much more than that. It is symptomatic of the slow but profound process of the revolutionising of the British Labour Movement that is taking place before our eyes."[34]

Bramley's anti-communist speech was therefore of no consequence, would have no bearing on the struggle unfolding in Britain because he was in favour of "international unity". The CP leadership was in denial. This "international unity" was, in fact, a smokescreen behind which those like Bramley could hide from the British workers their right-wing policies at home. Instead of praising his "remarkable speech", the CP should have been pointing to the glaring contradiction of verbal radicalism abroad and a diametrically opposed policy when it came to the great issues which confronted the working class in Britain.

The consequences of this policy were on full view at the Scarborough conference of the TUC in September 1925. Left and even militant resolutions were accepted by comfortable majorities so long as they were on general and international issues. The

Congress accepted a resolution on the establishment of "well-organised shop committees" but only "in principle" and with 1.7 million votes against! A resolution which called for the "overthrow of capitalism" was passed. However, the closer that any proposal came to calling for action rather than general Left sentiments, the more the Right showed its opposition. The affiliation of trades' councils to the TUC was ruled out of order. The Right gave a glimpse, through J.R. Clynes, secretary of the General and Municipal Workers Union, of the role they were about to play when he declared: "I am not in fear of the capitalist class. The only class I fear is our own… We should put our trust in our leaders."[35]

Left resolutions were accepted but the Right was strengthened on the General Council, with Thomas coming back on after two years of absence and Ernest Bevin of the Transport Workers was elected. Yet in a report on this conference in *Labour Monthly* we read the following: "There can be no further doubt but that the Scarborough Congress has been the most important and momentous in the history of the British Trades Union Movement… The whole proceedings… have proved that there is now definitely in existence a growing revolutionary opinion which no intrigues or appeals to constitutional procedure could stifle… If the Left Wing on the General Council had boldly come out and asked Congress for complete power, giving the urgent reasons for the step being taken, it would have been a complete counter-offensive to the Right Wing… The speeches of Comrades Brown, Tomsky and Bramley indicated the importance of Britain to the international working class movement, and showed that, outside of Russia, the British movement is the real international leader…"[36]

It is true that some criticism of proceedings at Scarborough were aired in *Labour Monthly*. "The weaknesses were… the reluctance of the Left Wing of the General Council to come out openly and fight the Right Wing on every possible occasion, for there could be no doubt that the Right Wing leaders… had very effectively marshalled their forces… and they could have been completely crushed from the first day of Congress to the last if the Left Wing on the council had seized their opportunity… there is now the greatest opportunity in our history for those leaders claiming to be left-wingers to come out boldly and take a prominent place in the revolutionary movement – they must do this or they, too, will be forced to take up a position no different from that of the Right Wing."[37]

But these mild criticisms of the Left were not systematic and did not drive home to the working class, through Communist Party members, the real political deficiencies of the Left or indicate the role that they in particular could play in the event of a head-on collision of the classes. Yet the role of the Right, and particularly the Left, was clearly exposed at the Labour Party Conference in Liverpool barely a month later. Trotsky had commented about the Scarborough TUC *apropos* the Left: "This sort of leftism remains only as long as it does not impose any practical obligations. As soon as the question of action arises the Lefts respectfully surrender the leadership to the Rights."[38]

This is a feature of the reformist Labour Left, with the exception of some like Tony Benn, who did to some extent confront the Right in the Labour Party in the election for deputy leader in the 1980s. However, he still clings today to a discredited 'Labour Party', which has transformed into a capitalist party. The political weaknesses of left reformism were shown in the battle of Liverpool City Council in the 1980s. In the upswing of the struggle, when the mass of the working class poured onto the political arena, in Liverpool in particular,[39] and 25 left councils appeared to be standing in solidarity against the Thatcher government, the Labour Lefts and even some of those in the trade unions such as National Union of Public Employees official Tom Sawyer – who straddled both – appeared to be supportive. But at bottom they were as terrified of the determination of the working class to defeat Thatcher as the right within the Labour Party. Any movement of the 'uncontrollable masses' inevitably comes into collision with leaders whose political programme amounts to left phrases. One by one they peeled off from supporting the Liverpool struggle and most invariably ended up in the camp of the Right. Neil Kinnock, erstwhile Tribunite left winger, wielded the knife on behalf of the ruling class and the Labour Right at the 1985 Labour Party Conference. Although not completely obvious to everybody at the time – it was for Militant – this marked the beginning of the end of the Labour Party as a distinct workers' party. Former left trade union leaders joined in the witch-hunt of Militant, such as Jack Dromey, of the Transport and General Workers' Union and formerly an organiser of the low-paid Grunwick workers' strike in the 1970s, who became the hammer of the left and particularly of Militant.

Labour Party Conference

Those Lefts, who the Communist Party placed so much faith in, were to play as baleful a role at the 1925 Labour Party Conference as their descendants were to do at the 1984 and 1985 Labour Party conferences and after. In 1924, the Labour Party Conference had rejected the affiliation of the Communist Party to the Labour Party but a motion that no member of the Communist Party be eligible for membership of the Labour Party was only carried by a small majority. This provoked big opposition with something like 100 Constituency Labour Parties calling for its rescinding at the 1925 conference. From the outset of the 1925 conference, its chairman struck a different note to what had been heard at Scarborough just one month before. C.P. Cramp of the railway workers declared that he recognised the class struggle but the movement needed to be creative. He then went on to spell out what this meant: "In our practice as a political party we do actually transcend the conflict of classes; we direct our energies to constructive work and ask for the cooperation of all classes."[40] These honeyed phrases were uttered on the very eve of the greatest industrial conflict the working class was to experience. In the run-up to the conference, the opposition to the exclusion of the Communist Party amongst the rank and file was powerful.

Rhondda Borough Labour Party, for instance, held a special conference towards the end of February 1925 and considered the question of Communist-Labour relations. On the affiliation of the local Communist Party to the Rhondda Borough Labour Party the vote was: 12,090 for, 5,068 against. On the endorsement of Communist Party members as Labour Party candidates: 11,367 for, 4,437 against. On the question of the right of individual Communists to Labour Party membership, the conference unanimously voted in favour. Interestingly, the CP in a statement calling for resistance to the right-wing witch-hunting methods of the Labour leadership, stated: "The Communist Party stands for the maintenance of the federal principle of the Labour Party."[41] This, of course, is the general principle upon which the Labour Party itself was founded and is something which should be central in the formation of a new mass workers' party in Britain. However, the CP in 1925 was much more advanced and democratic than some erstwhile Left groups today, even some on the 'far left' like the Socialist Workers Party, who reject the federal principle in new formations of the working class.

In the 1980s it was Thatcher and Tebbit in the House of Commons, boosted by denunciatory articles of *Militant* in *The Times*, who demanded that the Labour leaders should act "responsibly" and drive us out of Labour's ranks. The same task was undertaken by the capitalist press in the run-up to the Liverpool conference of the Labour Party in 1925. *The Observer* played first fiddle in the witch-hunt against *Militant* with an infamous article by Nora Beloff in 1975 denouncing *Militant* as an alleged "party within a party" within Labour. In 1925, the same journal demanded: "If these resolutions [demanding the exclusion of the CP] are carried, Labour will have nailed its colours… to the Parliamentary mast. Its break with the Minority Movement in the trade unions will be complete."[42] Sir Alfred Mond, the leading bourgeois industrialist, fulminated that the Labour leaders "must decide whether they wish to be regarded as responsible statesmen or not". He asked "how much longer they were going to tolerate the canker which was eating at their hearts?"[43] The right-wing Labour leaders duly responded to this pressure, and the Left remained completely silent at this conference. We saw a similar display of Pontius Pilate-ism at the 1985 Labour Party conference when Kinnock made his infamous attack on *Militant*. The

Labour Left remained silent, with the exception of those like Eric Heffer and Tony Benn, while former Lefts like Blunkett danced to the tune of Kinnock.

In 1925, trade union leaders like Bevin were in cahoots with MacDonald in driving out the Communist Party after the Liverpool conference. MacDonald said: "As Mr Bevin assured you, he and I have a little bit of a row occasionally. Why not? Provided we are in the same spirit, holding the same view... Division on certain policies held by men with the same spirit, certainly within the same movement; but with different philosophies and different outlooks, no..."[44] Bevin's stance at Liverpool was not an accident and foreshadowed his role during the General Strike. The same goes for the erstwhile Lefts, who sat on their hands, remained silent, while their 'allies', the Communist Party, in the united front of the 'Anglo-Russian Trade Union Committee', were cast out of the Labour Party.

Liverpool, a warning

The capitalist press was beside itself in praising the decisions of the Liverpool conference. In an uncanny echo of the 1980s, they hailed the decisions to expel the CP almost in the same phrases that would be used in relation to the expulsion of *Militant* 60 years later. The *Financial Times* declared: "Investment [read the capitalists], evidently, is greatly relieved by the testimony afforded at the Liverpool congress to the fact that the Reds are not going to have things their own way."[45] *The Times* followed suit with "so far so good... Communism must not only be condemned; it must be cast out."[46] Thomas joined in: "Smash the Reds or they will smash us," he wrote.[47]

The Communist Party denounced the decisions of the congress. Harry Pollitt was to write later, in his autobiography: "The Liverpool conference contained the germ of the abject sell-out of 1931."[48] It could be added, also of the General Strike of 1926. And it was not just the Right but the Left leaders also, as we shall see, who were fully complicit in the sell-out which was to come. The Communist Party neither sufficiently criticised sharply enough the Left's role at Liverpool, nor did it draw all the conclusions necessary about their future role in a head-on collision of the classes. Palme Dutt was to write after the General Strike was derailed in June 1926 in *Labour Monthly*: "Every prediction, policy and warning of the revolutionaries has been justified by the events of May."[49] Unfortunately, that was not the case. Any 'criticisms' amounted, as we have seen from the above, to a mild slap on the wrists of Swales, Purcell, Hicks and Co. Palme Dutt in November 1925, said Klugmann, "stressed the complete silence of the non-Communist Left who allowed MacDonald 'to ride roughshod over them'".[50] And what is the comment of this historian of the Communist Party, many years after the event? "This was indeed a significant aspect of the conference. The left-wing trade union leaders, some of whom had taken a prominent part at Scarborough, failed completely to fight in the harder conditions of Liverpool."[51]

Contrast this mild rebuke from a considerable historical distance to what Trotsky wrote, as a means of a warning to the Communist Party, in January 1926: "At the same time as the British unions fraternise with the Soviet trade unions which are under the leadership of communists, at Liverpool the British Labour Party which rests upon these same unions expels British communists from its ranks thus preparing a government-fascist operation to smash their organisations. It would be criminal to forget for one day that Lefts such as Brailsford[52] and even Lansbury[53] in effect approved of the Liverpool conference resolution and blamed the communists for it all. It is true that when indignation with the reactionary police-state spirit of the Liverpool conference revealed itself from the lower ranks, the 'Left' leaders readily changed their line. But to evaluate them one must take both sides of the matter into account. Revolutionaries need a good memory. Messrs. 'Lefts' do not have a line of their own. They will go on swinging to the right under the pressure of bourgeois-Fabian reaction and to the left under the pressure of the masses. In difficult moments these pious Christians are always ready to play the part, if not of Herod then of Pontius Pilate and facing the British working class there are many difficult moments ahead."[54]

If the policy of political intransigence, recommended by Trotsky, had been adhered to consistently over a period of time, the British working class, particularly its most combative and politically developed layers, would have been much better prepared than they were in the events of the General Strike. Many of the middle-class Lefts, quite apart from those in the trade unions, had sympathy for Soviet power, for the Soviet trade unions and even, as we have seen, for a rapprochement with the Comintern so long as it remained at a distance. But they did not seriously challenge the hold of right-wing reformism in the Labour Party or seek to break out of the narrow limits of parliamentarianism. In this, as Trotsky pointed out, not *ex post facto* but in the course of the movements that unfolded in the course of 1925 and 1926, is an element of the deference that the middle class display towards a "strong state power". Trotsky added: "Of course the petty-bourgeois who has turned his face towards the Soviet Union is more progressive than the petty-bourgeois who goes on his knees before the United States. This is a step forward. But one cannot build revolutionary perspectives on such a deference."[55]

Working-class support for their class who had taken power in Russia was of a deep-going determined character and was demonstrated with the threat of a general strike that met and defeated Churchill's plans to intervene in Poland in 1920.

Radical middle-class leftism, characterised by the Left within the Labour Party at that stage, particularly gathered around the Independent Labour Party, was ephemeral and vacillating and could quite easily be turned into passivity when the Right attacked the Left, particularly the Marxists. It could even turn into a virulent anti-Marxism, as we have seen many times in the history of the British labour movement.

Within a fortnight of the Liverpool conference of the Labour Party, 12 leaders of the Communist Party were arrested and subsequently imprisoned. The expulsion of the Communist Party by Labour's right-wing political 'police' was the signal for the capitalist police and state to arrest its leaders. Something similar happened 60 years later when Kinnock engineered the eviction from the Labour Party of the leaders of the 47 Liverpool councillors, the 'Mersey Militants' like Tony Mulhearn, Harry Smith, who wasn't expelled then but was driven out later, and Paul Astbury, followed shortly afterwards with the removal of the councillors from office, hefty fines and a threat to sequestrate their homes if they could not pay. In 1925, by their silence and acquiescence the Left were as responsible as the Right but in November, one month after the Liverpool conference, the Left's failure to fight was put down to "bad organisation". *Labour Monthly* commented: "The Right Wing at [Scarborough] preferred, like Brer Fox, to 'lay low and say nuffin', rather than to fight for their programme openly. At Liverpool the opposite was the case. The work was conducted by a well-organised and well-oiled machine. But at Liverpool the extreme flank of the Left Wing – the Communist Party – came out into the open. The left element proved to be disconnected and badly organised both at Liverpool and at Scarborough."[56]

But in February 1926 some serious criticisms were directed at the reformist Left by William Paul (editor of the *Sunday Worker*). He wrote: "The determined attempt made at the Edinburgh, London and Liverpool Labour Party conferences to expel [the Communists] made a very deep impression upon those who imagined that they were left wingers because they used Left Wing phrases… When deeds were demanded the left wingers failed. None of the left wingers, outside of the small Communist group, dared to put forward an alternative programme [at the London and Liverpool conferences]… The main reason for the collapse of the Left Wing at the big conferences was their lack of organised contact and the absence of any common line of action. And this weakness, let it be emphasised, is still preventing the rise of a real Left Wing that means business… The Left Wing parliamentarians are not afraid to use bold phrases in the constituencies when they are amongst the rank and file. But they are not prepared to organise the rank and filers and give them a socialist policy."[57] If this approach had been consistently advanced and linked to concrete suggestions of what needed to be done by the Left and the working class, then it would have helped the working class to prepare for what was to come.

Battle lines drawn

The bourgeois were encouraged by the shift to the Right, and the open quiescence of the Left to this at Liverpool, as well as the quasi-Left phraseology at Scarborough, not backed by action. Nevertheless, they also prepared to build up their forces for a head-on collision if the trade union and Labour tops were not capable of derailing the movement. In October Churchill, irritated by the many threats of future trouble made by Cook, replied to him in a like manner: "Mr Cook had said openly that he would force a general election in the spring by means of a strike, or that he would force nationalisation by means of a strike. If those were the counsels which were to prevail they had to be fought to the fullest extent."[58] Churchill had been explicit in July about why the government retreated on Red Friday: "We decided to postpone the crisis in the hope of averting it, or, if not of averting it, of coping effectually with it when the time came."[59]

Not only were the eyes of the world working class turned towards Britain, international capital was taking a keen interest in events here. The *New York Times* wrote in August that the government must "Seek to arm itself with legal powers to deal with a nationwide strike not only in coal mining, but in transportation and engineering services, in shipbuilding and the textile trades. For, behind the immediate threat of a coal strike, there stood visible to the eyes of Mr Baldwin the menace of the one big union quitting work and paralysing the industrial and commercial life of England. The government has been, and is now, without weapons to meet such an emergency."[60] The same journal, two weeks later, returned to the same theme, "urging not merely legal protection against future general strikes, but the formation of a citizens' volunteer brigade such as Sweden had established during the great strike of 1909".[61]

A rabid right-wing journal, *La Revue de Paris*, wrote in retrospect after the General Strike: "Had the trade unions ordered the General Strike at the date originally fixed by the Soviets, of 1 August 1925, the British government would have been conquered." It went on to say that public opinion would have been with the government but would have been insufficiently organised. "Mr Baldwin, reckoning the disproportion between the forces of order and of revolution, played for time."[62] Interestingly Crook, an American writer on the General Strike, wrote that "the French notion that all large-scale industrial disturbances must mean revolution… is probably not far from the facts."[63] Leave aside the hyperbole about the "Soviets" being behind developments in Britain, nevertheless there is an understanding in these lines that, in Britain at least, a general strike could open the floodgates to revolution. There was to be much discussion later on the issue of the General Strike as to whether it was a revolutionary opportunity or not. But the serious representatives of capital, both in Britain and worldwide, had no doubts about the potential revolutionary situation that could flow from this titanic conflict between labour and capital.

One week after the Labour Party conference, the Tories met in Brighton and Prime Minister Baldwin informed them that the government was considering prosecuting the leaders of the Communist Party. The capitalists were eager to remove serious organisations capable of acting as a rallying point for the working class. Although it was small, insufficiently critical of the leaders of the Left, and thereby had not prepared fully politically from a Marxist point of view, nevertheless the CP did conduct energetic propaganda and agitation on the issue of factory committees, councils of action, raised criticisms of the Right and warned about their lack of preparedness for the coming conflict. One week after Baldwin's speech, the police raided the Communist Party headquarters and twelve of the principal leaders of the party were arrested. They were arraigned at the Old Bailey on charges of seditious libel, for "publishing the writings of Mister Lenin". [64]

Jailings

Just as in the 1980s the attack on the Liverpool Militants encouraged the state to persecute the heroic 47 councillors there and those in Lambeth, fine them and drive them from office, so too the shift to the right in the Labour Party in the 1920s opened the way for repression, with its first victims being the CP leaders. This was just the start because within a week of their arrest, militant miners, members of the South Wales Miners' Federation, working in the anthracite mines of the Amman Valley, were also in the dock. In fact, this area of South Wales was the scene of an incredible movement of the miners, reflected in the strike of the anthracite miners in 1925. the historians of the South Wales miners wrote: "New forms of action emerged. There was an unusual aggressive willingness: to escalate their strike; use mass mobile picket lines; a network of spies (which penetrated the police), riots and disturbances. It led to the control of the town of Ammanford [by the miners] for a week. There was a remarkable and widespread acceptance of prison sentences and gaoled leaders were feted like heroes."[65] In all 167 miners were tried over a three-week period, being accused of "terror" towards "His Majesty's subjects". The jury was composed of the Welsh landed proprietor class, with colonels, three majors, a captain and a knight dominating it. Fifty miners were sentenced to terms of imprisonment with one receiving 17 months behind bars.

However, the arrest and imprisonment of the 12 Communist Party leaders, taken together with the actions against the miners, indicated to the working class movement that general repression was in the offing against all those who stood in the way of the capitalists and their government's plans to crush them. An unprecedented solidarity mood and campaign resulted from this involving more than 70 Labour MPs as well as literary figures such as George Bernard Shaw standing bail for the CP leaders. The mood generated on this even affected those who had remained silent while the CP was driven out of the Labour Party just one month before. Big meetings and mass marches of up to 15,000 to Wandsworth prison were organised demanding the release of the "class war" prisoners.

Leading Left figures in the Labour Party like George Lansbury – he was one of those who disgracefully stepped aside when the CP was expelled – were now compelled by the pressure of the working class to join in the campaign for the release of the prisoners. A "huge solidarity rally"[66] was held in London's Albert Hall, hired in the personal name of Lansbury on 7 March 1926. Lansbury later declared this "was one of the biggest meetings ever held in London."[67] *Militant*, in the 1980s, held two rallies in this venue, with a capacity of 5,000, until it became too small and we were forced to move to Alexandra Palace. Of the 1925 meeting Lansbury recalled: "I got the whole audience to stand and repeat after me the slogans for which the Communists were sent to prison. To call upon the workers not to go into the capitalist army or navy or air force, for no worker to join the military, and for those who were in the military or navy not to fire on their comrades who are workers."[68] Cook and the Communist Party had published leaflets demanding that soldiers "don't shoot". This was denounced as vehemently by the right-wing Labour and trade union leaders as the capitalists themselves.

The CP was not only "seditious" but was, according to the capitalist press, in the pay of Moscow financed by its "gold", etc. This was as ludicrous then as the similar accusations against *Militant* in the 1980s. The pressure from below compelled trade union leaders like George Hicks to comment that the persecution of the Communist Party put them "in the same position as the trade unions were during the early part of last [nineteenth] century."[69] A.J. Cook, just before the arrests, in a message to the *Sunday Worker*, issued yet one more warning to the right wing in the labour movement: "I warn the right-wing leaders in our movement to cease their attacks upon the left wing. They are encouraging every element of reaction in this country to destroy our militant fighters. If these are beaten, the path lies open for the propertied interests to smash those who call themselves moderate."[70] The "moderates", however, when push came to shove, would prefer to defend the "propertied interests" rather than risk going outside the bounds of capitalist society.

It is true that some right-wing Labour leaders like MacDonald were compelled to mumble that it was "a disservice" (to whom?) to prosecute the Communist Party at that stage. His main complaint, however, was that the CP's "potentialities for sedition", that is having an effect on the working class, had only been increased by the imprisonments![71] J.R. Clynes, Home Secretary in MacDonald's government, complained bitterly that the Communist leaders were being "lifted to the level of martyrs".[72] R. Page Arnot, who was to play a significant role in the General Strike in the North East of England, points out in his book that the "arrests and persecutions [of the CP leaders] were judged to be part of the government's preparedness for the coming offensive; it was an attempt to strike terror."[73]

Fascists

If there was any doubt just how seriously the British ruling class were preparing dictatorial measures, if they should prove necessary, listen to the words of Foreign Secretary Austen Chamberlain as he excused the Mussolini regime in Italy at that time: "I believe [Mussolini] to be accused of crimes in which he had no share, and I suspect him to have connived unwillingly at other outrages which he would have prevented if he could."[74] Churchill, Chamberlain's co-member of Baldwin's cabinet, was also to talk in the 1920s and 1930s of his "admiration" of Mussolini – "your movement has rendered a service to the whole world" – and hoping that Britain could find a similar figure in its hour of need![75] Without a doubt, as we have seen with the formation of the OMS, the British bourgeois taste faced with a similar dilemma as their Italian counterparts would not have hesitated to lean on fascistic methods, if not the small fascist organisations themselves, if they could have got away with it, in order to defeat the working class. As early as 1923, 'The Patriot', the Duke of Northumberland's paper, carried an advert from a Miss Rotha Lintorn-Orman, founder of the British Fascists, asking for recruits to a "British Fascisti" to act as an organised force to "combat the Red revolution".[76] In November 1925, the British Fascists in a manifesto described itself as: "A body of patriotic citizens who will place their resources at the disposal of a constitutional government in the maintenance of law and order, and will be capable of resisting, by force if absolutely necessary, any attempt at a revolution which aims at the forcible overthrow of the British Constitution and the Empire." It declared its intention to enforce "severe measures against disloyalty, to suppress the Communist Sunday Schools, to abolish the dole and to uphold the fundamental principles of free speech provided it was not seditious".[77] As Florey pointed out, "at about the same time" as these comments were made, a headline appeared in the *Daily Express*: "Mussolini gags Italy – newspapers and parties to be suppressed – fascist 'purge' – the death penalty extended"![78]

The more militant fascists left the parent body to form the National Fascisti in 1924: "They were a tougher, far more arrogant group from the middle and upper class."[79]

It was they who kidnapped Harry Pollitt in Liverpool. When they dissolved into the OMS they were welcomed with open arms by the state. George Lansbury asked Baldwin on 16 November 1925, whether he was aware no action was being taken by the Director of Public Prosecutions in connection with the admission of an attack on a motor van of the *Daily Herald*, mentioned earlier. He also asked the Home Secretary if he was also "aware of the existence of certain fascist and other organisations and societies organised in armed forces – drilling – in uniform."[80]

However, the "Chief Constable of Liverpool was not worried"[81] about the wanton and mischievous exploits of the British fascists. According to *The Times*, "Liverpool will be the starting point of a new move on the part of the Fascisti. Arrangements have been made for members in the Liverpool area to become special constables and to drill at the hall of the city police. Captain W.J. Lewis, Commander of the Fascisti in the Lancashire and Wirral area, stated that officers of the organisation were to take the oath at police headquarters today, and the swearing in of other members would follow in due course. It was expected that between 2,000 and 3,000 would thus be enrolled… 'We are trying to show the way to the whole country, but so far Liverpool is the only place where arrangements have been made with the police,' [said Lewis]… An official of the Liverpool police said on Saturday if members of the Fascisti offered themselves as special constables there was no reason why they should not be enrolled, provided they were suitable and met the requirements laid down. If they joined they would be drilled in precisely the same way as the constabulary was drilled now."

As we have explained above, British fascism was a very small and inconsequential force at this stage. Fascists were seen as auxiliaries by the state forces who were themselves preparing harsh measures, potentially dictatorial in character, against the working class in Britain. Therefore the pressure from Lansbury and other Labour leaders for prosecution of the fascists, even when their crimes were recognised, was ignored and the charges were dropped: "The reason given was because the evidence was insufficient to support the charges."[82]

4 On the eve of battle

owever, the repression against the Communist Party leaders and the anthracite miners went ahead and were clearly meant to intimidate the working class as a whole. The resistance, however, to these measures produced consternation in the ranks of the ruling class. The membership of the Communist Party increased and the Communist Party and the Minority Movement did warn, in general terms, of the dangers that lay ahead. There was disquiet within the ranks of the miners, echoed by the trade union movement as a whole, on the lack of any real sense of urgency in the TUC by the General Council or the Labour Party. Cook himself began to raise the question that if the miners wanted any initiative they themselves would have to supply it. There was therefore an attempt made to revive the Industrial Alliance.

This proposal broke down because Thomas, in a quite provocative manoeuvre, proposed that membership of the alliance should be dependent on a scheme of fusing together all the unions in one industry. This, although couched in "reason-

The lockout begins - 1 May 1926

able terms", ostensibly stood for one industrial union. But it was aimed at dragooning the Associated Society of Locomotive Engineers and Firemen (ASLEF), the train drivers union, into a larger federation against its will and this broke up the discussions.

The miners then turned back to the General Council of the TUC, upon whom, allegedly, the miners were to become "dependent".[1] It was correct to exert pressure on the General Council to organise union support for the miners but as important was the need to turn to the rank and file of the unions. The General Council, for its part, urged the miners to wait for the decisions of the Samuel Commission, on which, it must be remembered, not a single miners' representative sat, unlike the Sankey Commission which preceded Red Friday. This commission was stuffed with establishment figures, starting with Sir Herbert Samuel himself, a top Liberal politician from a finance capital background and a former under-secretary in the Home Office. After 1919 he was British High Commissioner in Palestine. Fellow commissioners included a managing partner in a banking house, the chairman of Lloyd's cotton firm, Sir William Beveridge – who would later become famous through his report in the Second World War into the proposals for the welfare state – but who had been a former leader writer on the *Morning Post* newspaper and a member of the Board of Trade. We shall see just how 'sympathetic' this individual and the other members of the Commission were to the miners' case.

To go over the role of the General Council on the eve of the greatest battle between the classes in Britain, particularly in the months of late 1925 and early 1926 before the General Strike, is to reveal the breathtaking complacency, if not sabotage, of these 'leaders'. Walter Citrine, general secretary of the TUC, admitted later in 1927 at the conference of trade union executives called to draw up the balance sheet of the strike, that "it was known [by the TUC leaders] that preparations had been made so elaborately by the government as to make the possibilities of success much less than in 1925".[2] Yet nothing was done with this knowledge to prepare the working class. This wing of the TUC, the Right, was therefore the architect of the defeat, which they believed would therefore discredit "once and forever" militant class struggle policies in the trade union movement.

A bluff?

Even Bevin probably believed that pressure from the mobilised trade union movement could repeat the "trick" of 1925 and compel the government to retreat. Essentially empirical, he therefore was undisguised in spelling out later the unpreparedness of the General Council on the eve of the battle. At the same conference where Citrine spoke, Bevin stated: "With regard to the preparations for the strike, there were no preparations until April 27 [1926] and I do not want anyone to go away from this conference under the impression that the General Council had any particular plan to run this movement. In fact, the General Council did not sit down to draft the plans until they were called together on April 27, [six days before the General Strike started] and it is better for everybody to know the task was thrown upon us from April 27 to May 1, and when that task is understood you will be able to appreciate, not the little difficulties, but the wonderful response and organisation we had."[3] The "wonderful response" had nothing to do with the abilities of the General Council but the marvellous combative fighting spirit that was unleashed amongst the working class once the General Strike had been called.

How did the Left and the Communist Party prepare in these vital months? The *Workers' Weekly* is full of calls for the working class to be prepared. On 1 January 1926, the main headline on page one of the paper was "1926 – great clash coming".[4] It called for resistance to all wage cuts, to set up factory committees. It also demanded that the General Council call an all-union executive conference to prepare, demanded the setting up of a workers' defence corps and the release of class war prisoners. It also echoed A.J. Cook's demand of "Not a penny off the pay: not a minute on the day". But again, the slogan of 'All power to the General Council' was put forward when it was clear what the right wing would do with this power in a "great clash". Rather than just denouncing the right wing, the Communist Party, even with a small force, should have been consistently and insistently warning about what the Right was likely to do, and demanding and criticising the Left for not adopting a clearly different, fighting, active approach from the Right. Sometimes the Left were criticised but without naming names. For instance, in the *Workers' Weekly* of 15 January 1926, in the report of the CP's Executive Committee, it refers to "self-styled 'left wingers' who are afraid to associate with the Communists in joint effort… because Mr MacDonald and the right wing will be displeased with them will always find excuses for refusing to put up a real fight for socialism".[5] This is fair enough as it goes but it contains no definite or concrete criticisms of the TUC General Council Left for not coming out with a serious programme of opposition, of action, against the right-wing General Council.

Moreover, it still carried uncritical and favourable reports of these left wingers on international issues. For instance, a few columns away from the foregoing criticisms of 'left wingers' we read: "Defending the necessity of world unity, Purcell said that the European and American workers were faced with two alternatives: 'Either they would raise the workers of the colonial countries – China, India, etc. – up to their own level or they would be forced to sink to theirs'."[6] This is the same Purcell who remained silent, as we have seen, when the Communist Party was expelled at the

Liverpool conference of the Labour Party. It was the same individual who was preparing to bloc with the right wing during the General Strike.

The columns of the *Workers' Weekly* also revealed the contradictions in the Communist Party's position on this struggle, how they were torn between support for Stalin who represented the bureaucratic elite which was gradually emerging in Russia and appreciation of Trotsky's political clarity, particularly in his analysis of the situation in Britain. We can read, for instance, in three articles by T.A. Jackson in editions of the *Workers' Weekly* in February and March 1926, a laudatory defence of Trotsky's *Where is Britain Going?* against the avalanche of bourgeois and reformist criticism that had met its publication. The first article was sub-headed: "Showing how Trotsky trounces the Fabians and all other Tories – making the official Labour critics to grimace and lie". Jackson writes: "Trotsky, as a man qualified to speak by years of study, and by an all but unique practical experience of economic and social crises, examines in his book first the general trend of Britain's development… and secondly the leadership immediately operating upon the British labour movement. He finds this latter, for reasons given, utterly inadequate to the immensity of the emergency before it."[7]

What Jackson doesn't explain is that Trotsky urged in his book and in his letters on Britain that the Communist Party should criticise not just the right-wing leadership but the Left as well. He states that Trotsky "sees salvation for Britain only in … the leadership of the struggle [given] to persons and bodies directly responsive to the struggling masses – with their consciousness sharpened and intensified as it will be by the actual practical struggle itself."[8] Jackson's conclusion was: "We, for our part, stand by Trotsky, not merely in his main line but in every essential detail… we see in [the] evasions and misrepresentations of the *[Daily] Herald* and of *Forward* a stronger proof of the truth of Trotsky's case than any that even he has produced."[9]

R. Palme Dutt was, at this stage, perhaps the Communist Party's leading theoretician before he later degenerated into an apologist for Stalinism. He wrote in a long, 18-page review in *Labour Monthly* a laudatory article about Trotsky's book. In answer to those who criticise Trotsky for failing to understand the English situation, Palme Dutt writes: "This self-ignorance of the reformist idealist school, which is so naïvely exposed in the reviews of Trotsky and their 'British' repudiations of his 'Russian' standpoint, can be illustrated in a very simple form. A challenge may safely be issued to the critics to name a single book by a single English author or politician, bourgeois or labour leader, which is as close to the essentials of the English situation as Trotsky's book. It cannot be done." He concluded: "The English working class has cause to be grateful to Trotsky for his book; and to hope that he will not stay his hand at this short sketch, but will carry forward his work of interpretation, polemic and elucidation, and elaborate his analysis further, which is so much needed in England. For despite all the national Philistines, the problem of England, more than of any other country, will only be served by the united force of the whole international movement."[10]

Palme Dutt would become more than a little embarrassed by his praise for Trotsky when he later learnt to bend the truth in Stalin's school of falsification about Trotsky's ideas and role. The trends were evident in the *Workers' Weekly* in 1926 as to how the Communist Party would develop in the future, given the theoretical weaknesses precisely on the 'international' issues that Palme Dutt refers to. And there was no more important international issue than the struggle then under way between the bureaucratic conservative clique of Stalin and Co., and the Left Opposition, which was defending the international perspectives of the Russian Revolution as well as the programme of democracy within the Communist Party of the Soviet Union and in the state. Yet on 1 January 1926, the *Workers' Weekly* hailed a speech by Stalin at the Fourteenth Russian Communist Party Congress two weeks before: "The great speech by Comrade Stalin, General Secretary... lasted five hours and during the whole of the time he held the rapt attention of the 1,260 delegates present." In this speech, according to the *Workers' Weekly*, the "Congress hailed with a burst of applause Stalin's declaration that the party would liquidate as painlessly, and with the same unanimity, as it conquered Trotskyism", the "richer peasantry".[11] What the *Workers' Weekly* fails to add is that it was the very policies of Stalin and Bukharin – with the latter urging the peasants to "get rich" – that had precisely allowed the pro-capitalist sentiments to develop in the Russian villages reflected in the rise of the rich peasants. Trotsky and the Left Opposition had warned against this. These policies of Stalin led to a virtual civil war between a state increasingly dominated by a rising bureaucratic elite and the challenge that it met from the rich peasants – 'kulaks' – who threatened the social foundations of the October Revolution.

These international issues were not just noises off stage, of no relevance to the burning questions in the British labour movement and particularly the General Strike. A rising bureaucratic centrist elite around Stalin and Bukharin stood for diplomacy and unprincipled compromises with the Lefts who were their allies on an international level in the Anglo-Russian Trade Union Committee. Trotsky, as we have seen, stood for a policy of political intransigence, of criticism and political preparation above all for the inevitable retreat of reformism. The Communist Party, through the *Workers' Weekly*, could not be faulted in its criticisms of the General Council, particularly of the Right, in the run-up to 3 May. It called in its issue of 15

January for the "organisation of workers' defence corps". It also called for the summoning by the General Council of a conference of trade union executive committees, in accordance with the Scarborough decision. But the rider to this was for this conference once more to "give wider powers to the General Council to lead the whole workers' industrial army".[12] This inevitably engendered illusions that the General Council, dominated by the Right, with the compliance of the erstwhile Left, was capable of seriously preparing for the collision to come.

Samuel responds

This was evident even at the Minority Movement conference of March 1926, two months before the General Strike. Present were 883 delegates representing almost one million trade unionists. Once more the NMM advanced radical demands, for instance, for the trades councils to constitute themselves as councils of action. Yet this was undermined by the call for the "concentration of trade union power in the General Council of the Trade Union Congress – [which] will prove the wisdom and far-sightedness of our policy."[13] This conference met just a few weeks after the Samuel Commission finally reported. The Commission had been set up in September 1925 and opened its proceedings to the public in the following October. The looming clash with the miners as the flashpoint dominated discussion at every level of society. So great was the interest in the Commission's findings that its final 300-page report, originally published at one shilling (5p) a copy and then reissued at threepence (1p), sold over 100,000 copies, the official best seller of this kind of publication until then. However, Samuel soon regretted his return from the tranquillity of Lake Garda in Italy, bemoaning in private the class polarisation he witnessed: "I can do nothing, as far as I can see at present."[14]

In an attempt to break the deadlock and in the well-worn tradition of the British ruling class of holding a club in one hand while at the same time uttering soothing words, he met the miners' leaders Herbert Smith and A.J. Cook to inform them of the Commission's recommendations. The miners had made it absolutely clear that there must be no reduction in wages and stood for the "mines for the miners". They had approached the famous socialist historian, R.H. Tawney, who was also, coincidentally, Beveridge's brother-in-law, and had been a member of the Sankey Commission, to prepare a scheme for nationalisation. At the same time, the Labour Research Department, under the influence of the Communist Party, prepared their own nationalisation scheme for the miners. But over an "agreeable meal" for Cook and Smith, the miners' leaders were informed that the commissioners would not feel it right to recommend any renewal of the coal subsidy after 30 April. "Sacrifices" on the part of the miners were suggested. All of this was, of course, couched in terms of "temporary" increases in hours or a cut in wages. The commissioners complained later that Smith's mind was like "granite" and that Cook was a "drunken dragonfly" because he repeated the "dreary rigmarole" of "not a minute off the day not a penny off the pay".[15] Yet the attitude of Smith and Cook was no less firm than that in the mining areas and amongst the working class as a whole.

Unfortunately, neither Smith nor Cook took these revelations out to the public opinion of the working class movement. Therefore, the masses were not adequately prepared for the Commission's proposals, which rejected nationalisation (but which nevertheless repeated the Sankey Commission recommendation for the public ownership of coal royalties). The Commission went over the long-term crisis in the coal industry and even admitted that they were "not well impressed by the existing organisation of the industry". Beveridge wrote later about the mine owners as a body: "I found myself saying harsh things about them."[16] The report admitted that many mines were old, badly designed, inefficient and badly run. In sanitised language, the report even called for "improvements" in the miners' working conditions. As well as this they admonished the owners and called on them to discontinue charging the miners as a body with deliberate attempts to destroy the prosperity of the industry, in order to compel its nationalisation, and to stop accusing the miners of restricting output. Despite all of this, however, they rejected nationalisation: "We are not satisfied that the scheme proposed to us [by the miners, the Labour Party and the TUC] is workable or that it offers a clear social gain."[17] The Commission predated Blair by 80 years in its approach to industries ruined by the capitalists. The diagnosis is devastating, the remedy, however, is to continue as before! It took 20 more years of ruinous private ownership before the Labour government of 1945 was compelled to step in and nationalise the mining industry with, of course, overcompensation to the ex-owners.

The Samuel Commission proposed reorganisation of the industry at some indefinite date in the future but suggested immediate reductions in miners' wages. It was not the bosses or the well-heeled but the poverty-stricken million-fold miners of Britain who had to take a temporary step down today, the commission argued in effect, in order to advance two or three steps tomorrow. Such is always the refrain of capitalism when confronted with the crisis of their system. The 'jam tomorrow' never really materialises. In any case, this is a system controlled by the capitalists; they should bear the burden of any 'sacrifices'. Instead, Samuel spoke of the need to "cut costs" – i.e. decrease wages and increase the hours – of the working class, in order to boost the "inadequate profits" of the industry.

Official reaction to the report, including at the top of the labour movement, was initially restrained. Desperately hoping for some kind of class compromise,

MacDonald eventually waxed lyrical about the Samuel Commission's conclusions: "It is a conspicuous landmark in the history of political thought and is indeed one of the strongest indictments of private enterprise that has ever been issued as an official paper. The stars in their courses are fighting for us. The miners' leaders have very wisely advised that tongues should be silent for the time being."[18] However, the miners' tongues, particularly that of Cook, were not silent for long. The aim of the report, with the compliance of right-wing Labour and trade union leaders, was clearly to split the working class away from the miners and to picture them as "unreasonable" unless they accepted the recommendations of the commission.

However, the Labour Rights' attempted embargo on discussion could not hold, as Arthur Cook declared in South Wales on 14 March, that there would be no wage cuts to miners' wages "whatsoever". The National Minority Movement and the Communist Party came out implacably against any acceptance of the main demands in the Samuel Commission report. But even then, while making many militant demands, the congress of the NMM in March 1926 still repeated that, "The real central body through which we must function is the General Council of the Trades Union Congress."[19] Yet as one historian of the strike commented later: "There could have been little doubt among Communist and Minority Movement leaders that most members of the Industrial Committee and probably also of the General Council, were determined to prevent not simply a revolutionary strike, but a large-scale strike of any kind. It was believed – or more accurately, hoped – that the left-wing trade union leaders would be able and willing to assert themselves when the time came."[20] The language of Left trade union leaders, as R.P. Dutt, editor of *Labour Monthly* observed optimistically after Red Friday, "is the clearest indication of the advance of the British working class to revolution".[21]

No room for manoeuvre

A mood of expectation and even a certain eagerness for the coming battle developed amongst the miners and the broader working class. This put pressure on the General Council to stand firm behind the miners, particularly in view of the fact that on 19 February, before the Samuel Commission had reported, the Industrial Committee had issued a statement of support for the miners: "There was to be no reduction in wages, no increase in working hours, and no interference with the principle of national agreements. This is the position of the trade union movement today."[22] This was not whistled out of the air but reflected the overall consciousness of the workers on the railways, in engineering, etc., who clearly understood that if the miners were defeated they would be dragged down as well. The right-wing trade union leaders like Thomas attempted to renege on the February statement of solidarity with the miners by immediately declaring after the

Commission had reported that it was the basis for an "equitable settlement of outstanding difficulties". Thomas also urged the General Council not to "acquiesce in a mere slogan" by which he meant the trade union movement's opposition to a reduction in wages.[23]

The miners' leaders approached the General Council, following a crucial national delegate conference of the union, and had sought reassurances of continued support, but they were met with prevarication and pressure for further "negotiations". The Industrial Committee of the TUC re-stated: "Its previous declarations in support of the miners' efforts to obtain an equitable settlement of outstanding difficulties." But it also reaffirmed that negotiations "should be continued without delay in order to obtain a clear understanding with regard to the report of the Coal Commission and to reduce points of difference to the smallest possible dimensions."[24] In reality, there were not "small points of difference" but an unbridgeable chasm which was opening up between the working class and the miners on the one side and the employers and the government on the other.

Throughout the winter of 1925-26 a gathering storm of opposition and discontent was manifest in the ranks of the working class. The huge meeting against the imprisonment of the Communist Party members and the anthracite miners in South Wales, the open preparations of the government for a showdown, the growth in the Minority Movement, and the general politicisation that had gripped British society undermined the grounds for compromise, not withstanding all the efforts of the TUC. Wherever they went, the miners could feel the groundswell of support amongst the working class for their cause. Moreover, the government itself was not all that enthusiastic about the Samuel Commission's proposals and declared it would only accept its recommendations if the miners and the owners also accepted. Baldwin advanced, through his Minister of Labour, who was himself a coal owner, an ultimatum to the miners. It bluntly declared: "Beyond 30 April the subsidy cannot go on."[25]

At the same time as the government was preparing for an extra-parliamentary struggle, the other side, the General Council, were frantically looking for compromises, the basis for which did not exist. The working class, for their part, at least its most combative elements, through the Minority Movement, were pressing to work "vigorously and perseveringly for the full and complete rejection of the Royal Commission's report" and demanded "nationalisation without compensation and full workers' control" of the mining industry.[26] At the same time, the mine owners decided to break national negotiations and go for wage talks at district level. When this was rejected, they posted notices at the pit heads that employment "on existing terms would cease on 30 April, the day the subsidy was to end".[27]

This attack spurred even the Industrial Committee of the TUC to condemn the owners for creating "ill-feeling and suspicion at a critical time" and asked to see Baldwin. Thomas was to state baldly what was, in effect, the guiding philosophy of the summits of the TUC at this stage when he spoke in Monmouthshire on 18 April. He declared: "To talk at this stage as if, in a few days, all the workers of the country are to be called out is not only letting loose passions that might be difficult to control, but it is not rendering the best service to the miners or anyone else." Instead of organising, mobilising, and encouraging the feeling that war was inevitable, Thomas pleaded, let them concentrate on finding a solution honourable and satisfactory to all sides.[28]

Rather than organising to build the strike, the right-wing trade union leaders, in cahoots with the right-wing Labour leaders like MacDonald and Henderson, were 'organising' for a defeat of the miners because the acceptance of the Samuel Commission report meant precisely that. They acted like the rich, selfish passengers on the Titanic, scrambling for lifeboats, kicking everyone including women and children out of the way in order to save their skins. Baldwin had met the Industrial Committee of the TUC on 13 April. He was as intransigent as ever but the TUC warned that unless the deadlock was broken, Cook and Smith would try to gain support at the following weekend's meeting of the Miners' International in Brussels. Baldwin was "unimpressed"; Frank Hodges, secretary of the Miners International, "had already expressed his approval of the Samuel Report and his intense dislike of Cook was no secret." Baldwin informed the Committee that they were "mistaken… if they thought he had granted the coal subsidy out of a funk. He had granted it because he was a pacifist [!] but if a pacifist was pushed too far he could be very combative and obstinate, and the Committee were not to think that the country's money was going to be poured out indefinitely".[29]

This had the desired effect on Thomas and he met Baldwin later, who made it clear that if there was a general strike "the pressure to restrict the powers of the trade unions would become irresistible. He [Baldwin] would be driven to deal with the political levy, the strike ballot and the Trade Disputes Act, and the Labour Party's chances of coming to power would be thrown back for years." Thomas, in turn, flew to MacDonald "to tell him into what desperate straits the miners' intransigence was leading them all".[30] More concerned about legal threats and parliamentary shadow boxing than the real plight of the miners and the working class, all he could see in this stubborn resistance was the leaders of the mineworkers' "intransigence".

This was far removed from what was happening below in the pits, the pit villages and in the working class communities. The Communist Party, through *Workers'*

Weekly, echoed this mood as the day of battle approached. It stated bluntly: "General Council gets cold feet – Circular refusing to call meeting on greater powers". The last part of this, for "greater powers" was, as we have seen, a constant refrain of the CP in 1924 and 1925 and was now repeated on the eve of battle. It declared: "If ever there was a time when the trade union movement needed a strong, militant general staff provided with the fullest possible power and authority, it is now."[31] But how could a General Council, which gets "cold feet", and had shown before the whole of the movement how pusillanimous it was, how blatant Thomas had been in trying to derail the strike, be granted more powers to betray the working class? The CP should have emphasised much more the need to prepare through the trades councils for the setting up of councils of action.

Events in the North-East of England and elsewhere were to show during the General Strike what would have been possible on this front if the policy from below had been more energetically pursued by the Communist Party. Despite its limited numbers – about 5,000 or 6,000 – it could have had a much greater effect in solid working-class areas such as South Wales, London, etc. Even when a correct call was made for councils of action, it was hedged with advice to the working class to look to above for "guidance". Thus, Tom Mann, when he opened the conference of action organised by the Minority Movement, said: "Therefore, prepare at once. Let us perfect our relations with each other, let us have our industrial machinery ready for action. The real central body through which we must function is the General Council of the Trades Union Congress."[32] All unions should be loyal and cooperate loyally therewith. George Hardy, acting Minority Movement general secretary, wrote in *Workers' Weekly* on 9 April 1926 that members "should work for the establishment of councils of action in every area but that the councils of action were to see all decisions of the General Council and the union executives were carried out."[33]

But this was precisely what the bureaucratic conservative officialdom at the top and in the districts was striving for. Negotiations between the General Council, through its Industrial Committee, and the government assumed a tortuous character, with each side, like seals passing a beach ball in a circus, attempting to put responsibility for the coming conflict on the other. Even Arthur Cook was weakening in the run-up to the strike in the face of the intransigence of the government and the weak-kneed response of the General Council. He confided to one of Baldwin's advisers, Thomas Jones: "We are economically in the weakest position we have ever been in... And while a lot of our chaps won't agree with me, we shall have to have a national minimum not only with pluses above it, but minuses below it."[34] In other words, even the most militant trade union leader was prepared to contemplate "temporary" cuts as he stared over the abyss of what was involved in the looming conflict.

General Strike called

Unless there are rounded-out Marxists with a clear understanding of what is involved in action of this character, it is inevitable that there will be hesitation and a drawing back before the battle is joined. Indeed, on the eve of great events, such prevarication can express itself even in the most revolutionary party. In Russia on the eve of the October Revolution, Zinoviev and Kamenev, supported by Stalin behind the scenes, disagreed with the preparations for the taking of power and even went public in denouncing Lenin and the Bolsheviks. Someone like Arthur Cook, very well meaning, a good fighting militant, passionate about the cause of the miners, in a polarised situation and without a revolutionary understanding and a mass party to back him up, inevitably hesitated and even posed the need to retreat.

Whether the miners would have accepted this is another thing entirely. Yet Cook, while expressing private hesitation, still publicly declared: "We have got the whole of the trade union movement in the country pledged to defend the miners' hours, wages and national agreements. Abroad, we have made agreements that no coal shall come into this country. The government and the owners know that we have got the organisation that can fight and win. My last word to the government is count the cost. The cost of a strike of the miners would mean the end of capitalism."[35] This once more underlined the illusions that Cook had in a strike, even a general strike, almost automatically ending capitalism. He went further in a meeting in South Wales: "Let me warn the government there is a new mentality in the police, the army, the navy, and the air force. Ninety-seven per cent of the recruits for the past two years have come from the working classes, and thousands of them miners, who will not shoot against their kith and kin when the order comes, and we shall not be afraid to advise them: this is a war to the death, and it is your death they are after."[36]

But this had little effect on the government. Baldwin, if anything, hardened the terms upon which an agreement could be made to end the prospects of a strike. The mine-owners also mapped out a savage policy of retrenchment of wages to be implemented after 30 April. Shift rates were to be reduced in a whole number of coal fields and in Durham and South Wales the proposed wages were to be lower than those in 1914! The Durham miners were to lose 18 shillings and fourpence (92p) a week and their comrades in South Wales would see their weekly earnings reduced from 78 shillings (£3.90) to less than 46 shillings (£2.30)! Baldwin made no attempt to stick to the proposals of the Samuel Report for the reorganisation of the mining industry but he proposed longer hours to solve the crisis. The Samuel Report "had stressed that sacrifices were not to be asked of the miners until agreement had been reached on the means for improving the industry's organisation and increasing its efficiency."[37] Yet the talk was exclusively of the "sacrifice" to be made by the miners.

The terms offered to the miners were those of surrender and were rejected not just by the miners but compelled the TUC to call a conference of executives of affiliated unions on the day after the miners were due to meet, Wednesday 28 April. Little concerned at these developments, Baldwin, it seems, busied himself with matters concerning cricket in the days leading up to the General Strike! Fiddling away while Rome was about to burn, we are also informed that at this time, "Baldwin bought *The Times*, the *Daily Telegraph* and *Morning Post*." Jones suggested that, with the coal crisis on, he should have bought the *Daily Herald*, "but the prime minister settled down happily with the *Telegraph* crossword, which he finished just as we steamed into Baker Street."[38]

Baldwin met the Industrial Committee but offered no concessions, not even saying that he had pressured the coal owners to accept some of the conditions on the reorganisation of the mines recommended in the Samuel Report. Even bourgeois commentators, such as J.L. Garvin in *The Observer*, repelled by the brutal visage of the bosses, wrote: "The owners have been tactless and irritating to the last degree. No responsible body of men has ever seemed more lacking in the human touch... Now, as last July, if they wanted to 'Get the men's backs up' and keep them up, the owners could not have gone about it better."[39] Baldwin relentlessly pushed the line in meetings with the TUC Industrial Committee that "there would be enormous unemployment" if wages are not reduced in the exporting areas. Yet the Industrial Committee "had no suggestion to make as to how the difficulty was to be overcome".[40]

Thomas actually indicated in these discussions that the General Council would not oppose wage cuts if reorganisation of the mining industry was undertaken. At the conference of TUC executives, Thomas declared: "My friends, when the verbatim reports are written, I suppose my usual critics will say that Thomas was almost grovelling and it is true. In all my long experience, and I have conducted many negotiations, I say to you – and my colleagues will bear testimony to it – I have never begged or pleaded like I begged and pleaded all today, and I pleaded not alone because I believed in the case of the miners, but because I believed in my bones that my duty to my country involved it."[41]

In the latter part of April, the policy of the General Council was to try and force the mineworkers' union to accept in substance most of the Samuel Report, which involved wage reductions and a longer working day. Why they were prepared to do this is perhaps summed up by Thomas. He wrote later: "What I dreaded about this strike more than anything else was this: If by chance it should have got out of the hands of those who would be able to exercise some control, every sane man knows what would have happened… That danger, that fear, was always in our minds, because we wanted at least, even in this struggle, to direct a disciplined army."[42] The danger of an "uncontrolled" movement from below was a constant fear of the right-wing General Council in the run-up to the General Strike. Their problem was the implacable opposition of a million miners to accepting any reduction in their already pitiful living standards.

The miners' leaders were forced to reflect this mood. On 27 March, speaking in Cardiff, A.J. Cook declared: "The government, no doubt, would consider longer hours with pleasure, but that pleasure will never be theirs. We have got to prepare ourselves for the control of this industry. I will not accept joint responsibility for private ownership. There can be no cooperation with capitalism as far as I'm personally concerned."[43] Lord Londonderry, leading Irish coal owner, writing to Baldwin on 13 April, stated: "Cook and Smith dare not take up any other attitude… They know there are many others ready and willing to take their places if they appear to falter."[44] In other words, an irresistible force existed, the determination of the miners – with the rest of the working class behind them – to defend their position. It was confronting an immovable object, the coal owners' and the British ruling class's equal determination to reduce living standards.

This determination of the miners and the rest of the working class compelled the right-wing General Council to preside over this coming clash. Having no alternative but to go down this road, they were equally determined to steer it into safe channels, to keep centralised control in their own hands if possible, and to betray it at the most opportune moment. Any conciliators on the government or employers' side also came up against the irresistible pressure of the coal owners and their support- ers in the Cabinet, like Churchill and Birkenhead, to cut wages and to organise a lock-out if necessary. On 21 April, Jones, after discussions with the South Wales coal owners, revealed to Baldwin their "plans to impose savage reductions". He added that they were "spoiling for a fight. The publication of terms like these would swing public opinion to the men".[45] But in discussions with the trade union leaders in late April Baldwin himself had in effect repudiated even the Samuel Report, which had demanded "reorganisation" of the mining industry at the cost of wage cuts.

No alternative to strike

The miners had called a special delegate conference for Wednesday 28 April and the General Council convened a meeting of trade union executives for the following day. In the meantime, Thomas and the rest of the right-wing General Council tried desperately to arrive at an agreement with the government. He begged the prime minister to do something before the situation got out of hand: "For ten days we negotiated, for ten days we said to the government, 'You force the coal owners to give us some terms, never mind what they are and however bad they are. Let us have something to go on'." The reply to Thomas was, "No, it cannot be done."[46] Despite all the attempts to seek a compromise they came to nothing as both sides shaped up for a battle. At the special conference of trade union executives on 29 April, a decision was taken to call a general strike at midnight 3/4 May in support of the miners. The decision was agreed almost unanimously by more than three-and-a-half million votes in favour to 49,000 against. (Some trade unions abstained because they had not had time to consult their members.) Only the seamen's union, led by its strikebreaking leader, Havelock Wilson, voted against. In the roll call of unions, the Union of Asylum Workers were the first to vote 'yes' but "No-one laughed. All were too deadly serious!"[47]

While this decision was met with acclamation, Cramp, Thomas's principal lieutenant in the NUR, leaned over and declared: "Pure fatalism – we can't win."[48] Thomas, his leader, was even more hysterical when speaking to Walter Citrine: "I am perfectly convinced, Walter, there is absolutely no hope. Stanley Baldwin talks to me just like a pal. There is going to be trouble and I can see no way out of it... You must remember there is a lot of Russian money in this country. The government are well informed. By God, you don't know! When I was in the government the railway sectional strike was on – you know, Bromley's strike. Well, do you know that I had on my desk every morning full details, photographs of letters that had passed, speeches made at private meetings – oh my God! They have tested the feelings in different parts of the country, and they have made up their minds that there will be trouble. They are going to smash it. It won't last more than a few days. A few people will get shot, of course (indicating the General Council members and the miners), more of them will get arrested. The government will arrest the remainder and say it is a case of putting them away for their own safety. Of course, the shooting won't be done by them direct, it will be those damned fascists and those fellows."[49]

Why then did Thomas and his union vote for the strike? Because of the massive pressure amongst railwaymen on even right-wing leaders like this. If Thomas had gone against this in a crude fashion, he would almost certainly have met the fate of a later NUR leader, Sid Weighell, who refused to accept the demands of his own union on the issue of Labour Party democracy in the 1980s and was forced to resign. In his later account of what happened, Thomas said he "urged and pleaded with the NUR executive to keep out of it. Many asked me afterwards why I didn't resign my position as leader of the railwaymen when I realised my advice would not be taken." His answer was that he could not let the miners down and "side with the government".[50] But that is precisely what he did during the strike. His removal before the strike would have opened the floodgates to a more radical leadership at all levels of the unions and that is the reason why he remained, in order to derail the struggle of the miners, the railwaymen and the rest of the working class.

The mood at the 30 April meeting of the executives was electric, which even affected some of the less than radical trade union leaders. Bevin declared: "We look upon your yes as meaning that you have placed your all upon the altar for this great movement, and having placed it there, even if every penny goes, if every asset goes, history will ultimately write up that it was a magnificent generation that was prepared to do it rather than see the miners driven down like slaves."[51] And yet, while the cheers still rang in their ears, straight after this conference the General Council's Industrial Committee tried to persuade the government to negotiate a way out. In fact, even in the course of the discussion at the executives' conference, Herbert Smith, who had negotiated with Baldwin the night before, implied that he was prepared to negotiate further and even suggested that "the miners might accept wage cuts in return for reorganisation". This was too much for Arthur Cook who sprang up and shouted that "his president 'had gone too far'".[52]

Ramsey MacDonald expressed the fears of the parliamentarians and hoped for a settlement even after the decision had been taken for a strike. He still held out hopes that in the next week, "something will happen… which will enable us to go about our work cheerily and heartily and hopefully".[53] The Right on the General Council certainly took steps to fulfil MacDonald's "hopes". Just before the vote on the General Council's scheme for action, the chairman of the conference of trade union executives, Pugh, stated: "The scheme requires that the Miners' Federation hand over to the General Council the conduct of this dispute."[54] The miners' leaders welcomed the support of the General Council but clearly understood that they would be fully involved with the negotiations and obviously with the expectation, naively as it turned out, that the General Council would remain firm.

Immediately the conference was out of the way, the General Council began to move every muscle to try and avert the strike by negotiations with the government. Delegates had left London, including crucially most of the miners' delegates, with the exception of A.J. Cook. Citrine wrote to Baldwin, in the name of the General Council, stating that all the unions, including the miners, had decided to hand over the conduct of the dispute to the General Council, and that the General Council was ready for any further discussion with the government. There was much to-ing and fro-ing by the trade union leaders to Downing Street. Eventually, a formula was accepted, which A.J. Cook, who knew nothing about it at the time, said "meant a reduction in wages and district agreements – conditions against which the TUC had themselves declared".[55] The General Council were prepared to betray before battle was joined, figuratively at one minute to midnight.

In the discussions with the government, Birkenhead, a government minister, had drawn up a formula which read: "We, the TUC, would urge the miners to authorise us to enter upon discussions with the understanding that they and we accept the [Samuel] Report as a basis of settlement and we approach it with the knowledge that it may involve some reduction in wages." Despite the "could", the clear intention was to accept the cut in wages which the government and mine-owners stood for throughout. So eager was Thomas to get out of the commitment to a strike that he declared: "Never mind what the miners or anybody else say, we accept it." By "we", he meant the TUC. Pugh, at least, stated that they could not take a decision without the miners, while Swales, an alleged Left, who "might have been expected to protest against the formula, was the least vocal".[56]

When this was presented to the Cabinet, the "violence of its reaction against the formula was so great" that Hankey confessed "he had never witnessed a scene like it". All who were "not present when it was agreed reacted in the same way against it, and felt that it would be read by the whole country as a capitulation on the part of the government to the threat of a general strike."[57] It was clear that the 'hawks' in the government were spoiling for a fight with the working class. As an excuse to call off negotiations, they pointed to the telegrams from the TUC, calling for the strike, which had already been sent out. The government then declared: "Since the discussions which took place last night between ministers and members of the Trade Union Committee, it has come to the knowledge of the government that specific instructions have been sent under the authority of the Trade Union Congress directing their members in several of the most vital industries and services in the country to carry out a general strike on Tuesday next. Such action would involve a challenge to the constitutional rights and freedom of the nation. The government must therefore require from the Trade Union Committee an unconditional withdrawal of this threat before it can continue negotiations."[58]

To have accepted this ultimatum would have been "total and abject surrender", which even the right wing of the General Council could not accept, given the mobilisation that had taken place. Nevertheless, they still attempted to negotiate with the government on the basis of cuts for the miners. As Kingsley Martin, editor of New Statesman, admitted subsequently: "The TUC stood as a combatant in a war which had been forced upon it and which it feared to win. The forces of labour were commanded by socialist reformists and the forces of the government by class-conscious believers in the inevitable conflict."[5]

5 The Strike Begins

E verywhere the government had prepared and was thirsting for the fight. They were given the excuse for calling off negotiations with the TUC by the spontaneous actions of the *Daily Mail* printers. This was then, and is today, one of the most reactionary journals not just in Britain but in Europe and the world. It became infamous in the 1930s for its support for fascism – "Hurrah for the Blackshirts!" The writers on the *Daily Mail* invariably dipped their pens in mad dog saliva before writing rabid articles denouncing the working class and labour movement. It had already earned the deep-seated hatred of workers because of the role it had played, through its editor Thomas Marlowe, in the infamous Zinoviev letter, which had helped to defeat the minority Labour government of 1924. Now, in a vicious leading article entitled "For King and Country", it compared the General Strike threat with a foreign war and called upon all "law-abiding men and women" to hold themselves ready to help the "nation" against the attack of the Red rebels. It declared that the General Strike was "a revolutionary movement intended to inflict suffering upon a great mass of innocent persons in the community... It must be dealt with by every resource at the disposal of the community."[1]

Dock woker's picket

The printers objected to this article, although the secretary of the printers' union NATSOPA at the *Daily Mail* "would have nothing to do with a strike".[2] Marlowe then phoned the Cabinet. One of Baldwin's aides then phoned the King's assistant private secretary at Windsor: "The Daily Mail has ceased to function. Don't be alarmed. Tell His Majesty so he should not go off the deep end." There was no need for concern, came the reply from Windsor. "We don't take the *Daily Mail* or the *Daily Express*"![3] Notwithstanding this, the government seized the opportunity to break off negotiations with the TUC, who for their part responded by grovelling even more. Pugh and Citrine returned to Number Ten with a resolution repudiating the *Mail* strike and protesting at the government's peremptory refusal to go on with the talks. But Baldwin had gone to bed and they could only find the caretaker and a resident detective still on duty!

This incident is incredible for the light it throws on the hypocrisy of capitalism and the so-called "freedom of the press". Here is a great struggle about to be embarked on between labour and capital with all the cards, most of the weapons for influencing public opinion, controlled by the latter. A virtual monopoly was exercised by the capitalist press – with the exception of the *Daily Herald*, the *Workers' Weekly*, etc. And yet the action of one group of workers to veto a vicious, one-sided attack on the working class was taken as an attack on the "freedom" of the press. Just what this "freedom" amounts to under capitalism was shown later by the dictatorial actions of Churchill with his monopolisation of newsprint, the setting up of the *British Gazette* and the attempt to take over the BBC. The NATSOPA men, supported by the chapels in the machine room, foundry and packing departments, were prepared to print the paper if the offending leader article was deleted. The management refused and the *Daily Mail* was not printed that night.

Freedom of the Press

Most historians of the General Strike, including some who lean to the Left, argue that it was a "tactical error" for printing unions to come out in solidarity with the miners during the strike. In a "newsless world", it is argued, the working class movement would not be able to have its voice heard. Better to allow the 'liberal' press, at least, like the then *Manchester Guardian*, to reflect some of the workers and trade unions' views. It is suggested that, otherwise, these views would be suppressed by a news blackout. However, in all social upheavals, and 1926 certainly was that, the working class will find the means of communication no matter what obstacles are placed in their path. This sometimes takes the form of commandeering printing press facilities, from the private owners, to allow the voice of the working class to be heard. This is what happened during the 1917 Russian and 1974-76 Portuguese Revolutions. Capitalist papers were still produced but some of the facilities were now used by parties, in Russia, which enjoyed the mass support of workers and peasants. This is seen by the capitalists and their apologists as a violation of their God-given inherent right to own and manage "their property". It is a grave infringement of the much vaunted "freedom of the press".

But what does this "freedom", both in 1926 and now, amount to? A handful of millionaires – some, like Rupert Murdoch who does not even live in Britain – are able to mould public opinion, even attempt to determine the outcomes of general elections; "It was *The Sun* wot won it!". Yet the trade unions, still numbering seven million workers in their ranks in Britain, have no daily voice. Nor has the Labour Party, when it was a workers' party at the bottom, had a single daily in recent history, although at one stage it commanded the votes of nearly 14 million people. Nor can the labour movement, socialists and Marxists count on support from the "liberal" press. Trotsky once remarked that *The Times* newspaper – this was in its pre-Murdoch days when it was a 'journal of record' – told the truth nine times out of ten the better to lie on that one crucial occasion which was vital for the system and the class which it ultimately defended, capitalism. The same applied to the "liberal" press in 1926 as it does today. An occasional airing is given to the case of the labour movement – otherwise, the newspapers would appear to be too biased – but little of the case for socialism or Marxism is ever allowed. The average writer on these journals, even when they may privately stand on the Left, know that they cannot go "too far" in reflecting views which would be unacceptable to the powers that be at the top. Crude censorship is not necessary with a policeman standing over journalists only because one exists inside the head of most of them, telling the journalist what can and can't be written.

Forced to tolerate the lies of the capitalist media in "normal" times, in periods of social upheaval the masses invariably act against their slanderers. The courageous action of the *Daily Mail* printers was in this tradition. Instead of repudiating them, as the General Council did, it would, if it had been a serious workers' leadership, have praised and supported them to the hilt, as did the mass of the working class. Moreover, it should have used this action to strike a blow against the hallowed "freedom of the press" by calling for the nationalisation of printing and broadcasting facilities. Not in order to establish a union or Labour "monopoly" as the capitalists would charge. On the contrary, only by a measure like this would real democratic access to the newspapers and the media be possible. Then, parties including minority ones, perhaps according to their votes in elections, would be allowed proportional access and time to explain their case. This would not amount to a "government-controlled press", a monopoly of whoever happens to be in power at any one time, which Marxists and the Socialist Party implacably oppose. This would be not a measure to "suppress democracy" but would result in its flowering and growth. The General Strike would reveal the great initiatives from below in strike bulletins and newspapers, which showed flair and wit, produced working-class journalists who really knew how to write in popular language and, above all, tell the truth about the situation. This was in stark contrast to the official journal of the TUC, the *British Worker*, which was dull, bureaucratically conceived and executed and, above all, lagging way behind the development and the mood of the mass of the working class at each stage.

Daily Mail

Baldwin said of the action of the *Daily Mail* workers: "We felt that this was more than a threat. It was direct action, and direct action, in my view, of the worst kind because it was suppressing, or trying to suppress, the possibility of the dissemination of news to the public. In these circumstances and with infinite regret, we had to take the stand that we could go no further."[4] And yet he knew that the *Mail* strike had occurred not just without the knowledge of the General Council but directly contrary to their intentions, which was to keep the conflict in safe channels and under their direct control.

Churchill, in the Commons, declared that he could detect "no difference between a general strike to force some Bill which the country [read capitalists] does not wish for, and a general strike to force Parliament to pay a subsidy... it is a conflict which, if it is fought out to a conclusion, can only end in the overthrow of parliamentary government or in its decisive victory."[5] Baldwin developed the same theme, stating that the government had "found itself challenged with an alternative government... I do not think all the leaders, when they assented to ordering a general strike, fully realised that they were threatening the basis of ordered government, and going nearer to proclaiming civil war than we have been for centuries past... It is not wages that are imperilled; it is the freedom of our very Constitution."[6]

Here is the clearest statement from a capitalist point of view of what is actually involved in a general strike of the character which developed in Britain in 1926. It does mean, in embryo, there is an 'alternative government' in the forms of organisation of the working class, which fights not just on an 'economic' issue but is against the very foundations of the system. This, of course, is not the way that the Labour or trade union leaders viewed the question. Thomas, in the same debate in the Commons, declared that there was no political motivation in the strike and that it could not be construed as a threat to the constitution: "I know the government's position, I have never disguised that in a challenge to the Constitution, God help us unless the government won... but this is not only not a revolution, it is not something that says, 'We want to overthrow everything'. It [the strike] is merely, a plain, economic, industrial dispute."[7] MacDonald confided to Citrine that his hair had gone greyer in one morning! Moreover "with the discussion of general strikes and Bolshevism and all that kind of thing, I have nothing at all to do. I respect the Constitution".[8]

This was not the way the working class viewed the issue. The background to the meetings of the trade union executives on 30 April and 1 May was a great ferment in the working class with the giant London May Day demonstration passing by the hall in which the conference was deliberating. The only issue of the *Workers' Daily* appeared on 3 May and commented: "It was impossible to count the numbers that took part in the London demonstrations... In one procession alone the tail had not reached Hyde Park until the head had been there an hour." The demonstrators broke into the 'Red Flag' as the first section reached the hall and an observer said that 'You had never heard it sung like this before'."[9] Even the delegates at the special executives' conference were caught up in the mood and ended the conference with the 'Red Flag' being sung, which the leader of the Labour Party, MacDonald, joined in with gusto, "though he personally regarded Labour's anthem as 'The funeral dirge of our movement'."[10] Shades of Tony Blair today!

The right-wing leaders were caught up in a mighty wave from below which carried all before it. They had not foreseen either the mood of the working class as a whole nor the eagerness with which the government looked towards this struggle and its defeat as a means of teaching the working class a very brutal lesson. Even if the other unions had not joined in support for the miners, a movement of general strike proportions could still have developed without official control from the top. Bevin later commented: "It must not be forgotten that apart from the rights and wrongs of the calling of a general strike, there would in any case, with the miners' lock-out, have been widespread unofficial fighting in all parts of the country, which would have produced anarchy in the movement."[11] The government and the trade union leaders feared "anarchy", the spontaneous initiatives of the working class freed from bureaucratic restrictions. Ramsay MacDonald conceded that after the way in which the government had approached the negotiations over the miners' conditions, "it was perfectly evident that had no general strike been declared industry would have been almost as much paralysed by unauthorised strikes".[12]

A state of emergency was declared by the government. The signal for its strike-breaking organisation to move was one word: "Action." Food depots had been set up in places like Hyde Park and most ominously, even while they were discussing with the TUC, "military precautions [had been] agreed by the Cabinet the previous week."[13] All army and navy leave was cancelled and troop reinforcements were moved into London, Scotland, South Wales and Lancashire. Although the Cabinet had decided that troop movements were to occur "as unobtrusively as possible", in Liverpool two battalions of infantry landed from a troopship and marched through the city with steel helmets, rifles and full equipment, while the battleships Ramillies and Barham, recalled from the Atlantic Fleet, anchored in the Mersey. Warships also anchored in the Tyne, the Clyde and Humber and at Cardiff, Bristol, Swansea, Barrow, Middlesbrough and Harwich. Troops were to be used "as a last resort".[14]

"Salt of the earth"

All the preparations, however, of the bosses and the government were puny when measured against the colossal response of the working class to the call for a general strike. After the humiliation of unemployment and grinding poverty, millions of workers believed that "their day had come". This is best summed up by an Ashton, near Manchester, sheet metal worker who spoke for millions when he wrote: "Employers of labour were coming, cap in hand, begging for permission... to allow their workers to return to perform certain customary operations. 'Please can I move a quantity of coal from such and such a place' or 'Please can my transport workers move certain foodstuffs in this or that direction'. Most of them turned away empty after a most humiliating experience, for one and all were put through a stern questioning, just to make them realise that we and not they were the salt of the earth. I thought of the many occasions when I had been turned away from the door of some workshop in a weary struggle to get the means to purchase the essentials of life for self and dependents... The only tactic practised by some of them was bullying, and that was no use in the situation such as this; some tried persuasion, referring to us as *Mr Chairman* and *Gentlemen*, but only a rigid examination of the stern facts of the case moved our actions. The cap-in-hand position was reversed."[15]

There are many different kinds of general strikes. Some erupt spontaneously from below, taking by surprise not just the capitalists but also the summits of the labour movement who then have to run very quickly in order to keep up with the working class. One such example was the greatest general strike in history in France in 1968, when 10 million workers spontaneously occupied the factories. The spark for this struggle came from the students, which led to repression from the police, a mass demonstration of a million, which in turn led to the occupation of the factories, workplaces and offices of France and raised the spectre of revolution not just in France but throughout the whole of Europe. The historical and social soil of France and the consciousness of the working class in that country created a tradition of 'spontaneous' or semi-spontaneous movements from below. In this sense these occupations in 1968 were a revival of the great sit-down strikes of 1936.

However, in other countries, like Britain, the tradition of the working class has been to channel its protests through the official trade union and labour movement organisations. The national leadership, therefore, has held in the past, and to some extent still today, huge authority in the eyes of the working class. This was evident in the 1926 General Strike. The national leaderships of the unions, forced into calling a general strike against their will, were determined to keep a bureaucratic grip on how it developed. The response to the strike shocked them as much as it did the capitalists: "It soon became clear that the response to the General Council's strike call far exceeded even the Council's expectations. Tuesday, [4 May] dawned with uncharacteristic stillness in the streets and railway stations of the cities: there were no trains preparing to bring suburban cargoes to town and no buses getting ready to heave the city millions to their shops and offices... The main approaches to London were choked with cars stretching in unbroken convoys across the Thames bridges to the city centre and from Marble Arch to Piccadilly traffic moved at the rate of only a few yards an hour."[16]

Strike action by members of the NUR and ASLEF was unanimous on most lines and there was only isolated blacklegging by some members of the Railway Clerks Association, which was insufficient to allow anywhere near normal services. On the London Midland and Scottish Railway, only four per cent of normal passenger services and only one per cent of freight services ran, on the London and North Eastern Railway about the same number ran and on the Great Western Railway between three and five per cent. Despite all this, the government lied that "a limited railway service" was running from the north of England. On the London Underground, 15 out of 315 trains ran on the first day and only for short distances. Three hundred buses out of 4,400 were staffed by volunteer crews and blacklegs and by the end of the week this fell to 40. Only nine of the 2,000 tram cars in London were operating. The dockers joined their fellow transport workers and at the London docks an immediate crisis arose with the threatened shutdown of electricity to the vast refrigeration plant, where three-quarters of a million carcasses were stored. As one commentator put it: "It was not the kind of crisis which could be resolved by the jolly undergraduates and hearty middle-aged businessmen of the OMS. The Royal Navy had to sail to the rescue of submerged submarines which anchored in the King George V dock and rigged their own electricity supplies to the refrigerating plant."[17]

Solid strike

Another historian, Julian Symons, indicates the solid character of the strike: "The workers' reaction to the strike call was immediate and overwhelming. There can be no doubt that it completely surprised the government, as well as the TUC. From district after district reports came into the TUC headquarters in Eccleston

Square, sending the same message in various words: the men were all out, the strike was solid."[18] The TUC also stated on the first day of the strike: "We have from all over the country, from Land's End to John o'Groats reports that have surpassed all our expectations. Not only the railwaymen and transport men, but all other trades came out in a manner we did not expect immediately. The difficulty of the General Council has been to keep men in what we call the second line of defence rather than call them off. There are also no reports other than those acquired, orderly and good-tempered desire to keep the peace of all sections of the community."[19]

The greatest dissatisfaction amongst rank-and-file workers was the calculated, bureaucratic and frustrating decision of the General Council to fight this battle in 'stages'. The intention was to bring out a first line and hold back 'in reserve' key workers such as engineers and shipyard workers, for instance, who were held in check for another week. This was Bevin's brainchild and ostensibly it was because he feared that if everybody came out, the strike would lose momentum very quickly. It seems that Citrine and Thomas opposed this strategy. But all were concerned really to lessen the impact of the strike. Thomas admitted: "Up to the evening of the strike the government thought it knew our power, but the strike exceeded their greatest expectation. The position is that they are staggered."[20]

This prevarication of the TUC gave the government an extra precious week in which to perfect and reorganise its ragged, strikebreaking organisation. It also frustrated and dissipated the energy of the workers who were hammering at the door of the TUC to join the strike. Appeals to come out were not confined to the big industrial unions. For instance, operators at the Central Telegraph Office, the nerve centre of Britain's telegraphic system, were incensed that there were no plans at all for calling them out. Even the 310 members of the Goldbeaters Trade Society wanted to know what role they could play. The General Council's approach inevitably led to frustration, conflicts between different trade groups and a lack of coordination; at least as far as the TUC organisations were concerned. Even with the limited objectives set by the General Council, if all the organised workers had been called out at once, the government could have been completely paralysed, its strikebreaking organisations, including the armed forces, largely nullified and with every chance of bringing the government to its knees. Reform is a by-product of a radical or revolutionary struggle. A complete general strike had more chance – although not certain to succeed if it did not go further – than a limited one. Instead, what the TUC was organising was not a general strike but a 'partial' one, with workers brought out in stages. Nevertheless, two million came out on the first day, another half a million on the second day and the figure oscillated around this up to the end of the general strike. This meant two and half million were on strike at any one time and one million miners were locked out. In total, probably four million workers out of five and a half million organised came out on strike.

The inevitable confusion over which workers would come out on strike and which would stay to cover 'emergencies' – which was not always successfully carried out – arose from the decision of the General Council to keep power centralised in the hands of trade union officials in London. Its instructions were: "The General Council recommend that the actual calling out of the workers should be left to the unions, and instructions should only be issued by the accredited representatives of the unions participating in the dispute."[21] The pressure was for "trade union officials" to play the key role at all levels, thereby hoping to exclude rank-and-file worker participation in generalised councils of action or strike committees at each level throughout the country. The bureaucratic cast of mind which dominated the trades unions then and now is that everything must be prescribed from above. Yet history and experience have shown that in really successful strike struggles, improvisation and initiative of workers and their representatives, such as shop stewards' committees, are vital even in a trade union and labour movement as in Britain with its traditions of going through the official organisations.

The British Gazette, the BBC and the British Worker

The Communist Party did attempt – and in some areas very successfully – as well as other sections of the Left and the working class, to propose and set up councils of action around the trades councils in many areas. The CP raised the slogan: "A council of action in every town! Every man behind the miners!"[22] The National Minority Movement also proposed that the councils of action should be all-embracing, representing "every political, industrial, cooperative and unemployed organisation – no organisation should be left outside if we are to defeat the mine-owners and the government." However, even the CP, through the Minority Movement, suggested that if a workers' defence corps was set up, "They should be trade unionists of good character and under commanders who are trade union officials".[23] It also proposed that the local committees should work for friendly relations with the armed forces to explain to them the issues of the struggle, to show them how it was "the government which had declared war on the trade unions".[24] However, a clear call for delegates from the factories and workplaces – union and non-union – does not appear to have been made even by the CP.

The policy of the General Council and its conservative approach was summed up by its newly-created journal, the *British Worker*. On the fourth day of the strike it declared: "Meanwhile the mass of the labour movement is sound, sensible, straight-forward. It has folded its arms and quietly awaits the results."[25] The editor of this journal had declared that his aim was to keep out of the paper "anything which might cause uncontrollable irritation and violence." He went on: "Our task is to keep the strikers steady and quiet. We must not be provocative; our line is to be dignified, calm in our own strength; to make our statements forcibly, but with moderation of language. We shall print every day very prominently and in bold type, well-displayed, this 'Message to all Workers'; the General Council of the Trades Union Congress wishes to emphasise the fact that this is an industrial dispute. It expects every member taking part to be exemplary in his conduct and not to give any opportunity for police interference. The outbreak of any disturbances would be very damaging to the prospects of a successful termination of the dispute. The council asks pickets especially to avoid obstruction and to confine themselves strictly to their legitimate duties."[26]

This stands in stark contrast to the militant, pugnacious way in which the government set about mobilising all its force, with Churchill in the vanguard, determined to crush the strike and inflict a humiliating defeat on the working class. The London print workers had followed the lead of their comrades on the *Daily Mail* and had ceased work before they were officially called out. When the *London Evening News* tried to quote part of the *Mail's* 'King and Country' editorial, NATSOPA members halted production and both the *Star* and the *Evening Standard* failed to appear because the print workers objected to "the enthusiastic accounts which have been written of recruiting scenes [of strike breakers] in Whitehall". The National Union of Journalists on national newspapers in the main did not follow the instructions of their executive not to work with blacklegs. Only in Glasgow did the editorial as well as the printing staff walk out. Nevertheless, of the 1,870 newspapers in Britain at that time only 40 were published in small, limited editions.

Of course, the government capitalised on "this alleged infringement of freedom of the press", particularly in its attempt to mobilise middle-class opinion. Kingsley Martin, in his book *The British Public and the General Strike* (1926) wrote: "The freedom of the press today means the autocratic right of Lord Beaverbrook, Lord Rothermere and a few other private persons to select news and impose suggestions they desire upon as large a part of the population as they can persuade to buy their brand of news and accept their type of suggestion... Under these circumstances, Labour adherents feel that it is rather absurd to talk of the 'freedom of the press'."[27] Just what this meant was shown by the last shots fired by the press before they were closed down by the workers' action. The Daily Telegraph had one word on its placards: "War", declaring that a general strike was, essentially, "civil war", since it divided the nation into those who were "loyal" and those who were "disloyal". Moreover, they said that by ratifying the General Strike the TUC showed the "true flavour of their alien origin".[28]

The crippling and virtual closing down of the press, however, led to the decision of the government, under the editorship of Churchill, to set up its own organ for disinformation and lies. It turned to a number of newspaper proprietors to try and use their presses but was turned down by them all, apart from the ultra-right Duke of Northumberland who owned the *Morning Post*. Lord Beaverbrook, later on a friend of left-wing Labour figures such as Aneurin Bevan and Michael Foot, sent over a key printing superintendent who helped to get the *British Gazette* out. Its headline read: "First Day of Great Strike, Not So Complete as Hoped by its Promoters".[29] This was not true but Churchill never allowed the truth to get in the way of a good story. Even Lloyd George in the House of Commons denounced the *British Gazette* as a "first-class indiscretion, clothed in the tawdry garb of third-rate journalism".[30] Churchill's reply to any suggestion that the government should resort to 'neutral' reporting was that he could not "undertake to be impartial as between the fire brigade and the fire".[31]

In its first issue, Churchill wrote: "This strike is intended as a direct hold-up of the nation to ransom. It is for the nation to stand firm in its determination not to flinch." It then quoted Baldwin, "This moment has been chosen to challenge the existing Constitution of the country and substitute the reign of force for that which now exists... I do not believe there has been anything like a thorough-going consultation with the rank and file before this despotic power was put into the hands of a small executive in London... I do not think that all the leaders who assented to order a general strike fully realised that they were threatening the basis of ordered government and coming nearer to proclaiming civil war than we have been for centuries past." Churchill, the *Gazette* reported, had commented in the House of Commons: "Either the nation must be mistress in its own house or suffer the existing Constitution to be fatally injured and endure... a Soviet of Trade Unions with the real effective control on our economic and political life." At the same time, this government mouthpiece reported on the arrest of Communist Party MP Saklatvala: "Communist leader arrested".[32]

Mussolini admired

In its second edition, it invoked the spectre of fascism in the following headline: "Foreign views of the strike. Liberty and the State. The way of fascism." There was even a veiled warning from its correspondent in Rome: "The events in connection with the British strike are accepted in Rome as a proof that the old parliamentary regime has passed in the march of modern historical conditions... To effect the consolidation of the old and the new factors is Italy's task today under the fascist regime." It continued: "The [Italian] Cabinet, having yesterday completed a scheme for the creation of a new Ministry of Trade Corporations, is now hammering out administrative details whereby masters, unions and workers of the unions, province-wide, can be amalgamated in the framework of the State so that production can proceed with the highest efficiency consistent with the best conditions for the men and a reasonable return for the capitalists."[33] In other words, Italy's fascist 'corporate state' was invoked by Churchill – who we must remember praised Mussolini in the 1930s – in the midst of this conflict.

Baldwin was also unrelenting. In the second issue he declared: "Constitutional government is being attacked... Stand behind the government... The laws of England are the people's birthright... You have made Parliament their guardian. The General Strike is a challenge to Parliament and is the road to anarchy and ruin."[34] In the same issue, a short article on the Swiss press baldly states: "Capitalism at stake".[35] An unsigned editorial, probably penned by Churchill, starts: "Everyone must realise that, so far as the General Strike is concerned, there can be no question of compromise of any kind. Either the country will break the General Strike, or the General Strike will break the country."[36] At the same time, lying through his teeth, Churchill's journal reports: "The *South Wales Evening Express*, in an edition published on Tuesday, contained the following: 'It is all hopeless; we have realised that,' said Mr A.J. Cook."[37]

The *Gazette* consistently peddled misinformation about the "success" of government strikebreaking forces. Also in issue four, a poem by Rudyard Kipling was printed alongside a special notice which reads: "All ranks of the Armed Forces of the Crown are hereby notified that any action which they may find it necessary to take in an honest endeavour to aid the Civil Power will receive, both now and afterwards, the full support of His Majesty's Government."[38] The government was providing legal cover for any military suppression that may have become necessary. It was also calculated to further terrify the moderate trade union leadership. Churchill was not averse in playing on the fears and prevarication of the trade union leaders: "The responsibility of these trade union leaders is grievous. It is also a personal responsibility. They made no attempt to consult by ballot those who they claim to represent." At the same time the olive branch was proffered as he still appealed to these leaders to end the strike and "negotiate".[39]

A constant theme of the *Gazette* is how effective the strikebreaking measures of the government were. On 8 May, it reports "substantial improvement in train services" and in Liverpool "men returning to work". Yet the strike was maintaining momentum with increasing numbers joining it. This was indicated by Baldwin's statement: "I wish to make it as clear as I can that the government is not fighting to lower the standard of living of the miners or any other section of the workers. That suggestion is being spread abroad. It is not true. I do not believe that any honest person can doubt that my whole desire, is to maintain the standard of living of every worker, and that I am ready to press the employers to make sacrifices to this end consistent with keeping the industry itself in working order."[40]

So, the fact that Britain had been brought to the brink of "civil war" (Baldwin's previous statement) arose from a "misunderstanding"? Every worker in Britain understood that first it was the miners and then the rest of the working class who were facing savage cuts in their living standards. Moreover, the great majority of them, through the bitter experience of the whole period since 1918, had instinctively understood that the capitalist system itself was incapable of guaranteeing their present living standards never mind lasting improvements. The fact that Baldwin made this statement, more conciliatory than his previous ones, is an indication that the capitalists themselves were taking fright at the momentum that had been unleashed once the masses were on the move.

However, in the spirit of carrot and stick, in the same issue of the *Gazette*, Lord Balfour conjured up the spectre of an "anti-civilisation, barbaric revolutionary explosion". In an article headlined "Attempted Revolution – Its Purpose and Results", he declared that the capitalists were defending "the civilisation of which we are trustees". He stated: "Two hundred and thirty-eight years have passed since a revolution occurred in this country, whose object was to secure the supremacy of parliamentary government, and the traditional liberties of our people..." He was referring to the 1688 'Glorious Revolution', the 'safe' revolution as far as capitalism was concerned, and not the English Revolution of the seventeenth century! He went on: "We are now threatened, it seems, with a revolution of a very different kind... Its methods are being practised before our eyes. They are to deprive the people of food, transport, employment, and a free press... No revolution is going to compel the mine-owner indefinitely to carry on his industry at a loss. Revolutionary methods would be completely powerless except for evil... [This] is what I have called it – an attempted revolution."[41]

But the effectiveness of the strike sometimes crept accidentally into the pages of this biased government journal: "It became known today that workmen have been withdrawn from the House of Commons. The Speaker at the end of the sitting announced: 'I regret to say that it is the fact that men engaged in several of the principal services of the House have been withdrawn. I can assure the House that I shall not allow the House to be disabled from proceeding with its work by the actions of any persons whatsoever. If it is necessary, I will conduct the business of the House without any printing or without any electric light'"![42]

There were attempts to supplement the propaganda barrage that emanated from the *British Gazette* with the printing of limited editions of the London dailies and some of the regional press. But the other major wing of the government's propaganda barrage was the BBC, which had been effectively commandeered by the government as soon as the strike began. Churchill stated that it was "monstrous" not to use such an instrument as the BBC to the advantage of the government.[43] On the other hand, Ellen Wilkinson, then a left-wing Labour MP, declared after the strike: "Everywhere the complaints were bitter that a national service subscribed to by every class should have only been given one side during the dispute. Personally, I feel like asking the Postmaster-General for my licence fee back."[44]

Although the criticism of the BBC was well merited, this displayed a naivety in the extreme. Compared to the gross bias, for instance, of the Murdoch media – with Fox News being a virtual propaganda wing of the Bush administration – the BBC can often appear to be more balanced. But in periods of extreme social conflict, like in 1926 or the miners' strike of 1984-85, it becomes a propaganda tool of the ruling class. The fact that the government did not take over the BBC lock, stock and barrel was because, in effect, the BBC carried through a policy of self-censorship with a gross bias towards the government. Even the General Council, through the pages of the *Daily Herald*, warned on 3 May, that trade unionists should ignore all broadcasts and statements. Although the BBC was permitted to quote from the speeches of trade union leaders and from the *British Worker* – to show its fairness – it nevertheless echoed the government in the "large number of totally inaccurate reports of returns to work which were broadcast".[45]

Gulf between TUC and workers

Even when the Archbishop of Canterbury tried to mediate between the strikers and the government, produced a peace manifesto and requested that it should be broadcast on the BBC, he was flatly turned down. The Archbishop had approached Baldwin, who told him he would "prefer that the manifesto would not be broadcast". To reinforce the point, his aide visited Sir John Reith, Director-General of the BBC, insisting that the manifesto could not be reported and, in effect, threatening that if it was it would trigger a complete government takeover of the BBC. The puzzled Archbishop wrote to Reith: "Are we to understand that if the Churches decide to put something forth" then it would be 'censored'? It did not enter this shepherd's mind that his 'flock', which presumably included some striking workers, was similarly denied. When, however, the Catholic Archbishop of Westminster broadcast a denunciation of the General Strike – "There is no moral justification" – this was covered extensively by the *British Gazette* and the BBC. Ramsay MacDonald, representing the Labour Party, in complete breach of the

TUC's boycott of the BBC, requested that he should be allowed to broadcast. He even offered to make "any necessary alterations" to his speech if this was requested. Once more the government stepped in, through Churchill, and vetoed MacDonald, although Thomas was allowed to broadcast... after the General Strike had finished.[46]

Compare the capitalists' approach to the General Strike with the insipid approach of the General Council of the TUC. Its official strike newspaper, the *British Worker*, was only launched in answer to the foundation of the *British Gazette*. The latter fired the verbal and literary bullets, keeping in reserve real weapons, while the trade union leaders acted like a giant fire hose, more eager to stamp out the revolutionary fires burning below than to carry through the strike to a victorious conclusion. Trotsky drew a comparison between the *British Worker* during the strike and *Pravda* (Truth), the organ of the Bolsheviks during the Russian Revolution. Both were small, just four pages, but there the comparison ended. On *Pravda* he stated, "What four pages!" The mood of the masses was reflected at every stage as well as the direction the revolution needed to take.

There was no comparison between this journal and the sterile, lifeless *British Worker*. The latter was rigidly controlled from above, instructing local committees to keep to the statements issued by the TUC and "do nothing in the way of comment or interpretation". Typical was the following in an early issue of the *British Worker*. In a list of "Dos" for "difficult days", the advice to strikers was: "Do all you can to keep everybody smiling: the way to do that is to smile yourself. Do your best to discountenance any ideas of violent and disorderly conduct. Do the thing that's nearest: this will occupy you and will steady your nerves, if they get shaky. Do any odd jobs that want doing about the house. Do a little to interest and amuse the kiddies now you have the chance. Do what you can to improve your health: a good walk every day will keep you fit. Do *something*. Hanging about and swapping rumours is bad in every way."[47] To the charge of Baldwin that the General Strike was a challenge to parliament and the constitution, the *British Worker* declared: "No attack on the constitution". Referring to Baldwin's government: "They talk and write wildly about an attempt to upset the constitution, to usurp the authority of ministers, to set up a rival to the House of Commons... That is untrue." As to being "political", the *British Worker* declared indignantly: "No political issue has ever been mentioned or thought of in connection with it. It began over wages and conditions of working; it has never been concerned with anything else."[48]

This revealed the gulf that existed between Eccleston Square, the TUC's headquarters, and the mass of the strikers and the working class as a whole. On 10 May, the *British Worker* declared: "All's Well!" It went on to state that in the second week of the

General Strike, "Nothing could be more wonderful than the magnificent response of millions to the call of their leaders." It particularly praised the alleged "strict obedience to the instructions to avoid all conflict". This while ferocious battles were unfolding in different parts of the country between on one side strikers, pickets, despatch riders for local councils of action and the forces of the state on the other. The conclusion on 10 May was: "The General Council's message at the opening of the second week is 'Stand firm. Be loyal to instructions and trust your leaders.'"[49] The next day, the *British Worker* once more declared: "No slackening."[50] This was true of the working class but not of the General Council, who were to sell out the strike in a matter of days. The following day, the day before the calling off of the strike, even the *British Gazette* had to admit that "there is as yet little sign of a general collapse of the strike".[51]

That day, 12 May, was the day with the highest number of strikers, with a new wave of enthusiasm amongst workers rolling from one end of the country to the other. It is a basic tenet of all strikes, not just general strikes, that the working class, dragged out of its normal routine, learns more in one day about the realities of class society than in years of peaceful development. This applies even more to a one-day general strike, which if properly prepared can fuse the working class together, give them the consciousness and sense of their own power. Obviously a general strike is on a higher plane, one step removed from an actual taking of power by the working class. The General Strike of 1926, although "partial" in character, gave the working class this sense, of being pitted against the power of capitalism as a whole. Each day of the strike reinforced this feeling and began to breed the confidence that the working class could win.

Yet it is absolutely incredible that when the full panoply of the capitalist state had been mobilised to ensure victory for their class, the trade union leaders were mouthing outworn phrases to the effect that the strike was not political. What is politics if not "generalised economics", the class struggle taken from one factory or industry and onto a national plane, confronting not just a national group of employers but the government itself? The Baldwin government was quite conscious that this was a political confrontation with its constant intonation about the threat of "civil war", while the "Generals" of the TUC lamented such sentiments. Indeed, the government was actually planning to arrest the trade union leaders – Thomas, Bevin, the lot, Right and Left – if they had continued the strike any longer. "Swales believed that warrants had been issued for himself and Bevin" halfway through the general strike.[52]

6 The Workers Organise

ut the answer to the intonations of the General Council that the strike was not "political", that at bottom it did not represent a striving on the part of the working class to replace a government and a system that kept them in the mud, is given by the reaction at rank-and-file level of the working class. Everywhere, there was an enthusiastic response. In some areas, however, notably in the North-East, in parts of London, Liverpool and elsewhere, the formation of local councils of action, with the trades' councils at their heart, created elements at least of dual power. This term is used by Marxists to describe a situation where two rival organisations vie for power. The working class and its organisations begin to acquire powers which it does not possess in a 'normal' period, such as controlling transport, food and, in effect, vetoing the actions of the bosses and the government. The government loses power but not enough to allow it to be changed or overthrown. This situation is a period of 'double sovereignty', which does not usually last for a long time and is resolved by the victory of one power over the other. This kind of situation had not been seen in Britain possibly since the time of the English

Scottish Worker, strike bulletin

A pass for a TUC Despatch Rider

Revolution in the seventeenth century. During that revolution, which laid the basis for the rise of English capitalism, it took a territorial form, with the King and royalists concentrated in Oxford, and Parliament, representing the rising capitalists, based in London. In 1926, the 'dual power' was of a class character, existing through-out Britain, although more developed in some areas than others.

Councils of action

There were various reports given of the number of councils of action in Britain during the immortal nine days. There were approximately 400 trades' councils in operation and between 100 and 147 councils of action. Baldwin's aide Davidson wrote later: "The workers' reaction to the strike call had been much more complete than we had expected. The railwaymen were out almost to a man and London Transport came to a complete standstill. The Organisation of the Maintenance of Supplies which the Home Secretary had set up was quite unable to cope."[1] This was particularly true about the solid working-class areas. A.J. Cook also wrote in *The Nine Days*: "It was a wonderful achievement, a wonderful accomplishment that proved conclusively that the labour movement has the men and women that are capable in an emergency of providing the means of carrying on the country. Who can forget the effect of motor conveyances with posters saying: 'By permission of the TUC'? The government with its OMS was absolutely demoralised. Confidence, calm and order prevailed everywhere despite the irritation caused by the volunteers, blacklegs and special constables. The workers acted as one. Splendid discipline! Splendid loyalty!"[2] Nowhere was this more true than in the North-East of England. As one historian expressed it: "The General Strike in the North-East is especially interesting for at least two reasons. Firstly, it was in this area that an attempt was made by the strikers to organise themselves on a similar basis to that of the Government's Emergency Organisation... The strikers ambitiously attempted directly to counter the government organisation, establishing their own central strike committee for the area in Newcastle."[3]

R. Page Arnot, a leading member of the Communist Party, played a crucial role in the North-East and, later, also gave an indication of just how, with clear leadership, at least on an organisational level, the councils of action could have become a reality throughout Britain. He had been imprisoned for six months with other Communist Party leaders but on his release addressed a May Day meeting in the village of Chopwell in north-west Durham. He then "jotted down headings for a plan of campaign in the Durham-Northumberland area".[4] He clearly understood that because of its general character the strike should not be restricted to a section of the working class but should draw in all workers and organisations. Arnot suggested that local authorities with Labour majorities could effectively disrupt the government's plans by refusing to carry out government proposals. At a meeting in Chopwell it was decided to divide into 13 sections the apparatus needed and the tasks that had to be accomplished if the primary aim of the campaign, the defeat of the Civil Commissioner and his organisation, was to be achieved. The plan set out, in effect, the machinery for organising working class control of the region. Arnot insisted that it should be "simple, easy to throw up" and crucially "all inclusive".[5]

All the activities in each locality were to be centralised in a single body called the Council of Action, Strike Committee, Trades Council or some other name. Control of food supplies was considered to be crucial: "Who feeds the people wins the strike".[6] Stopping transport was also vital: "The effect on the mind of the workers out on strike of any transport was found to be bad; the mere rumble of wheels was something that weakened the morale of our men and correspondingly cheered the other side."[7] In an incredible feat of organisation, the committee, organised without any real serious preparation, began to guide the policy of a series of strike committees thrown up by the General Strike in the North-East of England. Anthony Mason, in his description of the strike in the North-East, gives examples of the degree of organisation and how it drew on the wellspring of working-class support. He comments on how the Strike Committee communicated throughout the region and cites the example of "Herbert Bell [who] was a motorcycle despatch rider for the Newcastle Strike Committee and he was able to recall journeys which he had made into Northumberland to local miners' lodges."[8]

Herbie Bell recounted his "escapades", as he put it, during the General Strike to me when I stayed with him in the 1960s. He was a heroic and legendary figure of the working class movement, a Marxist, a supporter of *Militant*, whose experiences included the First World War, the General Strike, the Independent Labour Party in the 1930s, the Trotskyist Revolutionary Communist Party during and after the Second World War and remained a Trotskyist till the day he died. He delivered strike bulletins to several places throughout the North-East. Herbie Bell and others confirmed that the communications from Newcastle were delivered throughout the region by despatch riders, who communicated the orders of the joint strike committee twice daily and were strictly obeyed. All who participated commented on how the strike committee "step by step... perfected its machinery."[9] The official TUC paper the *British Worker*, played very little role but the workers showed the power of initiative and improvisation, as well as humour, in the production of *Northern Light*, based in Chopwell and the Newcastle Trades Council's news-sheet the *Workers' Chronicle*.

As the strike developed, so did the militant mood throughout the area. This was influenced undoubtedly by the Communist Party, small in number but very energetic. The most impressive thing about the strike in the North-East was the complete failure of the government's blackleg machinery to work in the teeth of the colossal workers' power. Here were elements of a developed dual power. The Civil Commissioner, Sir Kingsley Wood, had to acknowledge this when he was forced to approach the Northumberland and Durham general council. R. Page Arnot wrote: "After 40 hours of the general stoppage [Sir Kingsley] came by night to negotiate personally with the strike committee. Sixty hours after the strike began, Sir Kingsley Wood, accompanied by General Sir Kerr Montgomery, were once more at Burt Hall [the strike committee headquarters], making a plea for 'dual control' of transport and food. This proposal was immediately rejected by the Joint Strike Committee ('we cannot agree to our men working under any from of dual control'), which at the same time decided 'that we now use the discretionary powers vested in us by the Trades Union Congress and withdraw all permits today'."[10]

The North-East was not the only area in which the working class showed its power. Tony Mulhearn described events on Merseyside during the General Strike in an article in *Militant* in 1976 to commemorate the fiftieth anniversary of the strike: "On Sunday, 2 May, the day before the strike was to begin, the Provisional Council of Action met and constituted the Merseyside Council of Action (MCA). As well as representatives from all the major trade unions it included a local sub-Council of Action from each area of Liverpool. Grouped around the MCA were the respective strike sub-committees for the transport, building and distributive trades which maintained contact with the Council of Action through liaison officers. This sophisticated structure of administration and organisation was to remain in continual session from the beginning of the General Strike until the end."

The strike was very successful: "The dockers were the backbone of the General Strike on Merseyside. By day three there were 100,000 workers on strike. These included 20,000 dockers, 20,000 railwaymen and 20,000 warehousemen. Council of Action bulletin Number 4 of 8 May reported that the 'strike is extending hourly. Men leaving work in sympathy with and without orders. Meat slaughtering centres all stopped'."

The bosses and their agents attempted to counter the strike's effects: "The Merseyside workers had to contend with a scab version of the *Liverpool Daily Post and Echo*. This was a two-page tabloid produced by scab labour. The print trade unionists were out to a man. Day after day this rag screamed out against the strike using all devices to try to demoralise the strikers and to whip up the rage of the middle class." There were also attempts at strike breaking. There were "reports of students scabbing on the docks. This was blown up by the *Echo* and described as 'near normal working' at the docks. The MCA bulletin refuted this declaring that only a handful of students were scabbing and, incidentally, only doing one quarter of the work per head normally done by the dockers. The MCA bulletin of 6 May reported '...non-unionists are assisting in picketing [the docks] and is frequently repeated'."[11] The General Strike remained solid on Merseyside until it was called off.

The South Wales coalfields displayed even more the potential for the revolutionary takeover of power by the working class. In *The Fed*, the history of the South Wales miners, the authors write: "The nine days of the General Strike and more especial-ly the seven-month lock-out revealed an alternative cultural pattern which had no comparable equivalent in the other British coalfields. The totality of commitment to the miners' cause was a form of class consciousness which translated itself into a community consciousness, so overwhelming were the miners in numbers and influence. It was a collectivist conception which burnt into the collective memory of the whole region and was most succinctly described by the poet, Idris Davies, in what he called 'The Angry Summer': 'We shall remember 1926, until our blood is dry.'"[12]

They further comment: "The industrial crisis of 1926 precipitated a polarising of class and community forces... It was as if the authorities deliberately stood to one side and seemed temporarily to allow the mining communities to carry on much as they wished. So overwhelming was the support that to contemplate not joining the strike would have been tantamount to committing social suicide. Not one miner is said to have been arrested, although there was much illegal action. It was not so much a question of 'dual power' as almost one of transference of power in some valleys. In such valleys as Bedlinog and Mardy, the miners through their strike committees and councils of action virtually ran their communities unchallenged."[13]

There was overwhelming support from the working class and the majority of the middle class in the north-east for the miners and workers' cause. The achievements of R. Page Arnot and the small membership of the Communist Party were particu-larly notable, given the fact that the party was weaker in this region before the General Strike than in many other areas of the country. However, because of its initiative and energy it grew rapidly as a result of the General Strike. It had one member in Chopwell in May 1926 and three weeks later there was no hall in the village which could hold the party membership. Page Arnot himself remarked that "I had to address nearly 200 Communists at Chopwell in a shallow amphitheatre of a hill amid the sunshine and the breeze of an August afternoon." Naturally attract-ing the attention of the police, he was forced during the strike to sleep in different houses every two or three nights and he also changed his name to "Mr Black".[14]

Chopwell

As a result of this intervention, Chopwell became a stronghold for the Communist Party with the *Morning Post* calling it "The Reddest Village in England".[15] Of course, this right-wing newspaper explained its "redness" by the alleged fact that "Chopwell has lived on the dole for a year". Newcastle was also described as, "The landing place of the Russian invasion". The *Morning Post* was trying to prove that the General Strike had been a "communist" inspired plot all along.

This rabid anti-socialist, anti-communist mood was reflected in the comments of the judiciary when they passed sentence on strikers. For instance, one of those charged with circulating the *Northern Light* was told by the magistrate: "If you think that the Council of Action can hold up the inhabitants in a state of tyranny you are very much mistaken. Why you and those associated with you don't go to Russia, I don't know. I am sure the government, and I personally, would subscribe willingly to get rid of the whole lot of you and let you go and live in that country where everything is so blissful and happy. We don't want you. Nobody wants you. You are just a source of danger to the community, and the sooner you make up your minds to either reform or get away, the better for all concerned."[16]

This hysteria contrasted with the sober confidence of the workers, with one correspondent commenting: "The Dawdon men have constituted a kind of Soviet and have intimated to the police that they are going to take possession of the roads to help the police and to ensure the safety of the public. No cars will be allowed to pass unless they have a permit from them. The police told me that this threat has not yet been carried into effect, but the men state they are proposing to begin tomorrow, and permits are certainly being issued by them to those people who have been to ask for them. This is, of course, a quiet way of assuming control."[17] An historian of the strike in the North-East, Mason's comments on this are pertinent: "Given another week, such organisation might well have increased in confidence and efficiency."[18]

On another occasion, a newsagent at Houghton-le-Spring had been allegedly visited by a "Bolshevist County Councillor" and his friends who informed him that "as the newspapers are now being set up by non-unionists, he would not be allowed to sell any. The newsagent has since exhibited a notice in his window announcing that no newspapers will be sold during the strike."[19] This hyperbole about "Bolshevist" councillors – the CP, as far as is known, had no councillors here – disguises the fact that the working class in this area was bound to exert pressure on and receive support from intermediary layers like shopkeepers. Their customers were miners and other workers in the main. The 1984-85 miners' strike also showed that they could be drawn behind the working class in struggle. These elements of workers' control were loathed by the government's supporters.

The workers combined a seriousness of organisation with humour, especially when it came to the forces of the state: "The lowest aim in life is to be a policeman. When a policeman dies he goes so low he has to climb up a ladder to get into hell, and even then he is not a welcome guest."[20] This mood from below was in stark contrast to the summits of the TUC whose attitude had changed decisively since the events of 1919-20. Then, as mentioned earlier, the TUC and the Labour Party organised a Council of Action, a soviet in outline, to prevent Churchill's intervention in Poland. Now they were bending over in all their efforts to prevent such developments in Britain and were living in terror that the strike might be converted into a political or even a revolutionary strike.

They would have been encouraged by the attitude of some strikers – a minority – under the influence of TUC officials, to proceed very cautiously. One French observer was incredulous when he learned that a football match between strikers and police had taken place in Plymouth: "The British are not a nation, they are a circus."[21] The Mayor of Lewes put up a prize in a public billiards match between strikers and the police. At Banbury, joint concerts were arranged and both sides competed in a tug-of-war. However, a much more ferocious and sometimes violent trial of strength was taking place in the majority of areas affected by the strike. There were clashes with the police in the East End of London and at the Elephant and Castle. In the *Manchester Guardian Bulletin*, its London correspondent reported: "Things seem more serious today with the streets much emptier through the taxicab drivers joining the strike. There are more buses now, each with one or two policemen beside the driver. A new strikers' plan borrowed from the French syndicalists has been tried this morning in Camberwell; some women laid their babies on the road in front of commercial vehicles and when the cars stopped, a man jumped on the footboards and turned out the drivers and smashed the machinery of the cars."[22]

Workers intervene

This supposedly "well-ordered" strike, pacific and marching to the "moderate" drumbeat of the General Council, nevertheless resulted in more than ten thousand workers being arrested and imprisoned during the course of the strike. This was comparable to the numbers arrested during the great miners' strike of 1984-85. However, this was not at all what the bureaucratic machine wanted. This led the leaders in some areas, like Cardiff mentioned earlier, to "Keep smiling". But this was not at all the mood or the actions which flowed from this in most parts of the country. On 4 May, most of the trades' councils had set up bodies, which included their own executives, delegates from the strike committees of the various unions, and representatives of local working-class organisations such as Labour Parties, ILP branches, the Communist Party and Cooperative Guilds. These were not soviets – workers' councils – in the strict sense in which they developed in the Russian and other revolutions. The councils of action which developed in the 1926 General Strike were in the main composed of labour movement organisations, trade union leaders and some rank-and-file participation. In the north-east of England and elsewhere they were broader and had some of the features of a soviet.

One of the reasons why workers' councils did not develop on the scale witnessed in the Russian Revolution was the bureaucratic dead hand and fear of the General Council of the TUC. However, if the strike had gone on, the trade union officialdom could have been pushed aside, and the councils of action and 'strike committees' would have broadened out to include delegates from workplaces. The Communist Party, as we have seen, was agitating widely along with the Minority Movement, for the setting up of councils of action. Moreover, in Glasgow, Edinburgh, Barrow, Doncaster, Sheffield, Liverpool and Birmingham, an outline of councils of action had been functioning, with the influence of the CP, for almost a year. The Liverpool 'Provisional Council of Action' had existed since March 1926. Therefore, when over 50 towns had improvised through the trades councils bodies of this character, they came into collision with the TUC. Moreover, many of the local union officials echoed the fear of the TUC. For instance, in Dunfermline the council of action had to rename itself the "strike committee" and the editors of the Cambridge strike bulletin were forbidden to mention "government provocation and the words 'council of action'".[23]

One historian has commented: "In other areas, the determination to avoid any kind of revolutionary connotation took more dramatic forms."[24] In Widnes, for instance, the NUR branch ended its meetings with 'God Save the King' and the Dover strike committee requested strikers to sing 'Rule Britannia' instead of the Red Flag when marching through the streets! But this was not at all typical as a perusal of the improvised strike bulletins demonstrates. In Sheffield, the "engineers welcomed the General Strike with special warmth because they saw a successful strike would break the hold of *all* employers, of miners, engineers, railwaymen, the lot."[25] In the Sheffield area there were some 20,000 miners and a considerable body of railwaymen "who had formed a council of action over a week before the General Strike started".[26]

In Oxford, the Council of Action strike bulletin stated: "There is no constitutional crisis! Stand firm workers!" Employers in Oxford had urged young people to "throw in their [union] membership cards". Moreover, the employers announced that they would "decline to put pressure on any individual who may wish to continue [working] or resume his employment as a non-union member".[27] The strike committee was moderate in Oxford, having disaffiliated from the National Minority Movement the previous February. But nevertheless, it attracted figures who subsequently became quite important. A.J.P. Taylor, the famous historian for instance, was an undergraduate at Oriel College at the time and a member of the Communist Party. He mentions in his autobiography that new recruits had joined him, including Tom Driberg, a future Labour MP. Hugh Gaitskell, then a university student, also offered his services to the Oxford Strike Committee. He subsequently became the right-wing leader of the Labour Party but the fact that types like this could be drawn in behind the strike in an area that was relatively weak is an indication of the effect that the strike had on sections, at least, of the middle class. Even in Shrewsbury, it was reported: "Huge meetings, everyone amazed at the way in which the call has been answered. Prominent members of local Conservative Party among the strikers… Everyone said, 'Nothing like this could have been imagined in Shrewsbury'."[28] Non-unionists joined the strike. From the most unlikely places the call was answered.

But the heart of the strike was in the solidly industrial areas. In Bolton, for instance, where the council of action was "the sole authoritative body all through" nine separate committees were set up to handle office staff, organisation, transport, publicity, finance, public representatives, picketing, vital services and messengers. By the second day of the strike, 2,280 pickets had volunteered for duty. Each was provided with a white silk ribbon and worked in shifts for four hours a day, and 29 cyclists and 57 motor-cyclists maintained daily contact with practically every town in Lancashire. At Merthyr, the Central Strike Committee formed six committees and four district committees, each with four sub-committees of its own. In Scotland, the Methil Council of Action also formed six committees and a courier service with three cars – few workers possessed these at this stage. An information committee was established throughout the whole of Fife and a panel of 30 speakers was drawn up, and meetings in support of the strike were always addressed by a miner, a railwayman and a docker.[29]

From below

In Stepney, the Town Hall was placed at the disposal of the council of action and meetings and concerts were held every night of the strike. Even in sleepy Canterbury, the strike committee reported: "The organisation here was perfect. No weakening whatever. Our difficulty was to keep the men not involved in work." In Coventry, workers struck without waiting for an official ruling on whether they were included in the 'first line' transport workers or the 'second line' engineers. In areas where it was not expected that the strike would be widely supported there was "often a spontaneous and powerful upsurge of working-class solidarity".[30] One such area was Johnstone, just outside Glasgow: "Never before has such solidarity been shown in an industrial dispute in this locality; even our political opponents, Orangemen, being active pickets and taking part generally in the struggle."[31]

It took a long struggle in Scotland, in which the great John McLean participated, to cut across sectarian religious divisions between Protestants and Catholics and unite the workers on class lines. Scotland, particularly Glasgow, remained politically at the head of the British working class, especially during the First World War and its aftermath. It was in this area that the effects of the Russian Revolution were most keenly felt by the working class. The National Minority Movement "made rapid headway in North Lanarkshire".[32] The polarisation on religious lines had begun to soften as the Orange Protestant workers moved towards Labour as a consequence of their trade union involvement. In 1921, a Labour MP was elected for Coatbridge but the most dramatic swing to the left in North Lanarkshire was the election of Walter Newbold, a member of the Communist Party, as MP for Motherwell in 1922. Robert Smillie, the Scottish miners' president, was a Belfast Protestant but was supported by Catholics in North Lanarkshire.

This was one area in which the Minority Movement outlined a plan for militant action in 1925 involving the setting up of councils of action. On the eve of battle, in April 1926, at a meeting of the Minority Movement in Hamilton, the conclusion was that time was running out, not just for the miners but for the working class: "Our only hope lies along the lines of solid, efficiently organised, militant action." The ruling class had come to fear the potential power of the miners and the working class in Scotland. During the 1921 lock-out, Lloyd George claimed: "The population of the Scottish mining villages are savage folk."[33] Official control of the strike rested in the General Council of the Scottish Trades Union Congress in Glasgow. But a series of local councils of action were organised throughout the industrial areas of Scotland, in which Communist Party members, although thin on the ground, played a key role. In Cambuslang, for instance, where there were 60 members of the CP, a local trades' council was formed and miners, steelworkers, transport and railway-men affiliated. However, once the council of action was set up on Sunday 2 May, other political groups and non-affiliated unions were allowed representation. The chairman and secretary were in the Communist Party. The widespread support for the strike was indicated in Cambuslang where there was "a wonderful feeling of solidarity not only among the strikers but also their families: the women played an exceptionally important part in the area".[34] When there was an attempt by the local

Labour MP, Wright, at a meeting in Eastfield public park to suggest that the strike was a mistake, he was "lucky to escape physical injury".[35]

"Tranquillity and peace"

Yet at the same time as this was happening, a national 'leader' of the strike, Thomas, was quoted prominently in Churchill's *Gazette* stating: "I have never disguised and I do not disguise now that I have never been in favour of the principle of a general strike."[36] There could not be a greater contrast between the mood on the ground and the treachery of the leaders at the top. The working class was becoming more and more radicalised as the strike progressed. Of course, there were different tempos, depending upon previous experience, size and power of the working class in an area and, crucially, on the political development and presence of capable leaders on the ground. In Scotland, "As the nine days progressed and the control of the councils [of action] increased they resembled embryo soviets. Their existence alongside the 'legal' authority created a dual power situation".[37] Moreover: "All of those interviewed confirmed this growing feeling of 'excitement', and 'power' even among those previously considered 'moderates'. Some saw the situation as 'pregnant with possibility'."[38] As we have seen, the councils of action in many areas were mainly 'embryos' of real generalised workers' councils, but there is no doubt that if the strike had progressed then the improvised councils would have been forced to extend their power, draw in representatives from the factories and the workplaces, organise more effective picketing and even a defence force to protect the picket lines and workers on strike.

Naturally, the "respectable" members of the General Council eschewed the idea of a workers' defence corps, which had been raised prominently by the National Minority Movement and the Communist Party during the strike. Yet up and down the country men were being arrested. On 11 May, for instance, the number of arrests had risen by 374; in Glasgow alone, the total since the strike began was over 200.[39] Strikers were arrested on the flimsiest excuses. In Accrington, for instance, a small boy was arrested for throwing orange peel at a "charabanc" (coach).[40] At Bolton, ten lads received up to three months in jail for drawing the draw-pin of a coal cart; and at Farnworth a man was sent to jail for a month for tearing down a government poster.

The government tried to create the impression – supported by the TUC – that all was tranquillity and peace but the reality on the ground was that as the strike progressed the inevitable collisions developed between strikers and pickets on the one side who were trying to prevent the employers from breaking the transport embargo, and the police on the other. In Newcastle, for instance, the employers would resort to the most underhand methods to break this embargo. They used permits to move non-essential goods and the TUC received many reports of lorries labelled 'essential food' containing anything from bedding for blacklegs to toy rocking horses! The *Westminster Worker* stated: "People are often found masquerading as loaves of bread."[41]

Workers' press

Humour and satire peppered the rank-and-file strike bulletins and newspapers as opposed to the official organ of the TUC, the *British Worker*, which was staid, dull and lagging behind what was taking place on the ground. For instance, the *St Pancras Bulletin* reported on 12 May that notices and posters on the walls of Highgate Cemetery called for volunteers and suggested that "it should be 'picketed by underground men'"! The *Kensington Strike Bulletin* announced on 7 May: "The strike is over. Only 400,000 NUR men are now on strike, plus one million miners and two million others. But three trains are running in Manchester and there is a five minute service every two hours on the tubes. A bag of coal has been brought from Newcastle today." The *Bristol Bulletin* read: "Early in the morning, per broadcast from London, see the little puff-puffs all in a row, D'Arcy on the engine, pulled a little lever, expansion of the boiler – UP WE GO!" The Eastern Valleys Joint Industrial Council in Monmouthshire published an imaginary conversation between a striker and his young son: "'What is a BLACKLEG Daddy?' asked the innocent lad. 'A BLACKLEG is a TRAITOR, my boy. He is a man who knows not honour or shame!' 'Were there many BLACKLEGS in the valley, Daddy?' 'No my boy! Only the stationmaster at Abersychan and the two clerks at Crane Street Station.'"[42]

Where the workers were strong mass pickets developed which stopped attempts to break the trade union embargo. This was the case in parts of Scotland, the north of England, as we have seen, and in London's East End. In Falkirk in East Scotland, blackleg drivers were formally "placed under arrest" by pickets before they could turn back and "much of the traffic in and out of Edinburgh was controlled by the local strike committee".[43] Abe Moffat, Communist Party member and future president of the mineworkers, described the situation in Cowdenbeath in Fife: "All motor vehicles had to get permission from the trades council before travelling up the Great North Road. We had pickets on in various parts of the road to ensure that no-one passed without the permission of the trades council. To ensure that no-one would pass, miners had a rope across the road. If a motor vehicle had a pass it got through, if it had no pass it had to turn back."[44]

Police and strikers

Of course, these were areas in the vanguard of the workers' movement; not all areas were as effective in preventing blacklegs from working and the employers from seeking to break the strike. In these areas the TUC did nothing effectively to extend the examples of the more militant areas to less militant ones. On the contrary, most of their efforts were bent towards constraining and restraining the more militant sections of the working class in areas which were in danger of getting out of hand. They were particularly terrified that the movement would extend to the establishment of viable workers' defence corps. Yet because of the experience of the working class, with attempts to break the strike and collisions with the police, such bodies of workers' police , or workers' defence corps, at least in outline, are "specifically mentioned in reports of Aldershot, Chatham, Colchester, Croydon, Denny and Dunipace, Methil, St Pancras, Selby, Sowerby Bridge, and Willesden".[45] They were spontaneously formed and in clear breach of the wishes of the TUC.

This force, sometimes, as in the case of Chatham and Colchester, took the form of special pickets for meetings. But in places like Croydon, Methil and Willesden fairly large forces were developed. At Methil in East Scotland, a corps which had been organised under the command of an ex-Sergeant Major with 150 men was raised to a strength of 700 as a reply to police charges on pickets and was used on regular patrol work. It was organised under ex-Non Commissioned Officers and they patrolled the area in columns of four, armed with pick-shafts. The result was, "There was no further interference by police with the pickets."[46] In Lincoln, "The police asked us to supply the whole of the special constables – which we did".[47] In Swindon, "When our autocratic Mayor sent two tramcars on the streets, the police allowed our strike leaders to take charge of the situation."[48]

The difficulty of mobilising special constables out of the general population who could be in turn affected by strikers often coming from the same community was recognised by the government in: "It was thought that a special constable, recruited from a given village, might feel some compunction about summarily arresting his best friend for seditious talk on the village green. Mobile fleets of special constables were therefore recruited far away from the possible danger zones, and they dashed through those zones as strangers."[49] Much the same methods were used by the Thatcher government in the 1984-85 miners' strike. In Yorkshire, for instance, the Metropolitan Police from London achieved notoriety as the 'bully boys' of Thatcher in the violent methods against the miners both in the coal fields and in the attempts to prevent pickets from travelling in support of the miners.

Strike breakers ineffective

The government could not rely in 1926 on the loyalty of the largely civilian forces that were drawn from areas inhabited by strikers. The leaders of the strike in the North-East were warning Eccleston Square that the clashes between the police and strikers were escalating. The tension was so high that several thousand workers in

Newcastle were baton charged by police on Saturday night, 8 May. Strike leaders warned that the situation could "get out of hand" and the military could be resorted to. The use of the police in the North-East arose from the frustration felt by the authorities at the grip increasingly exercised by the workers and their organisations, the councils of action. The government had, in effect, lost control in the region and "this would certainly account for a new determination to smash the strike by force".[50]

But the police force, particularly the special constables, could not fail but to be affected by stubborn resistance from the working class, which was evident in many areas. At Lincoln, the Chief Constable was "a consistent friend of labour and absolutely refused the assistance of either military or mounted police". At Ilkeston, the strike committee found the local police were "very good and sooner assisted than interfered with us". The Leyton Strike Committee – an area with a huge concentration of railway workers – had a "very pleasant relationship with the police". The Selby Strike Committee observed: "Police assistance could not be improved upon; our strike police and local police worked in company and harmony". Even in Yeovil, "There was a good feeling exhibited by the town police throughout." In Bath, the Council of Action was "complimented and thanked by the Mayor and Chief Constable for maintaining perfect order; advised Mayor first day of strike to disband local specials as superfluosities".[51]

But mass picketing in the main roads of London's East End resulted in fierce street battles, in which 30 civilians were taken to Poplar Hospital and one man, it was alleged, died of his injuries. Further baton charges took place and violent clashes resulted around the Blackwall Tunnel, where cars were smashed and set alight. Attacks on trams and buses also led to clashes in Leeds, Nottingham, Manchester, Stoke, Liverpool, Glasgow and Edinburgh. There were also clashes in the East End and at the Elephant and Castle mounted police attacked the crowd after a bus, which was trying to dodge strike pickets, had crashed onto the pavement killing a man.

There were a number of candidates for the role of "strong man" in forcibly suppressing the strike. One of those was Churchill and another was 'Mussolini minor', Joynson-Hicks (Jix), the Home Secretary. He had declared on a previous occasion, "We did not conquer India for the benefit of the Indians. I know it is said at missionary meetings that we conquered it to raise the level of the Indians. That is cant. We conquered India as the outlet for the goods of Great Britain. We conquered India by the sword and by the sword we should hold it."[52] Of course, the "sword" was inadequate once the national revolt of the Indian people gathered momentum during and after the Second World War. But the very fact that people like this were in the government, as well as Churchill, who posed the possibility of a serious confrontation including the use of troops, could have ignited the explosive situation which existed. Any number of incidents could have triggered this off.

The *British Gazette* had garnered to itself the lion's share of newsprint available but when pickets tried to prevent this from reaching its offices, the combustible Churchill demanded the despatch of foot guards with ammunition to confront the strikers. The government, however, held to its line that "troops should be used only as a last resort". But it was becoming quite clear that the 98,000 special constables enrolled throughout the country – with 11,000 in London alone – were incapable of holding back the growing movement of the working class. It was because of the inadequacies of these forces that Churchill provocatively carried his statement in the *British Gazette*, mentioned earlier, that the armed forces would be mobilised if necessary.

The General Council of the TUC, because of the embargo on transport, were accused of an organised attempt to starve the people and wreck the state. A decision was then taken to break the standstill which the strikers had implemented in the London Docks. In London itself, there was only 48 hours supply of flour left when the government decided to act. It broke the pickets around the docks with 105 scab lorries at 4.30 in the morning with Grenadier Guardsmen in the lorries and twenty armoured cars, crewed by men of the Royal Tank Corps, escorting them. The *New York World* reported that there was "enough artillery to kill every living thing in every street in the neighbourhood". To the *British Gazette*, the convoy looked like "the commissariat of a victorious army".[53]

Workers' defence force

After this incident a clear call for the organisation of defensive formations of the working class, a defence corps, would have received widespread support. So also would the idea of appealing clearly to troops – most of whom came from the working class – not to fire on members of their own class. The refusal to do this was to disarm the working class and strike in the face of rising threats and violence. A.J. Cook had raised this issue, Communist Party members had been arrested for suggesting this. A display of military force in London not only served to anger the working class there but in other areas also. Clashes occurred at Southsea, Swansea and Nottingham, where water hoses were turned on strikers. At Houghton-le-Dale near Preston, police baton charged strikers trying to stop buses and shots were fired at a train passing below a bridge at Crewe. In Preston itself, a crowd of 5,000 tried to storm the police station to rescue a striker arrested after earlier attacks on buses. In

Hull, which had seen early clashes, further "disturbances" occurred. At Middlesbrough, renewed fighting broke out around the railway station. In Glasgow, *The Times* reported: "The struggle was of the wildest description; pots and pans, iron bars, pickheads and hammers were used as missiles" against the police. Rioting took place over four consecutive nights and 269 strikers were arrested.[54]

At Nine Elms Railway Depot in London, a particularly significant incident took place in the second week of the strike when a special constable was stabbed following an incident provoked by the police themselves. The police took revenge with baton charges in an attack on the union headquarters. 'Specials', drawn from middle-class youth, set about strikers with their batons "without any discretion". The secretary of the NUR branch described how "a covered lorry drove up from which alighted two sergeants and about 50 constables. Without the slightest provocation, they drew their batons and on the word to charge being given, they unmercifully belaboured men, women and children, injuring many. It was a mercy that I moved my head in time or I should have been killed." Most significantly, he states: "I am very much afraid after what has happened the men will arm themselves and as there are about 20,000 on strike in this neighbourhood, should the police again attempt such a thing it would be them taken to the mortuary and not the hospital."[55]

In Poplar, where local Labour leaders were addressing a meeting of 500 dockers outside the Town Hall, a police tender swerved into the crowd injuring many. Then, 30 policemen swarmed out to baton charge the crowd, injuring many including a local clergyman who had approached the police with an upheld crucifix. The police then stormed the NUR headquarters in Poplar High Street, "batoning anyone unfortunate enough to be within striking distance".[56] The Mayor of Poplar, who was in the building playing billiards at the time, was admitted to hospital with serious head injuries.

Widespread prosecutions also occurred; one Lambeth worker was fined £5 for shouting "We want the revolution!" A Manchester businessman found in possession of copies of the *Workers' Daily* received two months imprisonment. When Communist MP Saklatvala addressed a May Day meeting in Hyde Park, he was arrested. This was for calling on the "army boys" to "revolt now and refuse to fight, and they will be the real saviours of the homes and the workers". He received a two months jail sentence. A young Communist school teacher in Pontefract was jailed for a similar speech but gave her address as "Moscow, Soviet Russia". In Liverpool, a Communist Party member had told an open air meeting that troops stationed at Chelsea Barracks and Aldershot had refused to entrain for mining areas, and that all transport in the East End of London had been stopped by the workers in spite of repeated baton charges by mounted police. He was also jailed for three months. The Communist Party came in for special treatment, with raids on its national headquarters and provincial offices, with an estimated 1,200 members brought before the courts.[57] A 17-year old girl was imprisoned for tripping up a strike-breaker!

War clarifies, strips away, the inessential and shows in brutal relief the real character of the combatants. It tests out the strategy and tactics as well as organisation of the opposing armies. Class war possesses the same essential features. It requires a clear revolutionary leadership, at the head of a mass party, acting as a lever to allow the working class to draw all the necessary conclusions from the actions of the capitalist class as well as its own. At bottom, the General Strike of 1926 shattered the perceptions of all stripes of reformism that the capitalist state was in some sense neutral, could be seized hold of and utilised to carry through fundamental changes in the lives and conditions of the working class, the majority. Marx explained that the government is the "executive committee" of the ruling class. That was evident in the case of the Baldwin government, which acted quite clearly and consciously to inflict a serious defeat on the British labour movement. In order to do this, it pursued a relentless ideological struggle, took hold of the main levers for the dissemination of information, the *British Gazette* and the BBC, in order to win the population, in particular the middle class, to its side.

The capitalist state

But the government was also prepared to use its state, if necessary, to forcibly crush the working class. Friedrich Engels pointed out that the state can ultimately be reduced to armed bodies of men and their material appendages, courts, prisons, army and police. In 1926, the police were used on a widespread scale in order to try and smash the picket lines. As the strike progressed, however, these were shown to be ineffective and the 'special constables' mobilised were incapable of smashing the workers' movement. In areas like Liverpool, where the fascists had been recruited as 'specials', they were not in fact used in the course of the strike. But behind the police was the army, navy and the air force, who were "on standby" for use if necessary.

These conclusions arising from events, however, were far from the minds of the General Council of the TUC. Ultimately, they were prepared to bow down before this state as events were soon to show. The state in the 1926 General Strike was not "above classes" as MacDonald and Co. believed. They peddled this myth, linking it to the idea that the strike was "economic", a purely "industrial" struggle. In reality, the strikers came up not just against the individual employer but the government armed from head to toe with the necessary repressive instruments to crush the working class. The BBC was unequivocally on the side of the government and the boss class as a whole. When *The Times*, for instance, found its newsprint commandeered by Churchill and the government, it protested. Churchill's reply was: "I do not at all agree with your idea that the TUC have as much right as the government to publish their side of the case and to exhort their followers to continued action."[58] His justification for this 'biased', not to say dictatorial, measure was that there was a large number of people who were detached from the conflict and awaiting to see whether the government or the trade unions "is the stronger".

7 A Revolutionary Situation

Working class people learn more in one day of action than in years or decades of peaceful development. This applies to a strike in a single enterprise, in a district or region, or national action. But a general strike is the greatest school for driving home the realities of class society and the nature of its state. We have seen that the General Council of the TUC was not capable of doing this. On the contrary, by the end of the first week of the strike, they were desperately attempting to rein it in and secretly opened negotiations with the government via Herbert Samuel. A.J. Cook wrote later: "It seemed that the only desire of some leaders was to call off the General Strike at any cost, without any guarantees for the workers, miners or others."[1] Allen Hutt says of this statement by Cook: "That is exactly what happened; except that it was not some leaders but the whole General Council, including the Purcell-Hicks 'Lefts'."[2]

This, of course, was what Trotsky had been predicting all along. But the Communist Party was unprepared for this development. Right-wing union leaders like Thomas, in the final analysis, were props of the capitalist system and all that went with it. J.R.

Manchester demonstration.

Clynes, at one with Thomas in the General Strike, explained: "J.H. Thomas, representing the railwaymen, found, early in the strike, that his duties took him to Buckingham Palace. King George asked him a number of questions, and expressed his sympathy for the miners. At the end of the talk, His Majesty, who was gravely disturbed, remarked, it is said: 'Well, Thomas, if the worst happens I suppose all this – (with a gesture indicating his surroundings) – will vanish?' Fortunately for Britain and the world, it did not come to the worst. The trade unions saw to that."[3]

Favourable opportunity for CP

But how then did the Communist Party fare in this situation? It was a small party but, as we have seen, even between Red Friday and the beginning of the General Strike it had substantially increased its forces and, moreover, had the authority of the Russian Revolution at its back. This hugely favourable factor for the CP should not be underestimated. The authority and prestige of the Russian workers' state was colossal in the eyes of the working class in Britain and elsewhere, confronted as it was with an endemic and chronic capitalist crisis. The revolution had not yet degenerated into the Stalinist bureaucratic dictatorship which repelled the world working class. An intense struggle was under way between the forces around Stalin and the Left Opposition on the future direction of Russia. The fact that the British trade unions tried to cover themselves with the authority of the Russian Revolution showed its attractiveness to the working class as a whole.

There are many examples in history of small parties growing rapidly when revolutionary events occur. The Bolsheviks went from roughly 8,000 members on the eve of the February Revolution in 1917 to over a quarter of a million by October. This gave them a mass base and allowed the party to lead the working class, with the peasantry behind it, to the overthrow of Russian landlordism and capitalism. The process of revolution was speeded up in Russia because of the First World War. It was compressed into nine months, largely because of the desperation of the masses to end the First World War; the revolution was literally a life or death question. This could only be achieved on the basis of the Bolsheviks of Lenin and Trotsky coming to power. In other revolutionary situations, however, the processes were more drawn out; in Spain, for example, between 1931 and 1937. Yet in this revolution, the POUM (the United Marxist Workers' Party) grew from less than a thousand members before July 1936 to tens of thousands in 1937. The Chinese Communist Party grew from a handful – 51 in 1921 – to a mass force that could have taken power six years later in the revolution of 1925-27.

Of course, there can be no exact parallels that could be drawn for Britain in 1926. National traditions, the character of the labour movement, the state of preparedness and consciousness of the working class and other layers of society all have to be taken into account. "Tradition is the dead weight of history which lies on the brain of the living," as Marx pointed out. For the oldest working class in the world, where the organisation of trade unions goes back to before the French Revolution, one of the "traditions" that weighed on the working class in 1926 was the existence of an encrusted, conservative trade union officialdom, which like barnacles on a ship drags it back and threatens it with paralysis. This stratum in "normal" times dissipates the collective strength of workers, invariably in defence of its own narrow privileges. In a period of social explosions, however, the authority of these "leaders" can be shattered. This can result in such a weakening of their influence, even in a labour movement where the official apparatus plays an important role. It can allow space for the rapid emergence of genuine revolutionary forces. For instance, in Germany in 1923, the official unions were pushed aside. The working class, in the course of a developing revolutionary situation, stopped paying dues to the official trade unions and looked to the shop committees which could have become the basis for genuine workers' councils, which in turn, with the right leadership, could have carried through a revolution. In order to ensure that such opportunities can be seized – unique and often only existing for a limited time – there must be clarity amongst the leaders and ranks on the character of the period. This is not an easy task in the rapidly evolving movement. Appropriate fighting slogans and organisations are necessary which can lead the working class forward, ultimately to take power.

The fact that the Communist Party in Britain in 1926 did not have an adequate analysis, slogans or organisation which met the situation was not entirely of their own making. Farman describes them as "reluctant revolutionaries"[4] But this was not true of the rank and file or most of their leaders. They were "the salt of the earth", as we stated earlier, the flower of the British working class. They had displayed not a little courage and self-sacrifice – particularly when contrasted to MacDonald, Thomas and Co. They were prepared to go to jail for their class and pursued heroic work amongst the working class before, during and after the General Strike. Their political weaknesses arose from the advice they received from the Comintern. They were imprisoned in the mistaken tactic of the 'Anglo-Russian Trade Union Committee', which was to have fatal consequences in the nine days themselves and afterwards.

In particular, there was a complete underestimation of the revolutionary possibilities inherent in the developing situation. For instance, in the *Workers' Weekly* of 30 April 1926, a few days before the greatest event in British working class history was to unfold, Communist Party leader J.T. Murphy wrote an article with the title 'Revolution not in Sight'. He pointed out: "Our party does not hold the leading positions in the trade unions... And let it be remembered that those who are leading have no revolutionary perspectives before them. Any revolutionary perspective they may perceive will send the majority of them hot on the track of a retreat... To entertain any exaggerated views as to the revolutionary possibilities of this crisis and visions of new leadership 'arising spontaneously in the struggle,' etc., is fantastic. Let us keep our feet well on the ground and our heads clear." He went on, demonstrating in the process a complete underestimate of what was about to happen, "This is not the revolutionary crisis which is haunting the minds of the ruling class, but one of a long series of crises attending the decline of British capitalism... If the trade unions were staffed and led by a mass Communist Party, welding the whole workers' movement to working-class principles behind the revolutionary leadership of the Communist Party, the character of the present crisis would be different, and the nervous heroics of Jix would be more justified. But we have not a mass Communist Party yet. We have not won the leadership of the trade unions yet. We have not beaten MacDonald and his supporters *yet.*"[5]

Revolution

This was a completely inadequate explanation of perspectives for the struggle which loomed. The subjective weaknesses of the Communist Party seemed to be the main criteria to measure the objective reality. It also seems that Karl Radek, a member of the Left Opposition at the time, was of a similar mind as Murphy. When he spoke to Robert Boothby the latter reported his comments: "It is more interesting now there [in Britain] than here. But make no mistake, this is not a revolutionary movement it is simply a wage dispute."[6] This, as we have seen, was the theme of the right-wing trade union leaders. It certainly wasn't the view of some of the Moscow leaders like Zinoviev who wrote later in the journal *Communist International:* "The masses gave evidence of marvellous organisation. During the first seven days the strike was developing on an upward grade. The masses formed the councils of action, which were in fact beginning to develop in the direction of district soviets of workers' deputies."[7] As we have seen, the councils of action were not soviets, had not begun, unfortunately, "to develop in the direction of district soviets of workers' deputies". There were elements of dual power but also, contrary to what Murphy, the Communist Party leadership and what subsequent historians of the party have tried to prove, the nine days objectively displayed some of the features of a revolutionary or pre-revolutionary situation.

Revolutionary opportunity?

Lenin gave four basic conditions for a revolutionary situation. Firstly, the capitalists cannot rule in he old way. The second condition is that the middle class are either hostile to the old regime or are neutral. Thirdly, the working class is prepared to go the whole way in confronting the system. The fourth and most vital condition is the existence of a mass party and the leadership able to lead the working class to take power. To see whether Britain in 1926 met all or some of these conditions it is necessary to understand what are the factors which distinguish revolution from 'normal' periods. One indication is when the masses step onto the scene of history and begin to take their fate into their own hands. This signifies the beginning of a revolution.

The working class of Russia in February 1917 made a revolution in overthrowing the Tsarist regime. However, they lacked sufficient consciousness of their own power then to carry through the socialist revolution. This only came after many ebbs and flows over nine months. The mass involvement of the *majority* of organised workers in Britain in the General Strike, drawing behind them the unorganised, signified the beginning of a revolutionary process. This would have been enormously facilitated by factory committees embracing non-unionists. Mass involvement was a key feature of the nine days. Moreover, the working class was rapidly beginning to generalise their experience within days of the General Strike breaking out. A typical report, carried in a number of histories of the strike, is the comments of the Dartford Divisional Labour Party: "After the third day of the strike, if you spoke about the coal owners the audience would listen with a polite indifference, but if you attacked the government, or even mentioned the word, you had the audience with you, and that with cheers and wild enthusiasm. The issue was the TUC and the government; the miners and the owners were secondary to this issue."[8]

James Klugmann, historian of the Communist Party, interprets this and other similar statements as just the "beginning". He states: "Nine days was not *nearly* enough to transform the hatred of the Tories, employers, coal owners, and the disgust with the General Council, into a positive, scientific, socialist, revolutionary outlook." He even chastises members of the Communist Party and sections of the Communist International who, he says, should "not exaggerate" the stage of understanding of the working class during the General Strike. He argued that there was a "readiness to strike, but [also] a deep feeling of *solidarity* prevailed".[9] Lenin once said that a revolution does not develop in a "pure" form with one army lining up on one side "for the revolution" and another opposed! Revolutionary conscious-ness develops when the masses, and not all at once, come to the conclusion that "they cannot live like this any longer".

That was unmistakably the mood which had developed in Britain in the run-up to and, particularly, during the 1926 General Strike. The worker referred to earlier from Ashton summed this up. He believed that, at long last, he and his class were now in the driving seat as the bosses came "cap in hand" looking for favours from the councils of action. The general mood was one of hatred for the system. There were elements of dual power and, as Churchill and Baldwin understood, a reaching out by the working class for an "alternative government". That consciousness was developing with every hour and every day of the strike, which was the thing that most alarmed the "leadership" at the top.

As to the development of councils of action, Zinoviev exaggerated the situation. He compared them to the "structure and functions of the departments of the St Petersburg Soviet in the period of so-called 'dual power'" (February – November 1917). Nevertheless these parallel sources of power would have developed by leaps and bounds had the example of the North-East and other areas been eventually taken up. This is tacitly admitted by Farman: "The strike committees were clearly intending to substitute their own authority for that of the government. It is probable that, if the strike had been prolonged, regional groupings of councils of action would have operated with an increasing indifference to the TUC and they may well have evolved into embryo soviets."[10] Not "embryos" but fully-fledged workers' councils with more and more power concentrated in their hands were posed if the strike had gone on. The development of such organisations, even in their embryo, is in itself an unmistakable sign of a profound change in the situation.

It is true that it would not have been possible to sustain them if the strike had not culminated in a complete victory and the taking of power by the working class, something which was not possible given the character of the right-wing leadership of the TUC. But if councils of action had developed, filled out, become more like British 'soviets', even if only for a short period, this would have established an enormous historical reference point for the working class in future battles. Just as the Russian working class took the example of soviets in 1905 and applied them in 1917, so too would the British workers use a similar example from 1926 in the future. It was for this reason that the right-wing General Council acted to stultify the developments of councils of action in 1926. Subsequently, with the help of capitalist historians, they have belittled them, their role and potential in 1926.

Another condition of revolution is that the ruling class cannot rule in the old way; it splits into factions and divides amongst itself. This was an unmistakeable feature of 1926. There was general agreement amongst the ruling class on the need to drive down living standards, as the condition for restoring the health of their system. They would have preferred to have done this by pressure on the trade union leaders but, given the wellsprings of discontent pushing the latter into opposition, the capitalists could not achieve their objective in this way. They therefore decided, quite consciously, to take on the working class and inflict a defeat hoping it would have lasting effects. Even then there was a 'hard' wing of the capitalists (Churchill and Jix) and a 'soft' wing represented by Baldwin.

This was compounded by the difference with the Liberals; Lloyd George was making demagogic speeches denouncing the government and even hinting at support for the miners in this battle. He floated the idea of joining with MacDonald and right-wing Labour in a new 'political realignment'. MacDonald was a discredited figure in the aftermath of the 1924 minority Labour government, both within the Labour Party and in the trade unions, even with right-wing figures like Bevin. If this 'realignment' with Lloyd George had taken place, it would have represented something similar to the creation of the Social Democratic Party in 1981, led by Roy Jenkins, Shirley Williams, David Owen and Bill Rogers. This split the Labour vote and ensured the victory of Thatcher in the 1980s. The very fact that this was discussed in the tumultuous events of 1926 was itself a barometer of the extreme crisis which this symbolised for capitalism and its different political formations.

Middle class

What then was the mood amongst the middle class? Trotsky once described British society as one of the most "proletarian in the world", with regards to both the numbers of workers and their specific weight in society. Such was the immense power of this class – three quarters of the population – they could have taken power by themselves. But one of the conditions for revolution is that the intermediate layers in society should either support the working class in the struggle or be at least 'neutral'. Where they line up behind the bourgeois, they are potentially a source of reaction, support dictatorships and, in the case of fascism, are mobilised as a battering ram to smash and atomise the organisations of the working class. But the middle class in Britain, a minority but quite substantial in numbers, were not solidly behind Baldwin in this clash. It is true that the 'gilded youth' – bourgeois or petty bourgeois young people out for a 'lark' – were, in some senses, mobilised. But as we have seen by the fate of the OMS, they were largely ineffective in breaking the strike. While on the surface, most 'respectable' public opinion, usually denoting the middle class, appeared to be with the government, it was nevertheless very tentative. Hence, the reining in of Churchill and others when they threatened to go "too far" in using repressive methods. A confrontation leading to deaths on a sizeable scale would have fuelled the flames of working-class opposition and risked alienating the middle class.

The, at best, vacillating mood of the middle class in 1926 is indicated by the individuals who appeared on either side of the barricades. As mentioned earlier, A.J.P.

Taylor was on the side of the strikers, considered himself a communist, and even considered G.D.H. Cole somewhat of a reformist: "Mr G.D.H. Cole is a bit of a puzzle, with a Bolshevik soul and a Fabian muzzle."[11] On one occasion, as the General Strike loomed, he drove with Tom Driberg, later a left-wing Labour MP, to the Communist Party headquarters in London, expecting orders for the "coming revolution". He recounted that he found the doors there bolted and barred. "After much banging by us, there was a rattling of chains and an elderly Scotch Communist called Bob Steward appeared. He said 'There's no-one here. I am only the caretaker. Get along hame with ye.' These were the only instructions I ever received from the Communist Party of Great Britain." Bob *Stewart* was a founding member of the CPGB! Taylor admitted later that his experiences during the strike had had a deep effect on him, as the result of which he developed a great admiration for the British working class and felt that he should devote his life to their service. He also commented: "That was not all; the General Strike destroyed my faith, such as it was, in the Communist Party. The party that was supposed to lead the working class played no part in the strike except to be a nuisance."[12]

Other subsequently famous figures who were on the side of the working class included Cecil Day Lewis, the poet, who became a member of the Oxford University Strike Committee, John Betjeman and even Hugh Gaitskell, as mentioned earlier. The great W.H. Auden was also friendly towards the strikers and the labour movement. G.K Chesterton, the author, also showed sympathy, writing: "There are many things we should like to know about the free hand given to 'specials' during the recent crisis. We should like to know, for example, how many of them had seen service in Ireland as Black and Tans, and if any person in authority knew that they proposed to serve the English strikers as they had once served Irishmen. We know that the ruling classes had determined on a civil war, but we should like to know how far the police were prepared to go in helping them."[13] Surprisingly, Graham Greene, who later moved towards the Left, was recruited into the 'Special Constabulary'. He commented: "There was a wonderful absence of traffic, it was a beautiful, hushed London that we were not to know again until the Blitz, and there was the excitement of living on a frontier, close to violence... Our two-man patrol always ceased at the south end of Vauxhall Bridge, for beyond lay the enemy streets where groups of strikers stood outside the public houses. A few years later, my sympathies would have lain with them, but the great depression was still some years away: the middle class had not yet been educated by the hunger-marchers."[14]

Although the 1930s were to deepen the alienation of the middle class from the establishment, and sections of middle-class youth were drawn in 1926 to the 'specials' as a kind of extension of a "rather violent rugger match", nevertheless this did not denote a deep-set mood of support for the government by the middle class as a whole. Some, undoubtedly, were "prompted by a class instinct as powerful as that which motivated the strikers, well-fed young men from the fashionable clubs, universities and business institutions responded to Jix's appeals in their thousands".[15] The headmaster of Eton, and fifty of his assistants, and the 85-year old Earl of Meath, founder of the Empire Day movement, joined the government side. But this was hardly a powerful club with which to batter into submission working class resistance. The mass of the middle class was watching and waiting. Decisive action and the continuation of the strike for any length of time would have undermined their support for the government with the possibility of the middle class being drawn over to the side of the working class.

Mass revolutionary party vital

This, it is true, was not a fully 'mature' revolutionary situation in the classical sense of the term, nor was it a "normal" situation, a struggle just for wages. Three out of the four conditions for revolution existed, at least in outline. The capitalists were split, the working class was looking for a way out and were in revolt against capitalism. Moreover, increased social tension overflowed from the safe parliamentary channels which had been skilfully used by the ruling class in the past to contain them. The main arena was not parliament – which was a sideshow to the main drama which was played out in the 'street'. The middle class were not firmly behind the government and decisive action by the working class would have won them over to their side or at least neutralised them. It was the fourth condition, the subjective factor, the leadership and the mass party that was absent. Given its small number of members, it is true, as J.T. Murphy implies, that the CP would not have been able by itself to change the outcome of the strike. But it could have and would have come out of the strike immeasurably stronger with correct policies. Moreover, and more decisive in the long term, the understanding and consciousness of the working class would have been far higher in preparation for future battles.

Revolutions, in reality, rarely develop in a 'classical' form or in one act. Revolution is a process involving different phases. 1926 was a heightened stage of class polarisation. To have matured into a classical revolutionary or pre-revolutionary situation would have required the presence of a mass party and mass leadership. J.T. Murphy was correct that the Communist Party was not yet this force. But it was prevented from becoming the basis of such a force by the theoretical, strategic and tactical limitations which were on display during the General Strike. From an overall point of view, the Communist Party militants, devoted as they were to the working class and playing a key role at rank-and-file level, were not fully prepared for the situation.

This is not to say that even the best revolutionary party can always be prepared for all eventualities. Only Lenin and Trotsky fully understood the significance of the February Revolution in October 1917 – the majority of Bolshevik leaders on the ground, Stalin, Kamenev, etc., supported the capitalist 'Provisional Government'. This was, in effect, support for a 'popular front' government before coalitions between workers and capitalist parties were known by this name. However, the Russian working class had the priceless corrective presence of Lenin and Trotsky and the Bolshevik rank and file cadre which had been prepared by Lenin during the whole preceding period. This, unfortunately, was not the case as far as the young British Communist Party was concerned. Peter Kerrigan, a member of the Communist Party and chairman of the Central Strike Co-Coordinating Committee in Glasgow, later wrote: "For the nine days of the strike I was to be busy, almost to the exclusion of all other activity, with the work of the Central Coordinating Committee, of which I was first vice-chairman and then chairman. People ask me today: did I expect the betrayal of the General Strike? I always have to reply that, amid the struggle, I never thought of it."[16]

This was typical of the position of Communist Party fighters at the time. The responsibility lay not on their shoulders but on the fact that they had not been adequately politically prepared, either for the kind of social rupture which the General Strike constituted or for the strategy and tactics to ensure its victory. Even as a small party, it is incumbent on a revolutionary party to pose the question of what is needed to ensure victory, to criticise the inadequacies of the leadership, both Right and Left, and, above all, to seize the opportunity presented to build a powerful platform which can become the base of a mass revolutionary party later. J.T. Murphy, while pointing to the numerical weakness of the Communist Party, nevertheless projected before the strike the possibility of it growing to at least 100,000. This was not a Utopian target given the explosive character of the events that were unfolding, and the points of support, small though they were, which the Communist Party had at that stage. With a different policy, even after the strike was terminated, this would have been possible.

8 TUC leaders capitulate

rom day one, the General Council was trying to find a way of ending the strike. After the first week and as soon as they witnessed the ever-growing success of the strike, frantic efforts were made to derail it via negotiating channels with the government. From Saturday 8 May onwards, behind the scenes "soundings" to end the strike were undertaken. This was leaked to the international capitalist press, which was freer to report on such developments. The *New York World* carried a dispatch on 8 May from its London correspondent "revealing that Ramsay MacDonald had given a private interview to reporters in the House of Commons in which the Labour Party leader had stated that he was keeping in constant touch with Mr Baldwin and was 'hourly in conference, regarding settlement of the strike". The editors of the *British Worker*, once they discovered this report, were forbidden to publicise it for obvious reasons.[1]

The conduit to the government was none other than Sir Herbert Samuel, the chairman of the so far failed Coal Commission. All of this was done behind the

Labour Leaders

backs of the mineworkers' union. It is incredible that during the General Strike when the miners were supposed to be the *cause celebre*, they did not even have representation on the General Council. From 9-11 May there were days of numerous meetings. Only once, however, in all these discussions, were the miners called in, on 10 May. Smith and Cook flatly rejected the suggestion that the strike should be called off so as to allow negotiations to continue on the basis of wage reductions. Cook, in *The Nine Days*, wrote: "These discussions and pow-wows had reached the stage when the Negotiating Committee and the leaders of the Labour Party felt that something tangible had been secured to justify a move towards calling off the General Strike."[2] The miners were pressed relentlessly to accept cuts in wages, the very issue on which the General Strike had been called. First fiddle in this wage-cutting chorus fell to Thomas, of course, but with the majority of trade union leaders, supporting him. The miners were pressed to agree to negotiations, so much so that Cook wrote: "It did seem terrible that we had to fight not only the government and the coal-owners but certain labour leaders as well."[3]

At the same time, international interest and support for the General Strike was huge. There was an enthusiastic response of the Russian trade unions. This reflected the fact that the heads of the workers there had been raised in the expectation and the hope that the English workers were going to make a breakthrough and link up with the workers' state in Russia. Through factory collections amongst a very poor working class, two million roubles (£200,000) were donated. But the TUC rejected this donation, shamefully recording in the *British Worker* on 8 May: "The report in the foreign press yesterday that an offer had been made by the Russian Trade Unions was confirmed this morning by a definite contribution being offered to the General Council. The Council has informed the Russian Trade Unions, in a courteous communication, that they are unable to accept the offer and the cheque has been returned."[4]

But this kind of support was necessary and correct from a working-class point of view. The capitalists of Europe were themselves watching with keen interest events in England, were commenting in a most hysterical manner, and fervently wishing for the General Strike's defeat. *Le Temps* in France, for instance, was of the "considered opinion that the English strike is directly due to Zinoviev".[5] This was an attempt to link the strike to the forged Zinoviev letter which brought down the Labour government of 1924, as we have seen. It was one indication that if the strike had succeeded it would have shaken the whole of capitalist Europe, including the dictatorship of Mussolini in Italy. On the same day that the TUC turned down financial aid from the Russian workers, the *British Gazette*, basing itself on reports from Italy, claimed that the strike in England was not "causing unrest" among Italian workmen! But contradicting this, it quoted Italian authorities warning against "industrial suicide". It called on "masters and men to collaborate" and contrasted this to the strike in England which was clearly threatening the class collaborationist corporatism of the Mussolini regime. It also said that a joint meeting of workmen sent the "following message... to Signor Mussolini – 'While in England there is a strike, we have after a ten-hours sitting concluded a series of agreements for the provinces of Leghorn in the spirit of collaboration with the firmness of imperial Italy and the invincible Duce.'"[6]

This was a sign that the British bosses, and particularly Churchill were yearning for a state like Signor Mussolini's, which would dispense with strikes of all kinds and particularly a general strike. On 12 May, the *British Gazette* also discovered a "vast Soviet scheme". It reported: "Arnold Rechberg, a German businessman, writing in *The Nation* this morning, states that he has evidence that the English strike is only one side of a vast Soviet scheme... [The trade union leaders] thought they were merely defending the economic interests of the working class."[7] The *British Gazette*, not content with the retreat of the TUC on the issue of Russian donations, stated in the same issue: "FOR WHOSE BENEFIT? A question for trade unionists. The Council of the TUC make a great virtue of returning the Soviet's cheque for thousands. So money to subsidise the strike in this country was offered from this source! Why? Was it to serve a British interest?"[8] Instead of replying to these accusations, as *Militant* vigorously did in the 1980s when challenged about being bankrolled by "foreign capital", the General Council capitulated to this pressure. The TUC and the miners had the right and duty to request international support, including financial donations, from the working class throughout the world. The British miners in the 1984-85 strike sent countless delegations throughout the world – which *Militant* and the Committee for a Workers' International helped in some cases to organise – for collections for the miners to sustain their year-long struggle.

It was the right of the miners and the working class, and the duty of any leadership worthy of the name, to act in this fashion, to collect cash, to call for action, from workers worldwide in defence of British workers. The TUC should have thrown back into the faces of the capitalists the accusations of the press. It was rank hypocrisy. It has now been revealed that the modern Tory party of Cameron received donations and 'loans' from foreign capitalists to fight a British general election! The capitalists arrogate to themselves the right to borrow from foreign capital, from the International Monetary Fund, World Bank, etc., but attempt to deny a similar right for the working class to receive support from their compatriots throughout the world. *The Times* on 6 May 1926 had already provided what one historian called "a more rational account" of what had happened in relation to the offer of Russian trade unions' money. It stated: "Soviet support for strikers. Red trade unions throughout the USSR are organising contributions to support the British strikers. The money if accepted, could not have served the British Communist Party. The national leaders were arrested before the strike began, and throughout the strike raids were made on Communist rooms to get rid of local leaders."[9]

"Honourable settlement"

Notwithstanding the shameful rejection of the Russian offer, the working class internationally rallied to their British brothers and sisters: "Reactions to the strike on the part of the trade union movement elsewhere in Europe were enthusiastic. The International Transport Federation became the organising centre of a trade union boycott on all transport to Britain. The International Miners' Federation placed an embargo on the transport of coal. There were many contributions, including some of $5,000 from the International Federation of Trade Unions."[10] There was also a donation of $10,000 from collections made at mass meetings in Germany. The Indian trade union movement decided to take action against British ships, as did the Mexican Federation of Labour. In the United States the Amalgamated Clothing Workers sent a contribution of $10,000, although the American Federation of Labour (AFL) merely declared its sympathy for the miners.

Symons comments in relation to the attitude of the TUC: "It was rather an embarrassment for them to learn that there had been widespread demonstrations in support of the strike in the Soviet Union, that collections were being taken in all industrial centres, that many Russian workers had voted to contribute part of their wages towards a strike donation, and that all British ships in Russian ports had been held up."[11] The General Council sought to mollify bourgeois public opinion on the one side while restraining and constraining the strike on the other. A general strike is an 'either/or' situation. Either it goes forward, which means a deepening and widening of the strike and its organs, such as workers' councils, posing at least implicitly the question of power being taken by the working class, or it slackens, weakens and eventually disintegrates.

There are, of course, periods, as we have seen from our historical sketch earlier, where the ruling class, taking fright at the scale and success of a general strike, draws back and is forced to concede. Such was the situation in the historical upswing of capitalism prior to the First World War and even in the Kapp Putsch of 1920, which completely paralysed the organisation of the capitalist state – including strikes by the civil servants – which defeated the coup plotters around the banker Kapp. But the British General Strike was not one of those situations. It posed the question of power, which is the last thing that the General Council – Right and Left – was prepared to contemplate.

The success of the strike, combined with the more open display of capitalist state power, frightened the General Council. Troops were used, as we see in the case of the London Docks, to move food and attempt to break the strike. The police, in the second week of the strike, began to harass, arrest and baton charge workers. Many workers were sent to jail, particularly Communist Party members. The government even considered prohibiting banks from paying out money to any person acting in opposition to the "national interest". This was directly aimed at the union funds, with the government warning in the House of Commons that these were "liable to seizure". This even alarmed the King, who advised Baldwin that "anything done to touch the pockets of those who are now only existing on strike pay might cause exasperation and serious reprisals on the part of the sufferers."[12]

And, of course, some of the union leaders were taking fright at the possibilities of their own arrest. Purcell, an erstwhile left winger, asserted: "Definitely the government had issued warrants for his and Bevin's arrest, as Chairman and Secretary of the Strike Organisation Committee."[13] At the same time Thomas, in public speeches, was doing his best to demoralise workers, stating in Hammersmith that he had never favoured a general strike but at the same time brazenly spelling out the need for "compromise", i.e. betrayal of the strike: "The responsibility is indeed a heavy one. But there will be a graver responsibility on whichever side fails to recognise the moment when an honourable settlement can be arrived at. The moment must be accepted and everyone must work to that end."[14] Havelock Wilson, strike-breaker extraordinaire, and leader of the Seamen's Union, tried to do his bit for the bosses by successfully applying to the High Court for an injunction restraining his own union officials from calling on members to support the strike. (Some seamen had come out in favour of the miners.) The judge who heard the case claimed that the "so-called General Strike" called by the TUC committee is illegal and "contrary to law" and "those persons inciting or taking part in it are not protected by the Trades Disputes Act of 1906."[15]

Liberal M.P. Sir John Simon followed this up in the House of Commons by saying that the strike was of "a wholly unconstitutional and unlawful character... Every trade union leader who has advised and prompted breaches of contract by strikers is liable in damages to the uttermost farthing of his personal possessions..."[16] Even the *Solicitors' Journal*, a "legal weekly of established repute", entirely disagreed with Simons's conclusions. Of course, under Thatcher's vicious anti-union laws today, upheld by Blair and his New Labour government, the threat of sequestration, and action against the assets of unions and their officials, are used to prevent workers from taking solidarity action, as was the case in the 2005 'Gate Gourmet' dispute. This was also a threat made against the unions in 1926. Against the background, however, of millions of workers out on strike in 1926, such a threat had as little impact as a drop of water on a hot stove. Nevertheless, the government never let slip any opportunity to warn the trade union leaders of further anti-union legislation unless they came to heel. And the government proceeded to introduce anti-union legislation after they had defeated the strike.

Thomas's speech about an "honourable settlement" was seized on by the government and its organisations as an example of what it actually wanted, an "offer to capitulate".[17] The BBC used Thomas's statement every night on its nine o'clock bulletin and the *British Gazette* displayed it every day. Yet precisely when the right-wing negotiating Strike Organising Committee was prepared to crawl on its belly before the government, the strike was growing in numbers and cohesion, as was the confidence of the workers. "The feeling of the workers is that the General Council and the Labour Party must stand firmly for no reduction in the miners' wages. They declare they are out to win."[18] From Birmingham, the Welsh MP, Morgan Jones, said that the spirit of the strikers was a revelation and that he had attended a demonstration of 20,000 people on Sunday, 9 May. Kingsley Martin, with others in the report on the 'state of public opinion' in the Midlands, painted a very favourable picture, with even the Rotary Club passing resolutions for "peace" and the railwaymen "still one hundred per cent out... There were no disturbances... In Coventry they found the NUR and RCA almost one hundred per cent out, all tram and bus men out except inspectors, and no transport running except for a few independent buses." Even Oswald Mosley, then a Labour Party member, reported that in Birmingham the city was "astonishingly solid".[19] The same picture emerged everywhere, with workers who had not been called out on strike straining at the bit to do so. In London, Susan Lawrence, an ardent feminist MP for East Ham, addressed dozens of meetings in the East End on the Saturday and Sunday before the strike was called off and reported: "A glorious spirit, never again will the workers be trodden under foot as they are now – we are living in momentous times – a revolutionary reaction – a terrible time – perhaps – many of us in prison."[20]

"We are busted"

But this heady mood did not infect the leaders at the top. When Samuel returned from his sojourn in Italy on 6 May, he contacted Thomas a few days later and received a warm embrace, not just from Thomas but from others now willing to throw in the towel. Bevin was ready to negotiate away support for the miners. John Bromley, the ASLEF leader who was considered a 'left winger' and built up by the Communist Party before and during the strike as such, was ready to capitulate. He said to Cook on the evening of 10 May: "We are busted." A Labour MP, Rhys Davies, also stated later that many "'left-wing' leaders, such as Mr Bromley turned more 'right' during the strike than the original 'right-wing' leaders such as J.H. Thomas".[21] The sooner these Lefts had to move from phrases to action, the more they moved to the Right. This was not just evident in 1926 but subsequently as the experience of the labour movement in Britain at various stages since has shown.

In the critical periods of the 1970s, left-wing leaders such as Hugh Scanlon, of the engineers' union and Jack Jones of the Transport and General Workers' Union, particularly during the period of the Labour government of that decade, "looked over the abyss" and drew back. Scanlon had claimed at one stage to be a 'Marxist' yet he refused to contemplate a serious challenge to capitalism. Despite any good intentions that he and Jack Jones had initially, they reined in the working class from a full confrontation with the government and employers. Tom Sawyer, as we mentioned earlier, originally stood on the Left of the Labour Party but as it swung leftwards he swung right, ending up sitting on the red benches and decked out in ermine in the House of Lords. The crucial difference in the 1980s was that the Marxists, gathered around *Militant*, did criticise, in a positive way and warned of the inevitable role of left reformism and even centrism – which can be revolutionary in words and reformist in deeds – in a situation of heightened class conflict.

Although the miners had not been told of the negotiations with Samuel, by the end of the first week of the strike they were convinced that a furtive plot was afoot. In fact, the limited editions of the capitalist press had leaked that Baldwin and Thomas were in some kind of formal conversation. MacDonald also stated he was keeping in touch with the government. In fact, without any authority, the Labour leader had secretly visited Downing Street, with a leading engineering employer to press for a settlement based on temporary wage cuts of ten per cent pending final arbitration. Baldwin was looking over his shoulder at the ultras in his own cabinet led by Churchill. Baldwin's right-hand man, Jones, confessed later: "My policy was to split Eccleston Square [the TUC General Council] in two, with the aid of a gesture from the Prime Minister which would help the moderates." Churchill objected, fulminating in what Jones called "boiling eloquence" and railed at him: "We were at war… We were a long way from our position… We must go through with it. You must have the nerve."[22]

The government's uncompromising attitude was summed up in a letter dispatched to Samuel: "We have repeatedly stated that we cannot negotiate until the General Strike has been withdrawn. For if we did so… the true situation sincerely faced would be that we had procured the end of the General Strike by a process of bargaining. It is therefore plain that [the government] cannot enter any negotiations unless the strike is so unreservedly concluded that there is not even an implication of such a bargain."[23] In other words, the government were looking for complete surrender and the right-wing leaders of the General Council were going along with this. They were also trying to cover their tracks in order to shield themselves from the anger of the working class once the real implications of what had transpired were revealed.

The General Council was in an incredibly contradictory position, attempting behind the scenes to negotiate a way out and, at the same time, extending the number of workers called out. Thomas and Bromley both tried to argue that unless an agreement was arrived at with the government there would be a mass drift back to work on the railways. Bromley threatened: "Unless the strike is called off now there will be thousands of trains running. The result will be that there will be a debacle. It is no good; we cannot go on any longer."[24] He then threatened the miners that if the strike was not called off immediately he would order ASLEF members to resume work on Tuesday 11 May. This was the constant refrain of Bromley and Thomas but it was a complete myth. Official figures show that out of a total of 39,421 locomotive engineers employed on the four main railway companies, only 742 had reported for duty on Tuesday 11 May. The proportion of firemen and signalmen returning to work was similarly low, although there were substantial defections, it seems, from members of the Railway Clerks Association. Thomas argued later: "The criticism is – why do we not go on? We could not have gone on."[25]

Betrayal

The *British Worker* answered Thomas on 11 May, the day before the strike was called off when in block type it proclaimed: "The number of strikers has not diminished; it is increasing. There are more workers out today than there have been at any moment since the strike began."[26] Such "details" were unimportant to the right-wing General Council who were now in an unseemly scramble to terminate the strike and betray the miners. The General Council now insisted that no settlement was possible unless the miners accepted wage cuts. But Smith declared: "Our men in the coalfields have given us our instructions and we cannot depart from them."[27] Despite this, Thomas approached government plenipotentiaries and said that if the government would indicate, through a non-governmental representative, that the Samuel Report would be effected without delay, it was "possible" that the TUC might call off the General Strike and quite falsely indicated the miners would accept this. But when Baldwin received this proposal he rejected it and insisted that it remain for the TUC to call off the strike. However, hoping they could break the General Council, they delayed the introduction of further repressive measures such as the 'Illegal Strikes Bill'.

In a further meeting of the General Council, the miners were told that the government would accept the Samuel proposals on the basis that the strike would end and the lock-out notices were withdrawn. This would then allow the miners to return to work on the basis of the status quo, but with of course a reduction in wages to come after the resumption of work. A.J. Cook and Herbert Smith questioned as to what guarantee they would have that the government would accept the Samuel proposals. Thomas, as recalled in *The Nine Days*, said: "You may not trust my word, but you will not accept the word of the British gentleman who has been governor of Palestine?"![128] Cook wrote of this meeting that "an abyss [was] opening before himself and his colleagues".[29] Nevertheless, neither he nor Herbert Smith was prepared to go over the heads of the trade union leaders and call openly for the resistance of those on strike, make appeals for workers to come out and give a bold direction for the councils of action to be extended and developed on a nationwide scale.

Even while these discussions were taking place it was subsequently revealed that the Negotiating Committee of the TUC had arranged to see the Prime Minister that very night. Every effort, however, was made to pressurise the miners' leadership into accepting the Samuel terms of surrender but to little avail. When MacDonald, unbelievably, requested the right to speak to the miners' executive, he was told by Cook: "We do not want you to come to our meeting."[30] What a difference in attitude between the toadying right-wing general secretaries of most unions today, who are quite happy to invite New Labour ministers to their union conferences and even to the TUC, there to receive annual lectures on the need for them and their members to accept neo-liberal policies without qualms. When Herbert Smith asked whether the memorandum of Samuel could be discussed and amended, Pugh snapped: "No, you must take it or leave it." Smith declared bitterly: "Do you people realise the serious position you are putting yourselves in? Are you going back without any consideration for the men who are going to be victimised in this movement? Are you not going to consider them at all?"[31] But with the ground opening beneath their feet, it was preferable for the TUC leaders to betray the miners and refuse to take action than to prosecute the strike to a conclusion and challenge the very basis of capitalism.

The General Council decided to call off the General Strike on 12 May. Workers were putting out bulletins on this very day, one of which declared: "Cast your mind back only to 1914 onwards, and remember the pie-crust promises such as 'A Land Fit for Heroes', etc., *ad nauseum*. This is a trap set to catch any weak-kneed people there may be about. By the response there are so few as to be negligible. So much for their trick. It is conclusive proof of their inability to carry on. But we can carry on. Our organisations are our strength."[32] Nevertheless, the General Council trooped off to meet the government, no doubt expecting thanks from Baldwin. But they were met with a very cold reception at Downing Street. They met Baldwin's representative, Sir Horace Wilson, who asked them why they had come, "Had they come to negotiate, or to declare the strike off?" They tamely said the latter and then were taken to Baldwin, who with several other ministers, was waiting for them. Pugh, speaking much about the need for "negotiations", finished by saying: "We are here today, sir, to say that this General Strike is to be terminated forthwith." Baldwin declared brusquely: "That is, the General Strike is to be called off forthwith?" Pugh, Thomas and Bevin complied with the latter raising the issue of continuing negotiations with the miners. Baldwin was vague but "Bevin pressed a little, just a little and was gently rebuked". Not a word was said about the lock-out notices or about wages and hours, nor was the Samuel memorandum mentioned. Birkenhead, Neville Chamberlain and the rest smirked in triumph.[33]

Ben Turner, the textile workers' union leader, who had remained silent, noted in his diary: "General Council flabbergasted at nothing being settled about miners' lock-out notices. Retired and felt dismayed… left at 1.10 [p.m.] disappointed and disgusted. Papers soon out about TUC. Surrender."[34] Even when Bevin had pressed Baldwin for negotiations, the latter was peremptory in his reply: "I cannot say that, Mr Bevin. I think it may be that whatever decision I come to, the House of Commons may be the best place in which to say it." Farman comments: "Even Birkenhead felt something akin to compassion for the TUC leaders as they trooped dejectedly out of the Cabinet Room. Their surrender, he wrote later to Halifax, was 'so humiliating that some instinctive breeding made one unwilling even to look them in the face'."[35]

The conscious way in which Baldwin and his assistants, such as Jones, weighed up carefully the personalities on the General Council, their strengths and weaknesses, was shown in the following comments: "Bevin was the most powerful member of the TUC… the PM said… 'Ramsay [MacDonald] is a Kerensky and Kerenskys have lost control. [Kerensky was a member of the Social Revolutionary party (S.Rs.) in Russia, allegedly a radical, and in 1917 led the government, which defended landlordism and capitalism until it was overthrown by the Bolsheviks.]

Bevin may well picture himself as the Napoleon of the trade union movement. We must wait for the strike to wear itself out'."[36] In these remarks is the conscious weighing up by the representatives of the ruling class of figures in the labour movement. His hob-nobbing with the rich – much like Blair today – fitted out MacDonald to be a bulwark, a British Kerensky, against any threat to the propertied classes. He could be safely relied upon to derail a revolution if such a threat should be posed. His authority, however, in 1926 was peripheral. Far more important were the leaders of the trade unions. Baldwin, it seems, was cautious about Bevin but did not have a clear knowledge of the union leader's limitations. Ultimately, like MacDonald, he was not capable of taking a serious step outside the framework of capitalism. This was displayed very clearly in the winding up of the General Strike, in its aftermath and in the role that Bevin played in the trade union and labour movement after this.

Baldwin convened his Cabinet and then went to the House of Commons to announce his triumph as a "victory for common sense".[37] The British Worker ran three different editions on the afternoon and evening of 12 May but in not one of these did they give the real picture of the capitulation that had taken place.

9 Outrage

he first edition of the *British Worker* declared: "General Council satisfied that miners will now get a fair deal", while the second edition referred to the miners' executive resolution expressing "profound admiration" for the support of the rest of the working class. It merely carried a three-line reference to the fact that the miners were staying out, a hint, but no more, of the dissatisfaction of the miners with the role of the General Council.[1] Some unions, such as the Railway Clerks Association, sent letters with the headline: "Yours in victory". Cramp of the NUR sent telegrams to members of his union falsely declaring that "there are to be no wage cuts whatever for the miners".[2]

In Birmingham, the strike committee produced a special "*Victory Bulletin*". And why not? The strike had been solid here, the printers and the railwaymen had remained firm. By the end of the strike all the capitalist daily Birmingham papers were being produced in a four-page format – half their normal size – solely by management and apprentice labour. However, "Shortly after one o'clock on Wednesday afternoon [12

Striker's Picket

May], the sonorous tones of John Reith [of the BBC] announced over the wireless that the General Strike had been called off... The first assumption of the union movement in Birmingham was that the announcement marked a great victory for the miners."[3] Indeed there was no reason to think otherwise. The Birmingham ranks had held fairly solid and the second line of strikers had only come out that morning. Consequently, victory arrangements were put in hand: "Plans were made for the holding of a victory rally in Summerfield Park and the printing of a special victory issue of the strike bulletin." Workers, in other words, expected that they had won another Red Friday victory but on a huge scale. The reality, however, was that it was a serious defeat, far worse in its consequences than Black Friday.

Every serious historian, such as Symons, gives a clear picture of why the right wing of the General Council acted in the way they did. The issue of "intelligence" being received to the effect that the strike was weakening is dismissed. The "accuracy of [these reports] is not particularly relevant... if the strike was in danger of disintegration the General Council did not know it... It was not fear of a breakdown, but fear that the strike might get out of their own hands that primarily moved the most influential members of the General Council."[4] Charles Duke of the General and Municipal Workers (not a member of the General Council himself) said a few months after the General Strike: "Every day that the strike proceeded, the control and the authority of that dispute was passing out of the hands of responsible executives into the hands of men who had no authority, no control, and was wrecking the movement from one end to the other." Symons comments: "'The intensity of the struggle will increase' the leaders had been told. They preferred surrender to such an intensified struggle, with its implicit threat to their own power."[5]

Defeat stunned the working class. Even Islington and St Pancras, militant committees, initially thought there was cause to celebrate. Some reacted like Lenin when in August 1914 he received a copy of *Vorwärts*, the German social-democratic paper, which reported that the Social Democrat members of the Reichstag (parliament) had voted for war credits for German imperialism in the war. Lenin considered that it was a "forgery". At Long Eaton, the TUC's telegram "was thought at first to be a forgery because it came via the local police station". But in Manchester, where the news was communicated to the strike committee by Fenner Brockway, on the Left of the ILP, the latter reported that such was the perplexity, "One delegate even suggested that I had been 'got at' by the other side!" The first telegram from the TUC was really just the outline of the unofficial memorandum by Samuel, which the government had made clear was not binding on them or the employers. But when the real terms of surrender became known, "We could not believe our ears," said Brockway, "My first reaction was that the TUC General Council had become either demoralised or corrupted. With a heavy heart I sent the 'Special' of the *British Worker* onto the streets."[6] But when bundles were delivered to strikers in London "they were thrown back into [the] faces" of the TUC volunteers.[7]

At Oxford, there was "bitter disappointment" at the "cave-in". In Derbyshire, "Everybody furious when settlement was known." At Wolverhampton, "The whole of the workers stood solid and were prepared to fight to the bitter end, so that when the news came through... that the strike was over, it came as a shock." In Hull, there was, "Alarm – fear – despair – a victorious army disarmed and handed over to its enemies."[8] Even in an area that was solid, the North-East, there was a "belief that a victory had been secured [which] was initially also held by the publishers of the *Workers' Chronicle*."[9] When the BBC broadcast the end of the strike, this was considered to be black propaganda: "It is necessary to state that the British Broadcasting Company and the news agencies have been completely misrepresenting the end of the lock-out as a defeat for the General Strike. This is entirely untrue... The first general strike of modern times in Great Britain has proved a complete success."[10]

End of the strike

Given that ever more workers were joining the strike, that more and more power had been gathered into their hands, it is not unexpected that this would be the reaction. It was a mixture of anger, despair and, for many, wistfully wondering what could have been. One worker wrote that the Lewisham Council of Action "collapsed into wretchedness" when the General Council informed them of the terms of surrender. He commented: "It was too early to shout that we were betrayed but privately that was the only thing of which we were certain. That for which the strike had been called had not been achieved... We kept saying to each other, in an agitated way, 'We must keep calm' and we handed out this wonderful phrase to enquirers and repeated it at all the public meetings. But what were we going to do on the morrow? Go back to the boring daily round after this intoxicating taste of power?"[11]

This fairly sums up the general mood of disappointment but it also shows that the working class, at least the most conscious organised layer, were reaching out for "power". This gives the lie to those who argued at the time that this was just an "industrial dispute" – even those on the Left like the Communist Party went to some lengths to show it was all about "solidarity" and not a revolutionary challenge to capitalism. The dejection, however, was mixed with fury against the Right in particular on the General Council. Swansea Strike Committee forbade the distribution of the *British Worker* when they discovered the real position of the TUC while in Glasgow workers marched in procession carrying placards saying "Down with Thomas!"[12] That mood was deepened when the *British Gazette* shattered whatever illusions the TUC had tried to cultivate, that the defeat was not as great as feared, when it declared: "Unconditional withdrawal of notices by TUC. Men to return forthwith. Surrender received by Premier in Downing Street."[13]

Cold cruelty

This was a signal for the British ruling class to display that cold cruelty which it had used against its colonial slaves and was now deployed against its "own" working class. The boss class, freed from the nightmare of control exercised by the workers' organisations during the strike, now attempted to impose a dictatorship of capital in the factories. As one group of workers commented: "The bosses in all trades felt, in fact, that now they had the trade union movement at their feet and all they had to do was stamp on it."[14] This was summed up by a cartoon in *Punch*, depicting an employer greeting his workmen with the comment, "Glad to see you back, my lad; but you'll understand that in the circumstances we can't run to a fatted calf."[15] The situation was compounded by the fact that the General Council, while it was careful to restrain workers coming out on strike, preferring a drawn-out battle, made no attempt to have an orderly return to work. The consequence of this was that, without a lead from above, the workers looked towards the rank-and-file leaders and organisations.

Sometimes, the revolution needs the whip of the counter-revolution, as Marx commented. The employers refused to give assurances that there would be a return to the pre-strike situation. Consequently, the leaders were singled out and either, sacked – 200 LMS carters were dismissed in Birmingham – or only gradually taken back on the employers' terms. In some cases the ruling class used the courts to rub the noses of the working class in the dirt. In Birmingham, the Trade Union Emergency Committee members were put on trial on 14 May on a charge of "doing an act likely to cause disaffection amongst the civil population". This was after the formal ending of the General Strike. In their defence, their lawyer pointed out that four of the defendants were Justices of the Peace and two were city councillors and, moreover, publication of the news "Government Defeat" would not cause disaffection. He added: "To some it would cause pleasure, to others disappointment." This fell on deaf ears as Lord Ilkeston, the presiding stipendiary, found 18 of the 20 defendants guilty under the Emergency Powers Act. Oswald Mosley (later that year to win a by-election in Smethwick as a Labour candidate) intervened on the defendants' behalf. NUR members were dismissed and a "Miss Clark, a schoolteacher... was dismissed by the Education Department because of her conviction for her part in the publication of the *Birmingham Worker*". In Cadbury, every trade saw a loss of union membership and a long rearguard battle took place in the Birmingham labour movement in the years that followed to restore the pre-1926 situation.[16]

However, initially when the bosses tried to put the boot in, the working class in Birmingham reacted with determination and discipline. For instance, the vehicle builders in the tram depot, within a few hours of coming in, walked out again, claiming that they would not be returning until the principle of "all out, all in" was established. This set off a spontaneous movement of railwaymen and others in opposition to the bosses' policy of divide and rule. The bosses were bluntly warned in a message to the tramways department that if they continued to refuse to recognise the unions there was a considerable possibility of "guerrilla warfare" breaking out. The result of all this was that nationally 100,000 more workers were out than at any time before on the day that the General Strike was officially terminated. "It looked as though the end of the strike might be the beginning of the revolution," said Fenner Brockway.[17]

But the working class is not a tap which can be turned on and off at will. A general strike, by its very nature, has to proceed to an ever wider and larger gathering of strength and power into the hands of the working class or it stalls and falls back. The TUC generals had beheaded the workers' army. But Baldwin was alarmed by the vindictiveness of the bosses, as were the trade union leaders. This was in no way motivated by Baldwin's "distress" at the plight of the working class. He had a surer understanding than Churchill or Birkenhead that the bosses were going "too far", which threatened a new wave of struggle and even worse, was placing more power and authority into the hands of rank-and-file leaders. Farman comments: "It seemed also that the dreaded day of revolution was about to dawn. All over the country strike committees were reacting to the letter if not the spirit of the Communist Party's call for the continuation of the struggle independently of national union leaderships. In some areas, a rent strike was developing; in others, which had hitherto been peaceful, there were outbreaks of violence." The General Council received reports that "Feeling is running frightfully high all over the North." Even strike-breaker Thomas, together with the executives of the other rail unions, ordered their members not to resume work until previous agreements had been recognised. The General Council issued its own belated call to "Stand Together".[18]

Baldwin was so worried by these developments that, notwithstanding a fear by the Tory ultras that he was showing undue magnanimity, he saw the danger of these unofficial strikes developing, led from below. He therefore made a statement in the House of Commons: "I will not countenance any attack on the part of any employers to use this present occasion for trying in any way to get reductions in wages below those in force before the strike or any increase in hours." This was sheer hypocrisy because the whole purpose of the strike was to drive down living standards, firstly the miners, and then the rest of the working class. He was "opposed" to any attempts to destroy trade unions. The kind of trade unions the capitalists preferred, however, he spelt out: "There can be no greater disaster than that there should be anarchy in the trade union world. It would be impossible in our highly developed system of industry to carry on unless you had organisations which could speak for and bind the parties on both sides. We know that in all these great organisations there are some who are of little help. At a time like this there are some who like fishing in troubled waters. Let us get the workers calm as soon as we can."[19]

In other words: 'Don't provide an opportunity for the Left and militants to supplant right-wing trade union leaders, who in the final analysis are props of our system!' This is the real content of what Baldwin was trying to tell the average employer who did not possess the 'statecraft' of the representatives of the class as a whole, of knowing when to attack, when to conciliate and when to retreat. The British ruling class was not going to retreat after the General Strike, as events subsequently showed, but they were not prepared to push the situation immediately to the extent of provoking a further social explosion.

Hunger

But having ridden out the tide of working class revolt, all the bromides of Baldwin meant nothing in the end as the employers took revenge on the working class. The cynical bourgeois Fabian leader Beatrice Webb wrote in her diary a week after the strike that the British "governing class are as good-natured and stupid as the labour movement".[20] But this "good nature" was not very evident in the weeks, months and years after the General Strike. Some employers, it is true, did not want to immediately go "too far". For instance, the heads of the London, Midland and Scottish and Great Western railways told the permanent secretary to the Ministry of Transport that "they did not want to destroy the unions, they only wanted power to select the men who should return after the strike so as to eliminate undesirables"![21] Unbelievably, Thomas paid tribute to the "magnanimity" of the railway employers, declaring: "If any words of mine can help, may I say to every employer: 'Follow the example of the railway companies, do the big thing'." However, five months later Thomas was to admit that 200,000 railwaymen were working three days a week and 45,000, probably most of the "undesirables", were still waiting for their jobs back.[22]

London newspapers banned meetings of the chapels of the print unions during working hours and demanded "guarantees" against further interference with the contents of newspapers. All the employees of Outram Press in Glasgow were required to renounce their union membership and journalists were even forbidden to join union colleagues at a dinner. The Stationery Office was declared an "open" shop (i.e. open to non-union labour) and the *Manchester Guardian* imposed a company union. Even Bevin, with the power of the transport workers behind him, saw many workers dismissed or suspended but nevertheless claimed that "only" 1,500 workers had not been reinstated. More than 30,000 railwaymen, printers, engineers and dockers remained on strike in Hull until the 16 May in defence of 150 tramway employees who were demanding reinstatement. Similarly, 30,000 railwaymen marched through the streets of Manchester. But as Fenner Brockway wrote: "A spirit of fatalism came over the workers. The TUC had ordered them back; there was no hope of concerted resistance – so back they went... Of course a general strike must be revolutionary; it is of necessity a conflict between workers and the capitalist state. The strike of 1926 was led by a General Council who did not realise this when they reluctantly authorised the struggle. And they drew back from it as soon as they understood its full implications."[23]

Fenner Brockway, however, like others on the Left of the ILP which he represented, also did not draw all the implications of the meaning of a general strike and the role that was to be played, not just by the right wing but by the Left as well. The Communist Party, whose militants and leaders were undoubtedly courageous, and in some areas, as we have seen, gave a lead to the workers in the course of the strike, suffered repression. But they were hamstrung by their faulty analysis of the role of the Lefts. John Murray, in *The General Strike of 1926*, remarks on the mood of the working class when the strike was betrayed and particularly their attitude to those Lefts such as Purcell, Hicks and Co: "It was against these men that most anger was directed – particularly in the mining villages where gloom, depression and hunger were settling like a deadly cloud of poisonous gas."[24] In Lewisham, mentioned before, it was reported that the Council of Action "melted away". One of its members wrote: "Who was willing to work for it any more? The temporary unity of the local movement, a source of happiness and pride... collapsed. The right wing, for the most part silent during the struggle... were relieved to see the strike out of the way so they might continue once again the parliamentary work in which they believed."[25]

Lefts called to account

There had been isolated criticism of the Lefts on the General Council by the Communist Party but this was not systematic in character. Now, such was the indignation at the role of these Lefts amongst the working class – Purcell had participated in the negotiations to end the strike – that the CP was compelled to issue a strong public condemnation of the role of the Lefts. On 13 May, the Communist Party issued an appeal to "stand by the miners": "The General Council's decision to call off the General Strike is the greatest crime that has ever been permitted, not only against the miners, but against the working class of Great Britain and the whole world. The British workers had aroused the astonishment and admiration of the world by the enthusiasm with which they had entered upon the fight for the miners' standard of living... And most of the so-called Left Wing have been no better than the Right. By a policy of timid silence, by using the false pretext of loyalty to colleagues to cover up breaches of loyalty to workers, they have left a free hand to the Right Wing and thus helped to play the employers' game."[26]

This, of course, was too late, as was the call made by the party for a "national conference of delegates from strike committees". These were in the process of being dismantled, with the return of the workers to the factories and the workplaces. In the months that followed the defeat of the General Strike, in the CP's publications and those influenced by them, such as *Labour Monthly*, the criticisms of the Left and their role in the General Strike became more open, although still hesitant because of the continuation of the Anglo-Russian Trade Union Committee. Nevertheless, Palme Dutt, in July 1926, does criticise the Left: "It was conspicuously the case that the Left Wing which had developed an opposition tendency in the Trades Unions during the past two years, around the personalities of certain leaders of the General Council, such as Hicks, Bromley, Purcell, Tillett and others, completely failed to provide any alternative leadership during the crisis and in practice fell behind the Right Wing. This is an extremely significant fact, and it is all-important that the lesson from it should be learned. The trades union Left Wing had not yet in practice reached any basic differences from the Right."[27]

Page Arnot also underlined the point when he wrote in the same month: "The left wing had never for a moment believed that the government would do otherwise than it did in July 1925, that is, grant financial aid to industry. They had never seriously contemplated the General Strike, and had talked about it for purposes of bluff. Hicks now also joined the ranks of those who attacked Cook for landing them in this 'misfortune'."[28] Looking back on the lessons of 1925-26 he wrote: "Knowledge of the existence of this left wing was at once a stimulant and a narcotic for the masses. It gave them a rallying ground, lent confidence to their leftward mood."[29] However, no real attempt was made by the CP to lessen the impact of this "narcotic", to warn of its effects. Criticisms of the Left were not mentioned, at least not couched in the same way as here indicated, until after the end of the strike.

It would have been totally wrong, as some small left groups on the outskirts of the labour movement today do, to attack leading Left figures in a shrill and sectarian way, accusing them of betrayal at every opportunity. This has nothing in common with the genuine Marxist approach which seeks to educate and persuade, to "patiently explain", as Lenin said, even in radicalised or revolutionary periods, about the inadequacies in programme and tactics of those who are not rounded-out Marxists. To do this the Communist Party should have had a firm line of positive criticism and made demands that the Left take an independent position. They could not do this, saddled as they were by the Anglo-Russian Committee. Later historians of the strike, such as the official CP historian James Klugmann, argue that even these belated criticisms went "too far". On the one side he criticises the Left and their role in the General Council: "There was (on paper) a strong 'Left', on paper even a majority. These were men who at one time or another played a militant role in the trade union movement. But they were far from conscious socialists; their conceptions did not in the main pass beyond the field of trade unionism, they had no science of society, no perspective of transition to socialism and so they had no power to resist the reformism of MacDonald, and whilst the strike was on it ranged from a shameful silence to open support of the Thomas line. At best they were ineffective; at worst they abetted the sell-out."[30]

Nothing of this kind of criticism, couched in exceedingly mild terms, was made by Communist Party leaders or organs, we repeat, in a systematic manner, before or during the General Strike. On the contrary, we quoted earlier the comments of Palme Dutt on the need for "unity". This is absolutely correct, especially when talking about the organisational unity of the working class. But unity should not be of the "graveyard" kind with mouths closed to the political inadequacies of temporary allies. The best way to maintain the unity of the working class in action is on the basis of clear policies which offer the prospect of victory or at least the best results for the working class in the objective circumstances that pertain. Klugmann wrote about the "wretched role of the Left" group on the General Council but at the same time is critical of "some Communist statements [which began] to exaggerate the 'dangers of such a Left'".[31] It is the capitalists and their "labour lieutenants of capital" within the ranks of the working class, right-wing leaders of the ilk of MacDonald, who should be most energetically fought. Marxists would support all genuine steps towards the Left of those leaders who echo the spirit of opposition of ordinary workers against the Right. Yet the trade union 'Lefts' did have a formal majority, both within the trade unions and the Labour Party, at one stage, and they did not use this position but capitulated to the Right.

There was, undoubtedly, particularly in the criticisms made by Zinoviev and some figures of the Communist International after the termination of the strike, a sectarian strain in the criticisms of Hicks, Purcell and Co. Zinoviev had a tendency to swing violently from one extreme to another. He was the architect of the policy of conciliation of these Lefts and now, while exaggerating some features of the British General Strike, he had also lacerated the Left leaders. This, by the way, was at the same time as he strenuously opposed the breaking of the Anglo-Russian Trade Union Committee. In the theses on the British General Strike published by the Communist International, it came out for the "exposure of the left wing."[32] What cannot be disputed is that their role was vital in the mechanism of defeat by covering up the betrayal of the General Council. If they had clearly called during the strike for rank-and-file resistance, rejected the proposal for capitulation to the government, for a continuation of the strike, for a widening of the elements of workers' power, then this would have met a massive response from the miners and the rest of the working class. There may have been some chance of pressurising the Lefts in a critical situation to act in this way but there was absolutely no possibility of doing so if they were left free from criticism by the revolutionary wing, their inadequacies not systematically explained before the public opinion of the working class and all the necessary organisational inferences drawn from this. This, the Communist Party did not do.

CP gains

Nevertheless, the CP did gain support during the strike and afterwards. Membership doubled between May and October 1926 to 10,000, according to the CP leaders. This was a creditable achievement but nothing compared to what would have been possible. Moreover, after the initial gains were registered a decline had set in by the following year to just over 7,000, and half that figure by 1928.[33] The difficulties confronting the CP were compounded by the ultra-left mistakes made by the CP leadership under the direction of the Comintern. Trotsky, summing up the situation, was harsh but correct when he wrote in 1931: "The Minority Movement, embracing almost a million workers, seemed very promising, but it bore the germs of destruction within itself. The masses knew as the leaders of the Movement only Purcell, Hicks and Cook, whom, moreover, Moscow vouched for. These 'Left' friends, in a serious test, shamefully betrayed the proletariat. The revolutionary workers were thrown into confusion, sank into apathy and naturally extended their disappointment to the Communist Party itself which had only been the passive part of this whole mechanism of betrayal and perfidy. The Minority Movement was reduced to zero; the Communist Party returned to the existence of a negligible sect. In this way, thanks to a radically false conception of the party, the greatest movement of the English proletariat, which led to the General Strike, not only did not shake the apparatus of the reactionary bureaucracy, but, on the contrary, reinforced it and compromised communism in Great Britain for a long time."[34] The Minority Movement became a shadow of its former self and eventually collapsed. The working class, and particularly the miners, were those who reaped the bitter fruit of the defeat of the strike.

10 The Terrible Aftermath

Workers all over the country were facing victimisation in the aftermath of the strike. On Saturday 15 May, the TUC newspaper attacked its critics and defended its actions: "The General Council acted with courage in ending the stoppage."[1] It was only on Monday, 17 May in the final issue of the *British Worker*, that the newspaper carried a front page story revealing that the miners were still locked out. The government refused to implement the Samuel Commission's report; they had not promised anything else. The miners' leaders – A.J. Cook and Herbert Smith – had made a mistake in hinting that they would vote on the basis of the Samuel Commission recommendations but, as Cook pointed out later at the conference of trade union executives, there was never "any shred of a hope of the miners having an opportunity of accepting the Samuel Memorandum as a basis of negotiations".[2] The General Council, led by the right wing with the former Lefts in tow, compounded the betrayal of the General Strike by refusing to come to the aid of the miners. "Now began for the miners a long travail of misery and poverty."[3]

Hunger Marchers

With the termination of the General Strike, the miners were forced to continue the battle alone. In consequence there was terrible suffering in the mining areas. Yet most Tories were not prepared to accept that the miners were starving, cosseted as they were in their plush London clubs. Neville Chamberlain wrote in his diary on 20 June: "They [the miners] are not within sight of starvation, hardly of under-nutrition, so well are they looked after by the [Boards of] Guardians… They are not living too uncomfortably at the expense of the ratepayer, while the nation is gradually overcome by creeping paralysis."[4] The National Society for the Prevention of Cruelty to Children concurred with Chamberlain, as did the Fabian, Beatrice Webb, when she revealed that there was "no distress and some light-hearted enjoyment of the strike".[5] But George Lansbury more correctly described the plight of the miners: "One cold, brutal, inexorable fact stands out clear and distinct. Over one million mineworkers, together with their womenfolk and children are starving – yes, comrades, starving in the midst of plenty, starving in a land at the centre of which, here in this great Metropolis, wealth produced by the toilers of Britain is being poured out like water in an unparalleled orgy of wanton extravagance and luxurious pleasure."[6]

Moreover, the future right-wing Labour MP and member of the 1945 Labour government, Hugh Dalton, did not agree with Webb and Chamberlain. When he arrived in 1928 to seek the parliamentary nomination for the Labour Party in Seaham in County Durham, he noted: "Human values had depreciated almost to nothing. White-faced women who starved themselves to feed their children; children certified by doctors as 'suffering from malnutrition' – that meant having been half-starved long enough for it to become obvious – being fed at school; men sitting silent in Workmen's Clubs, too poor either to buy a drink or a smoke; every second shop in Newgate Street, the main street in Bishop Auckland, shuttered up and the shopkeeper ruined, because the people had no money to spend; old clothes and old boots being collected and distributed by charitable persons; others organising the departure of boys and girls, as soon as they left school, to be bell-hops in London hotels or kitchen maids in rich private houses."[7] This was after the strike had been terminated and if one compares this period to 1914 then average miners' wages were only 13 per cent over that level while the cost of living index had risen by 67 per cent!

The railwaymen also suffered a wage cut, notwithstanding Thomas's promises to protect them, and the misery of workers in general was intense. Every effort was made by the government in league with the coal owners to break the continuing miners' strike. Pickets and active strike supporters were arrested and jailed; there were baton charges of pit meetings and the beating up of miners. Steps were also taken to prevent funds raised at home and abroad from reaching the starving

miners and their families. Shamefully, the local authorities were warned by government agencies to withhold relief and suspend services like free milk for babies and
free meals for schoolchildren. The Ministry of Health was given powers to suspend
any board of guardians disobeying Whitehall's instructions to stop relief. Baldwin
tried to prevent the miners from garnering international solidarity and financial
support. On the eve of the departure of a miners' delegation to the United States, he
sent a letter to the American authorities stating there was no dire need in the British
coalfields. Nevertheless there were magnificent donations from the Soviet trade
unions of at least £1 million and the European trade unions, particularly the
Belgians, donated important sums to the miners' relief as well.[8]

Cook rescues General Council

The General Council of the TUC announced that it was calling a conference of
union executives in June 1926 to discuss the outcome of the General Strike.
They only did this reluctantly under the pressure of the rank and file and the
widespread discontent at the role of the General Council. There was great pressure
also, led by the Communist Party and the Minority Movement, for the TUC to issue
a levy on all working trade unionists and an embargo on the import of foreign coal.
Later, the levy was transformed into a 'voluntary' one. This raised limited sums and
the embargo on foreign imports of coal was never effectively carried out. The
conference of trade union executives was cancelled, to a wave of disappointment,
and this was with the agreement of the miners' leadership, ostensibly so that
nothing would undermine the struggle of the miners against the lock-out.

Unfortunately, Arthur Cook also agreed to suspend publication of his best-selling
booklet *The Nine Days*. The miners' leader felt compelled to do this probably
because of the pressure exerted by the General Council and the need to gain the
maximum broad practical support of trade unionists, which they mistakenly
believed was possible only by this compliance with the right wing. This 'June Pact'
effectively gave breathing space to the right wing before they had to face the wrath
of ordinary trade unionists and workers six months later. But while the miners were
expected to keep their mouths shut about the role of the General Council, this
dictum did not apply to the right wing who did not hesitate to attack the miners'
"attitude" and their "unwillingness" to be "reasonable". In the statement which was
to have been presented to the June conference, there is the following: "The strike
was terminated for one sufficient reason only, namely, that in view of the attitude of
the Miners' Federation its continuance would have rendered its purpose futile."[9]

This gave a completely false view of the miners' opinions and as we have seen, those
of the vast mass of the four million trade unionists who came out on strike. The

Communist Party was compelled to raise criticisms of the Left, though not at this stage of Arthur Cook himself. But because of their refusal to make the same criticisms before and during the General Strike, these were now largely ineffective. The CP also called for further action but this did not meet with a ready response because it had come too late. George Hardy, of the Minority Movement, admitted after the General Strike: "Although we knew of what treachery the right-wing leaders were capable, we did not clearly understand the part played by the so-called 'Left' in the union leadership. In the main they turned out to be windbags... We were taught a major lesson... the main point in preparing for action must always be to develop a class-conscious leadership among the rank and file."[10]

Anglo-Russian Committee

This was right but came too late; only now did the CP issue criticisms of the Left which sometimes assumed a sharp character. In the 18 June 1926 issue of *Workers' Weekly*, the headline read: "Small thanks to you, Hicks and Purcell... Apologists for Thomas." The article below it criticised these leaders: "Purcell knows very well that only last year the General Council had had the experience of preparing for a general strike, yet right up to the last day on this occasion (April 30) not a finger had been lifted by himself or any other alleged 'left-winger' to get preparations made for conducting the struggle. The General Council, right and left wingers together had deliberately avoided all preparations for fear of 'provoking trouble'!"[11]

Unfortunately, the Communist Party itself was guilty of the sin of 'not provoking trouble' by not criticising these left wingers in advance. Criticisms *ex post facto* were no substitute for preparing the working class in advance for the role of the General Council, in which the Left had been complicit. The Communist Party's press, both *Workers' Weekly* and its theoretical journal, *Communist Review*, together with the publications of the Comintern, were full of denunciations of Purcell, Hicks, and Co. in the aftermath of the strike. These invariably made correct criticisms of the Left, but very few of these were contained in their publications before the General Strike. *Communist Review* wrote: "Left-wing leaders who are afraid to associate themselves openly with those who fight for socialism (the Minority Movement and the Left Wing) will be afraid of insisting on a left-wing point of view even in a fight for wages. Every campaign of the Communist Party for a powerfully organised Minority Movement winning the leadership of the unions, for a powerful organised left wing winning the leadership of the Labour Party, has been amply justified."[12]

In July, it made criticisms of the Left in relation to the postponement of the June conference of executives: "Why is it that the 'left wingers' in the General Council were particularly in favour of postponing the conference? Because they were terrified of the alternatives which the conference opened up before them: either of exhibiting themselves to the workers at last as unashamed supporters of Thomas, or of coming out as a minority in the General Council on the side of the miners and fighting Thomas – which they have not the courage or the belief in the workers to do."[13]

There are many other statements in the *Communist Review* which are correct about the role of the Left. We will quote just one or two to illustrate how Trotsky's criticism, and that of the Left Opposition, if it had been followed would have prepared, through the Communist Party, the mass of the working class for the role of these Lefts. In the International Theses of the Communist Party, we read after the strike: "Left wingers ('centrists') who, thanks to their ambiguous attitude, political cowardice and policy of capitulation inevitably arising therefrom, inevitably go over to the side of the enemy at critical moments. The so-called 'leaders of the working class' manœuvre against the growth of revolutionary activity of the masses, both in their tactics and their ideology."[14] Again we read: "The 'left wingers' were in continual fear and trembling, had absolutely no independent position and were thereby doomed to be dragged along in the leading strings of the right wingers."[15]

Is this not a direct echo of Trotsky's comments before the strike on the role of the Lefts? Once more: "The 'Left' leaders of the General Council, who have the majority on it, not only offered absolutely no resistance whatsoever to the conscious betrayal of the Thomas element but all the time marched under the orders of the right wing… At turning points in the strike they sometimes acted no less shamefully than Thomas (for instance Hicks and the 'damned Russian money')." And again: "Only the tremendous pressure of the mass movement forced them to line up at its tail. Thus, the 'left wingers' in effect played a still more criminal role, for they had the majority and bore the direct responsibility for leadership of the strike."[16]

Yet in the very same document only a few pages earlier, we also read in relation to the Lefts and their participation in the Anglo-Russian Trade Union Committee, the following: "The withdrawal of the Soviet trade unions from the Anglo-Russian Trades Council should be considered absolutely undesirable. The workers of the USSR sent their representative to the Anglo-Russian Advisory Council, not by any means because they hoped to substitute negotiations with the higher opportunist leaders for the task of revolutionary transformation of capitalist countries… They entered the Anglo-Russian Council in order to strengthen the fraternal connection between the working class of Great Britain and the working class of the USSR… The task of the Leninists is not withdrawal from the Anglo-Russian Advisory Council but a struggle to change its composition, as well as a struggle to change the composition of all the leading organs from the General Council to the local trade union bodies."[17]

This was an answer to Trotsky and the International Left Opposition who had warned about the consequences of the Anglo-Russian Trade Union Committee before the strike had taken place. Now, in its aftermath, they demanded a complete break with the capitulators, both the Right and the Left, with the General Council as a whole. The Stalinist faction, the majority in the Russian Communist Party, refused to do this, thereby conferring the authority of the Comintern and with this the heritage of the Russian Revolution on those who were continuing to justify their strike breaking role. Moreover, they were doing nothing to assist the miners. Trotsky, on the eve of the General Strike, in a letter to the Russian Politburo, expressed the fear that the British Communist Party, like its Bulgarian counterpart in a critical moment of mass activity, might adopt a too passive or temporising attitude.

Moreover, before the General Strike, some of the Communist Party leaders had actually questioned Trotsky's analysis on the gravity of the economic and social crisis in Britain! "British comrades warned against overestimating the critical state of British capitalism. By this they revealed they underestimate the depth of the crisis and the imminence of social clashes."[18] He went on to state: "An incomparably less significant fact, namely the publication of my book with a preface by Brailsford [a leading ILP Left], was for me a further symptom of a willingness to compromise by an important section of the British Communists. They have not yet had experience of leadership by mass action. Taken together, all this aroused quite reasonable fears of excessive caution, lack of decision, and even passivity on the part of the powerful bureaucratic opposition in all the old administrative organisations of the working class."[19]

Trotsky's Criticism

Trotsky also quoted a report from British Communist Bob Stewart: "Unfortunately, in some of our regional organisations, it could be noted that there still remained in the party sectarian survivals; these organisations have not taken root sufficiently deeply in the trade unions; by which is also explained the fact that, during the strike, they lagged behind the masses."[20] Trotsky and the Left Opposition went further in July 1926, calling for a complete break by the Russian trade unions with the General Council of the British TUC and the break-up of the Anglo-Russian Committee. The TUC was temporising and postponing calling another conference of this committee. The Politburo of the Communist Party of the Soviet Union had followed a profoundly incorrect policy on the question of the Anglo-Russian committee over a lengthy period but Trotsky argued: "The point at which the working masses of Britain exerted the greatest opposing force to the General Council was when the General Strike was being broken. What was necessary was to keep in step with the most active forces of the British proletariat and to break at that moment with the General Council as the betrayer of the General Strike." He also pointed out that it would be "an impermissible error, bordering on the criminal, if we allowed the General Council in the future to move this question back, step by step, and to gradually and imperceptibly reduce the Anglo-Russian committee to nothing but to break with it themselves over some second-rate question, as over the statutes of the committee or the like."[21]

This is, in fact, how events turned out in relation to this "tactic" of Stalin and co. Trotsky and the Left Opposition did not in general oppose the tactic of the united front, even in relation to the General Council of the TUC. The question, however, was the relevance of this – in fact the dangers – in relation to the developing situation in Britain and on the issue of world peace and the defence of the Soviet Union. In fact, events were to show that this committee was not perceived by Stalin and his allies as a tactic to further the international class struggle. It was conceived as a "diplomatic" manœuvre to put pressure on the British capitalists and imperialism in general via the trade union and labour movement to prevent an attack on the Soviet Union. This was spelt out by Bukharin, Stalin's ally, who in the aftermath of the defeat of the General Strike argued for the maintenance of the Anglo-Russian Trade Union Committee from the point of view of a "diplomatic" counter-action to the offensive of imperialism against the USSR. The interests of the working class of Britain and the world were secondary to the state interests of the USSR.

But Trotsky and the International Left Opposition argued that war and, we might add, the prospect of war, are continuations of politics by other means. Opportunism always sees war as an "exceptional" phenomenon that requires the annulment of revolutionary politics and its basic principles. It was false to argue that it was necessary to maintain an alliance with the betrayers of the General Strike for a year after the Strike had finished, and while the miners were locked out, in order to "put pressure" on the British capitalists via the medium of the General Council. This merely allowed the General Council to continue to shelter in the aftermath of the strike under the umbrella of Russia and of the Comintern, and to choose the right moment to break on terms favourable to themselves.

There were three conferences of the Anglo-Russian Committee: in Paris in July 1926, in Berlin in August the same year and again in Berlin in April 1927. At each of these conferences the criticisms of the General Council from the Comintern and the British CP became more cautious, and the Left and their role were not even touched on. After the first conference in July 1926, the *Workers' Weekly* fully backed the Comintern's decision to maintain the Committee: "Has Anglo-Russian unity so far been justified?" Its answer was: "The conference of the Anglo-Russian Committee which has been agreed to by the General Council can still further justify itself in the work for international unity. It can take immediate steps to secure the embargo and to rally Continental workers to the aid of the British miners." However, the strike breakers of the General Council did not want to discuss "contentious" issues like this as indicated by the *Daily Herald*, which said that the Anglo-Russian Trade Union Committee must not "discuss the miners' dispute".[22]

Break with General Council

What was the answer of *Workers' Weekly* to this? "If this means discussing the fundamental questions of this dispute, we do not suppose that the British representatives [the right-wing General Council] would agree to this, or that if they did it would be possible to get agreement between them and the Russian trade union leaders. The Anglo-Russian Committee is, however, an international body [and at least] the next meeting of the Anglo-Russian Committee [should take] measures to assist the miners, and not measures to further divide and weaken the working class."[23] This shows just how desperate the Comintern was to maintain this unholy alliance, to the detriment of the Communist Party pursuing, in effect, a militant criticism of the General Council of the TUC and particularly on the Left.

The meeting was adjourned until the end of August. *Workers' Weekly*, commenting on the postponement of the meeting, said: "The Anglo-Russian Committee ended without results, and had to be 'adjourned' until the end of August." The French Communist Party daily *L'Humanité* was not so polite: "They [the General Council] hope the miners will be broken!" *Workers' Weekly* went on further: "Not the least dirty part in this sordid story was played by the so-called 'left wing' of the General Council, two members of which – Purcell and Hicks – attended the meeting. They have never made a public statement... Thereby Hicks and Purcell have fully justified the criticisms of them passed by the Russian unions: they have become screens and hand-rags for J.H. Thomas!"[24]

If this was the case, why did the British Communist Party, along with the Comintern as a whole, maintain its bloc with these strike breakers? Trotsky and the Left Opposition were referred to in the Communist Party's journals at this stage as "ultra-left" for wanting to break this unholy alliance at the top. Yet Trotsky and the Left Opposition also suggested: "At the same time, to intensify every effort to strengthen the united front, from below, relying above all on the ties that have been established with the mineworkers' union."[25] This approach had nothing in common with the ultra-left attitude adopted by the German Communist Party at the time of the rise of Hitler. Trotsky then demanded a united front between the German Communist Party and the Social Democrats.

Trotsky had proposed a united front both "above and below". The Comintern was for a "united front from below", ignoring the leaders of the social democracy who they characterised in an ultra-left manner as "social fascists". The united front tactic was at a different stage in 1926 than in Germany on the eve of Hitler coming to power. Trotsky explained his approach towards the situation in Britain: "The tactic of the united front still retains all its power as the most important method in the struggle of the masses. A basic principle of this tactic is: 'With the masses – always; with the vacillating leaders – sometimes, but only so long as they stand at the head of the masses.' It is necessary to make use of vacillating leaders while the masses are pushing them ahead, without for a moment abandoning criticism of these leaders. And it is necessary to break with them at the right time when they turn from vacillation to hostile action and betrayal. It is necessary to use the occasion of the break to expose the traitorous leaders and to contrast their position to that of the masses."[26]

But the Comintern and the British CP were maintaining this 'united front' while the leaders were 'not vacillating' but openly betraying the working class. The headline in *Workers' Weekly* read "General Council wrecking unity".[27] The British delegates had refused to discuss aid for the miners at the Anglo-Russian Trade Union Committee. Yet the *Workers' Weekly* in September 1926 still maintained the necessity for the alliance with the General Council. It even complains that there was a "British threat of a rupture" when in reality this rupture should have come from the side of the Russian trade unions themselves.[28] In the press of the British Communist Party there were criticisms made of the Left, but of a retrospective character. For instance, in the editorial of *Communist Review* we read: "Whom did the workers look to as their leaders, whom would they have followed in the event of a sharp clash between Right and Left? The men who had led the General Council on Red Friday last year – the left wing. By capitulating, by remaining silent, by taking the side of Thomas, the left wing left the workers temporarily leaderless and voiceless – save for our Party and the Minority Movement. And this treachery, unexpected [to whom – the CP? - PT] and fatal was greater than the certain and expected treason of Thomas. Yet if we cast our minds back to the part played by the 'left' wing at Scarborough – when they left all the fighting to the small Communist and Minority fraction – and last December, during the formation of the left wing – when they tried to disrupt the left wing because Communists were in it – we shall see that their treachery was not a sudden growth."[29]

Yet the bloc with these Lefts was still maintained through the Anglo-Russian Trade Union Committee. After the strike, we can even read sharp criticisms of Herbert Smith and A.J. Cook, the most prominent left-wing trade union leader. *Communist Review* in September 1926 states: "Cook and Smith had no business to weaken." The article criticised Smith and Cook "suddenly developing a respect for trade union etiquette". Cook had made a speech of 26 August on the possibility of longer hours for the miners. "Unless Cook and Smith are to be lost to the workers – and that would indeed be tragic, after the splendid fight they put up at first – the workers themselves must call them to order, and tell them to use their efforts in the sole direction whence victory can be brought: namely, the mobilisation of the whole British working class in active struggle on the side of the miners."[30]

Workers' Weekly made similar comments. Its banner headline in the 17 September edition read: "TUC leaders' united front against workers." It then goes on to state: "Cook helped them to get away with it."[31] This was a reference to the Bournemouth conference of the TUC that month in which the actions of the General Council were subjected to scrutiny but unfortunately were protected by the miners' leaders themselves. When Jack Tanner, a left-wing AEU leader, tried to move a reference back of the report of the General Council in order to get the General Strike discussed on the floor of the Congress (an NUR delegate seconded this) it was heavily defeated due to the intervention of Cook. He asked the Congress to respect the 'June pact', in effect a non-aggression pact between the miners and the sell-out General Council.

Cook's prestige was immense at this stage. Had he come out against the right-wing of the General Council, the floodgates of criticism would have been opened, which would have only reflected the mood which existed amongst the working class, particularly in the mining areas. Bob Smillie MP, an ex-miner and a member of the General Council, brought delegates to tears in describing the conditions in the mining areas and appealed for finance for the miners. In a monumental blunder, Bromley, collaborator of arch-traitor Thomas, seconded the motion but as soon as his name was announced uproar broke out with miners kicking over chairs and squaring up for a fight. The miners' delegates marched out of the Congress hall singing the Red Flag. It is incredible, however, that this Congress was allowed to pass without a serious discussion on the General Strike and the consequences for the whole of the working class which flowed from this. Only in January 1927 at a two-day special conference of trade union executives did the long awaited 'post mortem' on the General Strike take place. This was, however, after the termination of the miners' strike in November. The Right hoped that by this time they had ventilated the built-up anger and criticism of their role. This time Cook had no alternative but to criticise the General Council but the effect of this was blunted by the intervention of Citrine, who in a "brilliant" but anodyne contribution, appeared as the voice of sweet reason and "unity".

11 "Next time we will win without you"

The General Strike was a defeat and a serious one at that. The responsibility for this lay not with the miners and the working class as a whole. The ruling class took their revenge; the mine owners, without any pity, were determined to inflict brutal sacrifices on the miners and sought in the process to crush union organisation in the pits. Birkenhead boasted in private: "The discredit of the Miners' Federation is now complete."[1] However, the strike had been at some cost to the capitalists. Lost coal production alone amounted to the value of £97 million and a further £42 million had to be spent on imports of coal. *The Economist* put the total trade loss at between £300 million and £400 million. One hundred and sixty million working days were lost in strikes in 1926 as a whole, the highest ever in a single year, and only rivalled later by the upsurge of workers' militancy in the 1970s and 1980s. Trade union membership fell below five million for the first time since 1916, down from a figure of five and a half million before the General Strike. The number of TUC-affiliated unions fell even more steeply.

Strike meeting

For the miners, the government repealed the Seven Hours Act of 1919 and forced them to accept lower wages. They also introduced the anti-union 1927 Trade Disputes and Trade Union Act, which even the Liberal Lord Reading said offered "no single ray of light for British working men". It was, he said, to be "more vague, more indefinite, more lacking in precision in respect of the crimes which it indicates and the penalties which follow upon them, than any Bill I have ever seen or any Act of Parliament I have had to construe either as a law officer or as a judge". Symons comments: "More than any other single measure, the Trades Disputes Act caused hatred of Baldwin and his government among organised trade unionists. Its repeal in 1946, after the refusals to amend it of Chamberlain in 1939 and Churchill in 1945, had great emotional as well as practical significance for the labour movement."[2]

This Act has many of the features of Thatcher's later raft of anti-union laws. It illegalised "'anyone who declares, instigates, incites others to take part in or otherwise acts in furtherance of a strike declared to be illegal" and such a person "could be jailed for up to two years. The 'illegal strikes' phrase placed an enormous amount of discriminatory power in the hands of a reactionary government," and meant that anything like a repetition of the General Strike would have been classified as "illegal".[3] But the ban went further than this, covering all strikes which extended beyond a single trade or industry and was "designed or calculated to coerce the government either directly or by inflicting hardship upon the community".[4] As with the Thatcher acts, the threat of litigation was an integral part of this bill if trade unions decided to stage an "illegal strike". The Act also imposed restrictions on picketing, it prohibited civil servants from joining trade unions associated with the TUC and or Labour Party, and it forbade local authorities from making trade union membership a condition of employment. The Act was, as G.D.H. Cole pointed out, a "return to the old law of master and servant which had been swept away by the Employers' and Workmen Act of 1875".[5]

The Act also contained a clause providing that trade unionists who wanted to pay the political levy of their union would have to "contract in" rather than "contract out". This was meant, of course, to deprive the Labour Party of funds. The capitalists no longer need to legislate against workers collecting funds for the Labour Party because now, as the latest scandal over "loans" to Labour has shown, it is partly financed by big business. After 1926, the affiliated membership of the Labour Party fell from nearly 3.4 million in 1926 to just over 2 million two years later. Between 1927 and 1929, the Labour Party lost over a quarter of its total income from affiliation fees because of depleted trade union funds. The Tory hardliners led by Birkenhead, Churchill and Co had other trophies to their names from the defeat of the working class. Diplomatic relations were broken off with Russia on trumped-up charges of "misconduct" against the Soviet trade delegation in London. By this time, the Anglo-Russian Trade Union Committee had disappeared from the scene and the erstwhile "partners" of the Russian trade unions, the General Council, never raised a peep of protest.

Another consequence of the defeat of the General Strike was the divisions created in the Miners' Federation. A breakaway right-wing union was formed in the Midlands by George Spencer, leader of the Nottinghamshire Miners' Association; this "non-political" union was supported by the coal owners. This was to be mirrored later by the so-called Union of Democratic Mineworkers (UDM) created during the 1984-85 miners' strike. But it would be wrong to say that the working class – particularly its guiding layers – were cowered by these spiteful class acts of the ruling class. The 1927 anti-union act described as the "most reactionary sample of British labour legislation placed on the statute book since the evil Combination Laws of 1799-1800"[6] certainly had an effect in intimidating the trade union leaders and the TUC. Just over a month after its enactment, the Edinburgh TUC Congress revealed the unmistakeable shift to the right of the TUC and its leading figures. The president, George Hicks, a leading 'Left' in the firmament of the Communist Party and the Anglo-Russian Trade Union Committee, in his presidential address proposed co-operation with the employers "in a common endeavour to improve the efficiency of industry and to raise the workers' standard of life". In January 1928 the first joint meeting between a group of employers and the General Council took place. Its lone opponent on the General Council was Arthur Cook![7]

At the September 1928 TUC conference, the rejection of militant class struggle policies received further endorsement, which were characterised as "futile, certain to fail and sure to lead to bloodshed and misery".[8] 'Mondism', derived from the name of the Chairman of chemical firm ICI, Sir Alfred Mond, was embraced by the General Council. With Mond, they proposed to establish a "national industrial council" representing workers and bosses and a system of "compulsory conciliation". Emmanuel Shinwell MP, described it as the "blunt bargain" whereby "the trade unions keep the men in order; the employer, in return, agrees to employ union men only".[9] This policy did not go through without opposition but nevertheless it became, for a period, the official policy of the TUC.

In the aftermath of their victory in the General Strike, the capitalists appeared to be completely triumphant. In relation to Labour and trade union opposition to the 1927 Act, Birkenhead taunted: "Call all your meetings, blow all your trumpets, make all your speeches, unfurl all your red flags – and when you have done it all, the Bill is going through Parliament."[10] This Tory Lord was brutally frank in teaching the working class a harsh lesson. Parliamentary action alone, demonstrations, even passive general strikes, the ruling class in the final analysis can ride out. They will have to be removed from the scene of history by a mass movement of the working class and the weapon of the general strike is an important, indeed a vital weapon in the armoury of the working class, in carrying this task through to a conclusion. But this will only be possible by learning the lessons of 1926.

Lessons of 1926

The first and most basic lesson to be drawn from the General Strike is that the aim of capitalism as a system is to produce for profit and not for social need. Despite the noisy claims of the representatives of this system – as evidenced by Baldwin in 1925 and 1926 – about social peace and 'partnership', a constant struggle takes place over the share-out of the wealth produced by the labour of the working class. The battle to control this surplus, which Marx described as the unpaid labour of the working class, is usually called profit, and is the basis of the struggle between the contending classes. Capitalism seeks to maximise profits – by squeezing the working class even in the period of relative upswing, as we have seen in the 1990s and the first part of this decade – while the working class will fight to maintain and even improve its share. In periods of economic upswing, the capitalists may even allow some crumbs off its very rich table to fall into the lap of the working class. In the period of 1950-75, in Britain and throughout most of the developed capitalist world, a real advance in living standards took place. At the time, this was considered by capitalist commentators to be the norm, an indication that their system had overcome its contradictions. In fact, it was an exception to the usual state of affairs under capitalism.

This period was in marked contradistinction to the time of the General Strike. Then, as we have seen, a ferocious struggle took place between the capitalists and the working class. On the other hand, there are periods of relative social peace – usually when capitalism is going ahead – when the classes can 'rub along' and, generally, it does not result in explosive ruptures in society. There are, however, other periods when the class struggle takes a sharp form, as in 1926. The reason for this is not because of the personalities involved – who generally reflect class interests – but arises from the inherent contradictions of capitalism. The basic contradiction of this system is ultimately the inability of working-class people to buy back the goods they produce. Of the increased wealth they create, the working class receives only a portion in the form of wages. The capitalists overcome this problem by ploughing back the surplus into industry and production. This, in turn, generates even greater production, which creates the same problem again; what Marx called "overproduc- tion", a glut of goods and services which cannot be bought. When this happens, the capitalist system is afflicted by a recession or slump. This can coalesce with a protracted and generalised stagnation of the productive forces. Such a period occurred in the inter-war period in Britain and the capitalist world. It is in these kinds of periods when a sharpening of the class struggle can develop culminating sometimes in the kind of movement that took place in 1926.

The general strike did not drop from the sky but was the product of the period of 1918 to 1926 when, as we have seen, the capitalists, afflicted by a serious crisis, attempted to place the burden of this on the British working class. The working class resisted as best it could, saddled as it was with faulty leadership. They forced these leaders to declare a general strike which resulted in the grandiose conflict of the nine days. However, despite all their heroic efforts it was not victory but a defeat. On the anniversary of this great struggle, the best way to commemorate the tremendous efforts of the working class of 1926 is to ponder whether with a different leadership the working class could have come out of it victoriously.

And this is not just a historical question. In the light of the tumultuous events in France in early 2006, the working class is being pushed to the brink of a 'general strike'. In the first instance, this has taken the form of partial one-day strikes. The mood undoubtedly exists amongst the French working class for a complete one-day stoppage of both public and private sector workers in order to defeat the neo-liberal scheme of the Chirac government. But substantial sections see the need for a general strike. The French government is attacking the conditions of young people as a backdoor means of driving down the living standards of the working class as a whole. With sure instinct, the French working class has come out in a great solidarity movement in defence of young people. The French trade union leaders for their part, however, fear even a one-day general strike in France. Millions have poured onto the streets involving three million workers on at least two occasions. The trade union leaders remember, however, as do significant sections of the working class, what happened in 1968. Then, as now, it was the young people who were the first into battle. Students at the Sorbonne and elsewhere were in the vanguard as they are now. Only after the police had brutally attacked student demonstrations did the French working class come out on a one-day total stoppage. The strike was continued and what followed was the General Strike of May-June 1968 and the occupation of the factories, the greatest in history. At the time of writing, Chirac has been forced to withdraw the hated CPE young workers' contracts, with the proviso that the government will bring in unspecified new measures in the future.

Yet the features which have led to the recent social explosion in France are common to the rest of the countries of Europe. Even before the onset of a serious economic recession or slump, capitalism in Europe and worldwide is determined to ruthlessly pursue its neo-liberal agenda. It is being assisted in this aim by the shift to the right of the majority of the leaders of the trade unions and the abandonment of socialism by the leaders of the former workers' parties. Despite this, the working class is determined to ferociously defend the gains of the past. The accumulated experiences of the last two decades of neo-liberal policies, pursued with particular venom in Britain and the US, as well as the other 'Anglo-Saxon' countries, have reinforced this mood. Lodged in this situation, therefore, is the possibility of one-day general strikes and even of generalised struggles along the lines of 1926 in any number of countries in Europe, including Britain.

There are, however, some differences between the situations in 1926 and even France 1968, and the situation today in Europe. This is particularly evident on the issue of the political outlook, or consciousness, of the working class, then and now. In both 1926 and 1968, there was a widespread awareness and attraction to the ideas of socialism as the alternative to capitalism. Because of the collapse of Stalinism, and with it the planned economies of Eastern Europe, the capitalists were able to pursue a huge campaign against 'socialism'. This coincided with an economic boom and the lurch to the Right of the trade union and Labour leaders. This has thrown back consciousness. Also, the economic situation is not yet as severe as 1926 – 1968 took place, paradoxically, when the economic boom had not exhausted itself. On the other hand, the capitalists will pursue their neo-liberal agenda relentlessly unless they are checked by a resurgent labour movement. Inherent in this situation is therefore the possibility of a general strike. Because of all these factors taken together, this will probably mean that power may not be posed immediately in the minds of the working class. A 'general strike' today therefore could initially take the form of warning strikes to exert mass pressure to extract concessions. But these would be staging posts along the way towards strikes like 1926. This is why this event retains its importance today.

Britain has gone to the brink of such struggles on a number of occasions since 1926. In 1970, for instance, the newly elected Tory Prime Minister, Edward Heath, threatened the trade unions and the working class in a nationally televised broadcast with a 'general strike' unless they were prepared to come to heel and accept cuts in their rights and conditions. British capitalism was in the grip of a long-term crisis. The working class had shown under the previous Labour government of Harold Wilson that it was not going to swallow the 'sacrifices' demanded of them. In 1968, for instance, when Wilson and Barbara Castle introduced their infamous anti-trade union bill, 'In Place of Strife', it was resisted by mass demonstrations. The majority of the trade union and labour movement opposed it. This pressure compelled the Labour government to step back and these attacks were shelved.

Alarmed by the power of the working class, the ruling class had concluded that a 'strong' government was needed which could weaken and push back the power of the working class. However, they miscalculated and this resulted in a period of big strikes and social upheaval. It led to the mass occupation of the Upper Clyde Shipyards on Clydeside, which compelled the Heath government and British capitalism to stage a 'U-turn'. However, this did not prevent the Heath government from taking on the miners, in both 1972 and, particularly, in the 1974 strike. This latter strike resulted in the three-day week and led to a general election and the eviction of the Tories from office. This whole episode indicated just how the strategists of capital had pondered the events of the past, had seen what had happened in 1926 and were prepared, if necessary, to deploy the same means of defeating the working class. In the 1980s, under Thatcher, the issue of a general strike to topple her government was again raised. In a similar situation, which could occur in Britain and in Europe in the next stage, the capitalists will be drawing on the lessons from the past. The working class, for its part, must also explore the events like 1926 to see how best to prepare for a similar situation in the future. We hope that this book will be a step towards realising that goal.

The Future

The General Strike of 1926 was a magnificent display of working-class power. The attempt to trivialise and belittle its significance by references to strikers playing football with policemen and other secondary features of the strike is meant to diminish it in the eyes of the present generation. This is done quite consciously by capitalist historians together with the right-wing trade union leaders. They like to think that "never again" will a general strike occur in Britain. On the contrary, the situation that is developing in Britain will lead to a mighty collision, in fact a series of class conflicts between the classes which will put the issue of the general strike back onto the agenda.

One of the reasons why Britain has not yet repeated the experience of 1926 is the existence of a conservative officialdom that really does have the philosophy of Cramp, the NUR crony of Thomas in 1926 of "Never again".[11] If anything, their successors in the leadership of the trade unions today are more removed from the ideas of a general strike than in 1926. But ultimately their position depends on the ordinary members of the trade unions and the working class.

Baldwin was a consummate representative of big business. Despite all his phrases about class peace, he was quite clear that he was engaged in a war between the classes. He admitted later: "I provoked a general election in 1923 as a means of demoralising the labour movement and securing the commitment of the Labour

Party to our imperialist policy in deed and word. I provoked a general strike in 1926 as a means of demoralising the trade union leaders and breaking up the unity of the unions which had become so manifest in 1925. There is now no important organised political opposition either inside or outside Parliament. Whatever strength may be gained by the revolutionary forces, which as yet are very small, it will take some considerable time before they can seriously hamper any policy we wish to pursue."[12]

The strength of the capitalists in 1926 lay not in themselves but in the weakness of those at the top of the opposing army of the working class. The sell-out of the general strike was not accepted with equanimity by the working class, or by most of its organisations at the bottom and by the militants, the backbone of the British working class. At the Bournemouth conference of the TUC in September 1926, where the mantra of the Right was "never again", a significant contribution was made by a young miners' delegate, Peter Chambers. His final sentence was: "We will have another general strike without you, and we will win next time."[13] The "next time" has not come for 80 years but history has a way of confirming prophecies much later than when they were originally formulated. This young delegate was undoubtedly right, if not for his generation then for those workers who will move into action in this century. But to be "successful", in the sense of leading to a complete rupture with capitalism and a new democratic socialist society, it is necessary to absorb all the lessons of this strike.

Notes

Introduction

1. See Ken Smith's book on the Miners' strike 1984-85 *A Civil War Without Guns*.
2. Christopher Farman, *May 1926, The General Strike, Britain's Aborted Revolution*, p42.

1 British Capitalism's Postwar Crisis

1. Allen Hutt, *British Trade Unionism, A Short History*, p84.
2. William Keegan, *The Prudence of Mr Gordon Brown*, p276.
3. John Murray, *The General Strike of 1926 – A History*, p23.
4. Julian Symons, *The General Strike*, p5.
5. R.A. Florey, *The General Strike of 1926*, p13.
6. Leon Trotsky, *1905*, p105
7. A. MacManus and A. Inkpin, *The Communist*, 7 October 1920.

2 Red Friday

1. Walter Citrine, *Men and Work*, p77.
2. *Beatrice Webb's Diaries, 1924-32*, Margaret Cole (editor), p116.
3. Hutt, p98.
4. *Ibid*, p99.
5. Leon Trotsky, *Diaries in Exile*, p85.
6. Farman, p15.
7. J.M. Keynes, *The Economic Consequences of Mr Churchill*.
8. Wal Hannington, *Unemployed Struggles, 1919-1936*, p135.
9. Willie Gallacher, *The Rolling of the Thunder*, pp39-40.
10. *Workers' Weekly*, 30 January, 1925.
11. Farman, p41.
12. *Ibid*.
13. *Ibid*.
14. *Ibid*, p43.
15. *Ibid.*, p46.
16. *Ibid.*, p47.
17. *Manchester Guardian*, 4 August 1925.
18. Webb, p61.

3 The Nine Months

1. Symons, p18.
2. *Ibid..*
3. *Ibid.*, p20.
4. *Ibid*, p22.
5. Farman, p61.
6. Symons, pp25-26.
7. Originally gangs of reactionary young men who attacked republicans during the downswing of the French Revolution.
8. The *Daily Herald* was the daily paper of the TUC.
9. Aneurin Bevan, *In Place of Fear*, pp20-21.
10. *Offensiv*, 1975.
11. Trotsky, *The Middle of the Road, Trotsky's Writings on Britain*, vol 3, p103
12. W.H. Crook, *The General Strike*, pp295-6.
13. *Ibid*, p295.
14. Farman, pp49-50.
15. Crook, p295.
16. Farman, p71.
17. *Communist Review*, October 1924.
18. *Workers' Weekly*, 7 August 1925.
19. *Workers' Weekly*, 18 September, 1925.
20. Brian Norton, The Minority Movement and the Communist Party, *Militant International Review*, Summer 1986.
21. James Klugmann, *History of the Communist Party of Great Britain, 1925-1927*, p16.
22. *Daily Telegraph*, 12 May 1925.
23. *Workers' Weekly*, 28 August, 1925.
24. Klugmann, p46.
25. George Hardy, *Those Stormy Years*, p185
26. Leon Trotsky, *Europe and America*, p54.
27. M.N. Roy, The Empire and the Proletariat, *Labour Monthly*, January 1925.
28. The World of Labour, *Labour Monthly*, January 1925.
29. *Ibid.*
30. R Palme Dutt, Notes of the Month, *Labour Monthly*, September 1926
31. Two Deserters (Reply to Newbold and M. Phillips Price), Karl Radek, *Labour Monthly*, March 1925.
32. *the socialist*, 413, 27 October 2005.
33. Problems of the Labour Movement by P. Braun, *Labour Monthly*, June 1925.
34. Book Reviews by GAH, *Labour Monthly*, July 1925.
35. Farman, p52.
36. The Scarborough Conference, Harry Pollitt, *Labour Monthly*, October 1925.
37. Ibid.
38. Leon Trotsky, *Writings on Britain*, Volume 2, pp138-9.
39. See *Liverpool: A City That Dared To Fight.*
40. Klugmann, pp56-57.
41. *Ibid*, p54.
42. *The Observer*, 7 September, 1925.
43. Quoted in *Sunday Worker*, 20 September, 1925.
44. Klugmann, p59.
45. *Financial Times*, 1 October 1925.
46. *The Times*, 1 October 1925.
47. *Weekly Dispatch*, 11 October, 1925.
48. Harry Pollitt, *Serving My Time.*
49. R Palme Dutt, Notes of the Month, *Labour Monthly*, June 1926.
50. *Labour Monthly*, November 1925.
51. Klugmann, p66.
52. Henry Brailsford was a leading member of the ILP throughout the 1920s and editor of its newspaper 1922-26.
53. George Lansbury was a leading figure in the Labour Party throughout the 1920s and 1930s. He led the Poplar councillors against the Government in 1921. Nominally on the left of the party, he went on to lead it in between 1932 and 1935.
54. Leon Trotsky, *Trotsky's Writings on Britain*, Volume 2, pp139-140.
55. *Ibid*, p140.

56. P. Braun, Scarborough and Liverpool, *Labour Monthly*, November 1925.
57. William Paul, The Left Wing, *Labour Monthly*, February 1926.
58. *The Times*, 23 October, 1925.
59. R. Page Arnot, *The General Strike, May 1926, Its Origin and History*, p59.
60. *New York Times*, 3 August, 1925.
61. Crook, *The General Strike*, p298.
62. La préparation Bolcheviste de la grève Anglaise, *La Revue de Paris*, 15 May 1926, quoted in Crook, *The General Strike*, p297.
63. *Ibid*, p298.
64. Murray, p60.
65. Hywel Francis & David Smith, *The Fed, a history of the South Wales miners in the twentieth century*, p54.
66. Klugmann, p83.
67. *Ibid*.
68. George Lansbury, *The ICWPA*, p11. The ICWPA was the International Class War Prisoners Aid.
69. *Sunday Worker*, 29 November 1925.
70. *Ibid.*, 18 October, 1925.
71. Klugmann, p85.
72. *Daily Herald*, 17 October, 1925.
73. Page Arnot, p68.
74. Florey, p13.
75. *The Times*, 21 January 1927.
76. Florey, p14.
77. *Ibid*, p100.
78. *Daily Express*, Friday 5 November,.
79. Florey, p101.
80. *Ibid*.
81. *Ibid*.
82. *The Times*, 5 October 1925.

4 On the Eve of Battle
1. Klugmann, p93.
2. TUC General Council, *Report of the Conference of Trade Union Executives*, p26.
3. *Ibid*, p10.
4. *Workers Weekly*, 1 January 1926.
5. *Ibid*, 15 January 1926.
6. *Ibid*, 15 January 1926.
7. *Ibid*, 19 February, 1926.
8. *Ibid*.
9. *Ibid*.
10. Trotsky and his English Critics, R. Palme Dutt, *Labour Monthly*, April 1926.
11. *Workers' Weekly*, 1 January 1926.
12. *Ibid*, 15 January, 1926.
13. *Ibid*, 12 March 1926.
14. Farman, p75.
15. *Ibid*, p76.
16. *Ibid*, p77.
17. *Ibid*, p78.
18. *Forward*, 19 March 1926. Forward was the paper of the ILP.
19. Klugmann, p102.
20. Farman, pp82-83.
21. L.J. MacFarlane, *The British Communist Party: Its Origin and Development until 1929*, p155.
22. Farman, p71.
23. *Ibid*, p87.
24. Murray, p73.
25. Farman, p85.
26. *Ibid*, p88.
27. *Ibid*.
28. *Ibid*, p96.
29. *Ibid*, p90.
30. *Ibid*, p91.
31. *Workers' Weekly*, 19 March 1926.
32. Klugmann, p102.
33. *Workers Weekly*, 9 April 1926.
34. Farman, p93.
35. *Ibid*, p95.
36. *Ibid*, p95.
37. *Ibid*, pp98-99.
38. *Ibid*, p106.
39. *The Observer*, 25 April 1926.

40. Farman, p116.
41. *Ibid*, p126.
42. *Hansard*, 13 May 1926.
43. Farman, p92.
44. *Ibid*.
45. *Ibid* p96.
46. Murray, p79.
47. Farman, pp127-128.
48. *Ibid*, p128.
49. *Ibid*, p122-3.
50. *Ibid*, p127.
51. *Ibid*, p128.
52. *Ibid*, p129
53. *Ibid*.
54. TUC, *The Mining Crisis and the National Strike, 1926*, p33.
55. A.J. Cook, *The Nine Days*, p10.
56. Symons, p43.
57. Farman, p134.
58. *Ibid*, p136.
59. Kingsley Martin, *The British Public and the General Strike*.

5 The Strike Begins

1. *Daily Mail*, 3 May, 1926.
2. Farman, p140.
3. *Ibid*.
4. *Hansard*, 3 May 1926.
5. *Ibid*.
6. *Ibid*.
7. *Ibid*.
8. Farman. P145.
9. Klugmann, p111.
10. Farman, p130.
11. Klugmann, p180.
12. *Socialist Review*, June 1926.
13. Farman, p149.
14. *Ibid*.
15. *Ibid*, p204.
16. *Ibid*, p150.
17. *Ibid*, p151.
18. Symons, pp61-62.
19. *TUC Communiqué*, quoted in Page Arnot, p175.
20. Farman, p154.
21. Page Arnot, p162.
22. *Ibid*, p164.
23. Klugmann, p115.
24. *Ibid*.
25. *British Worker*, 7 May 1926.
26. Hamilton Fyfe, *Behind the Scenes of the General Strike*, p33.
27. Kingsley Martin, *The British Public and the General Strike*.
28. Murray, p122.
29. *British Gazette*, 5 May 1926.
30. Farman, p168.
31. *Ibid*.
32. *British Gazette*, 5 May 1926.
33. *Ibid*, 6 May 1926.
34. *Ibid*.
35. *Ibid*.
36. *Ibid*.
37. *Ibid*.
38. *Ibid*, 8 May 1926.
39. *Ibid*, 6 May 1926.
40. *Ibid*, 10 May, 1926.
41. *Ibid*.
42. *Ibid*, 8 May, 1926.

43. Farman, p184.
44. *Ibid*, p182.
45. *Ibid*, p184.
46. *Ibid*, pp185-190.
47. *British Worker*, 8 May 1926.
48. *Ibid*.
49. *Ibid*, 10 May 1926.
50. *Ibid*, 11 May 1926.
51. *British Gazette*, 12 May 1926.
52. Farman, p275.

⬛ **The Workers Organise**

1. Robert Rhodes James, *Memoirs of a Conservative. J.C.C. Davidson's Memoirs and papers, 1910-37*, p250.
2. A.J. Cook, *The Nine Days*.
3. Anthony Mason, *The General Strike in the North-East*, p11.
4. History Group of the Communist Party, *The General Strike in the North-East*, p2
5. Mason, p17.
6. *Labour Monthly*, June 1926.
7. C.R. Flynn, *An Account of the Proceedings of the Northumberland and Durham General Council and Joint Strike Committee*, pp6-7, quoted in Mason, p22.
8. Mason, p23
9. *Plebs*, August 1926, quoted in Mason, p24.
10. R. Page Arnot, *The Miners – Years of Struggle*, pp439-440.
11. Tony Mulhearn, Merseyside under workers' control, *Militant*, 26 March 1976.
12. *The Fed*, pp54-5.
13. *Ibid*, p55.
14. Klugmann, p163.
15. *Morning Post*, 15 June 1926.
16. *Newcastle Chronicle*, 21 May 1926.
17. Letter from Mr Dillon to Lord Londonderry, quoted in Mason, p87.
18. *Ibid*.
19. *Ibid*.
20. *Northern Light* 15 May 1926, quoted in Farman, p225.
21. Farman, p229.
22. *Ibid*, p231.
23. *Ibid*, p193.
24. *Ibid*.
25. Introduction by Bill Moore, *The General Strike in Sheffield*, p.xvii.
26. *Ibid*.
27. Robert S. Sephton, *Oxford and the General Strike*, p29.
28. Farman, p198.
29. *Ibid*.

30. *Ibid*, p198.
31. *Ibid*
32. John McLean, *The 1926 General Strike in Lanarkshire*, p7.
33. *Ibid*, p8
34. *Ibid*.
35. *Ibid*.
36. *British Gazette*, 11 May 1926.
37. McLean, p20.
38. *Ibid*.
39. Murray, p151.
40. Emile Burns, *Trades Councils in Action*, p73.
41. Farman, p204.
42. *Ibid*, pp203-4.
43. *Ibid*, pp204-5
44. Abe Moffat, *My Life with the Miners*, p45
45. Burns, p70.
46. Burns, *The General Strike of 1926*, p70
47. Burns, *Trades Councils in Action*, p72
48. *Ibid*.
49. George Glasgow, *General Strikes and Road Transport*, quoted in Burns, *Trades Councils in Action*, p73.
50. Farman, p227.
51. *Ibid*, p229.
52. *Ibid*, p234.
53. *Ibid*, p238.
54. *The Times*, 10 May 1926.
55. Farman, p244.
56. *Ibid*, p247.
57. *Ibid*, p248-9.
58. Symons, p166.

7 A Revolutionary Situation
1. Hutt, *op. cit.*, p112.
2. *Ibid*.
3. J.R. Clynes, *Memoirs 1924-1937*, pp81-82.
4. Farman, p209.
5. *Workers' Weekly*, 30 April 1926.
6. Robert Boothby, quoted in Farman, p213.
7. Theses of the Communist International on the British General Strike, *Labour Monthly*, July 1926.
8. Burns, *Trades Councils in Action*, p120.
9. Klugmann, pp186-188.
10. Farman, p215.
11. A.J.P. Taylor, *A Personal History*, quoted in Sephton, p53.
12. *Ibid*.
13. Farman, pp242-3.
14. *Ibid*. p241.
15. *Ibid*. p240.
16. J. Skelley, *The General Strike 1926*, p316.

8 TUC Leaders Capitulate

1. Murray, pp146-7.
2. Cook, p18.
3. *Ibid.*
4. *British Worker*, 8 May, 1926.
5. *British Gazette*, 8 May 1926.
6. *Ibid.*
7. *British Gazette*, 12 May, 1926.
8. *Ibid.*
9. *The Times*, 6 May 1926.
10. Symons, p136.
11. *Ibid.*
12. Farman, p263.
13. Symons, p196.
14. *Ibid.*
15. Farman, p259.
16. Murray, p152
17. Symons, p196.
18. *Ibid.*
19. *Ibid*, p197.
20. *Ibid*, p198
21. Crook, p397.
22. Farman, p268.
23. *Ibid*, p269.
24. Farman, p274.
25. Symons, p208.
26. *British Worker*, 11 May 1926.
27. Farman, p272
28. Cook, in Murray, p154.
29. *Ibid*, p155.
30. Symons, p205.
31. Farman, p277.
32. *Tottenham Strike Bulletin*, Wednesday 12 May, 1926.
33. Symons, pp206-7.
34. *Ibid*, p207.
35. Farman, p287.
36. *Ibid.*
37. Page Arnot, p218.

9 Outrage

1. Farman, p290.
2. *Ibid*, pp290-91.
3. *Nine Days in Birmingham*, p35.
4. Symons, pp210-11.
5. *Ibid*, p211.
6. Farman, pp291-2.
7. *Ibid*, p291.
8. *Ibid,*
9. Mason, p89.
10. *Ibid*, pp89-90.
11. Farman, p292.
12. Symons, p215
13. *British Gazette,* 13 May 1926.
14. Lansbury's *Labour Weekly*, 26 May 1926, quoted in Farman, p294.
15. Quoted in *Nine Days in Birmingham*, p35.
16. *Nine Days in Birmingham*, pp38-40.
17. Farman, p295.
18. *Ibid.* p296.
19. *Ibid*, p297.
20. *Ibid*, p301
21. *Ibid*, p299.
22. *Ibid.*
23. *Ibid*, pp299-300.
24. Murray, p168.
25. Farman, p300.
26. Page Arnot, pp233-4.
27. R Palme Dutt, Notes of the Month, *Labour Monthly,* July 1926.
28. 'Observer', Our First General Strike, *The Communist Review*, June 1926
29. Page Arnot, p244
30. Klugmann, p191.
31. *Ibid.*
32. *Communist Review*, July 1926, p133.
33. MacFarlane, p302.
34. Trotsky, *Trotsky's Writings on Britain*, p253.

10 The Terrible Aftermath
1. *British Worker*, 15 May, 1926.
2. Farman, p303.
3. Symons, p223.
4. Farman, p309.
5. *Ibid.*
6. *Lansbury's Labour Weekly*, 29 May 1926.
7. Hugh Dalton, *Call Back Yesterday*, p203, quoted in Farman, p320.
8. Murray, pp173-4.
9. *Ibid*, p176.
10. Hardy, p188.
11. *Workers Weekly*, 18 June 1926.
12. 'Observer', Our First General Strike, *Communist Review*, June 1926.
13. The Editorial View, *Communist Review*, July 1926.
14. Communist International Theses on the Lessons of the British General Strike, *Communist Review*, July 1926, p116.
15. *Ibid.* p118.
16. *Ibid*, p120.
17. *Ibid*, pp127-9.
18. Trotsky, The Future of the British Communist Party, *Leon Trotsky On Britain*, p251.
19. *Ibid*, pp251-2.
20. *Ibid*, p252.
21. Resolution on the General Strike in Britain, *Ibid*, pp253-4.
22. *Workers' Weekly*, 23 July, 1926.
23. *Ibid.*
24. *Workers' Weekly*, 6 August, 1926.
25. Trotsky, *Ibid*, p253.
26. *Ibid*, p255.
27. *Workers' Weekly*, 6 August 1926.
28. *Ibid*, 10 September 1926.
29. Editorial View, *Communist Review*, August 1926, p157.
30. Editorial View, *Communist Review*, September 1926, p157.
31. *Workers' Weekly*, 17 September 1926.

11 'Next Time We Will Win Without You'
1. Farman, p320.
2. Symons, p226.
3. Murray, p189.
4. *Ibid.*
5. G.D.H. Cole, *History of the Labour Party From 1914.*
6. Crook, p481.
7. Hutt, p115.
8. *Ibid.*
9. *Ibid*, p116.
10. Farman, p322.
11. Murray, p187.
12. *Ibid*, p199.
13. *Ibid*, p186.

Bibliography

- R. Page Arnot, *The Miners – Years of Struggle*, Allen & Unwin, London, 1953.
- R. Page Arnot, *The General Strike, May 1926, Its Origin and History*, EP Publishing, 1975 edition.
- Tony Benn, *The End of an Era: Diaries 1980-90*, Arrow Books, London, 1994.
- Aneurin Bevan, *In Place of Fear*, MacGibbon and Kee, London, 1952.
- Birmingham City Council, *Nine Days in Birmingham: The General Strike, 4-12 May 1926*, Birmingham Public Libraries, 1976.
- Emile Burns, *The General Strike 1926: Trades Councils in Action*, Lawrence & Wishart, London, 1975 edition.
- Walter Citrine, *Men and Work*, Hutchinson, London, 1964.
- Tony Cliff and Donny Gluckstein, *Marxism and Trade Union Struggle: The General Strike of 1926*, Bookmarks, London, 1986.
- J.R. Clynes, *Memoirs 1924-1937*, Hutchinson, London, 1937
- G.D.H. Cole, *History of the Labour Party From 1914*, Routledge and Paul, London, 1948.
- Margaret Cole (editor), *Beatrice Webb's Diaries, 1924-32*, Longman's Green, London, 1956.
- A.J. Cook, *The Nine Days*, Co-operative Printing Society, 1926.
- W.H. Crook, *The General Strike*, Chapel Hill University of North Carolina Press, 1931.
- W.H. Crook, *Communism and the General Strike*, Shoe String Press, Hamden Conneticut, 1960.
- Hugh Dalton, *Call Back Yesterday*, Muller, 1953.
- Clare Doyle, *France 1968: Month of Revolution*, Fortress Books, London, 1988.
- James Eaden and David Renton, *The Communist Party of Great Britain since 1920*, Palgrave, Basingstoke, 2002.
- Christopher Farman, *May 1926, The General Strike, Britain's Aborted Revolution*, Panther Books, St Albans, 1974.
- R.A. Florey, *The General Strike of 1926*, John Calder (Publishers), London, 1980.
- Hywel Francis & David Smith, *The Fed, a history of the South Wales miners in the twentieth century*, Lawrence and Wishart, London, 1980.
- Hamilton Fyfe, *Behind the Scenes of the General Strike*, Labour Publishing Co., 1926.
- Willie Gallacher, *The Rolling of the Thunder*, Lawrence and Wishart, London, 1947.
- George Glasgow, *General Strikes and Road Transport*,
- Wal Hannington, *Unemployed Struggles, 1919-1936*, Lawrence and Wishart, London, 1936.
- George Hardy, *Those Stormy Years*, Lawrence & Wishart, London, 1956.
- History Group of the Communist Party, *The General Strike in the North-East*, London, 1961.
- Allen Hutt, *British Trade Unionism, A Short History*, Lawrence & Wishart, London, 1975 edition.
- Allen Hutt, *The Condition of the Working Class in Britain*, Martin Lawrence, London, 1933.
- Allen Hutt, *Post-War History of the Working Class*, Gollancz, London, 1937.
- Robert Rhodes James, *Memoirs of a Conservative. J.C.C. Davidson's Memoirs and papers, 1910-37*, Weidenfield and Nicolson, London, 1969.

- William Keegan, *The Prudence of Mr Gordon Brown*, John Wiley & Sons, Chichester, 2003.
- J.M.Keynes, *The Economic Consequences of Mr Churchill*, Hogarth Press, 1925.
- James Klugmann, *History of the Communist Party of Great Britain, 1925-1927*, Lawrence & Wishart, London, 1969.
- George Lansbury, *The ICWPA at work*, British Section of the International Class War Prisoners Aid, 1926
- Rosa Luxemburg, *The Mass Strike*, Bookmarks, London, 2005 edition.
- L.J. MacFarlane, *The British Communist Party. Its Origin and Development until 1929*, MacGibbon and Kee, 1966.
- John McLean, *The 1926 General Strike in Lanarkshire*, History Group of the CPGB, London, 1976.
- Kingsley Martin, *The British Public and the General Strike*, Hogarth Press, 1926.
- Anthony Mason, *The General Strike in the North-East*, University of Hull Publications, 1970.
- Abe Moffat, *My Life with the Miners*, Lawrence and Wishart, London, 1965.
- C.L. Mowat, *The General Strike 1926*, Edward Arnold (Publishers), London, 1969.
- Bill Moore (Introduction), *The General Strike in Sheffield*, Sheffield City Libraries, 1986.
- Margaret Morris, *The General Strike*, Penguin, Middlesex, 1976.
- J.T. Murphy, *The Political Meaning of the General Strike*, Communist Party of Great Britain, London, 1926.
- John Murray, *The General Strike of 1926 – A History*, Lawrence and Wishart, London, 1951.
- R. Palme Dutt, *The Meaning of the General Strike*, Communist Party of Great Britain, London, 1926.
- Henry Pelling, *A History of British Trade Unionism*, Pelican, London, 1971.
- Harry Pollitt, *Serving My Time*, Lawrence & Wishart, London, 1940
- Raymond Postgate and others, *A Workers' History of the Great Strike*, Plebs League, 1927.
- Robert S. Sephton, *Oxford and the General Strike*, Oxford, 1993.
- J. Skelley, *The General Strike 1926*,
- Ken Smith, *A Civil War Without Guns*, Socialist Publications, London, 2004.
- *Strike Nights in Printing House Square*, Privately published, 1932.
- Julian Symons, *The General Strike*, Cresset Press, London, 1957.
- Peter Taaffe & Tony Mulhearn, *Liverpool: A City That Dared To Fight*, Fortress Books, London, 1988.
- A.J.P. Taylor, *A Personal History*, Hamish Hamilton, London, 1983.
- Leon Trotsky, *1905*, Allen Lane, Penguin Press edition, London, 1971.
- Leon Trotsky, *Diaries in Exile*, Faber and Faber, London, 1958.
- Leon Trotsky, *Europe and America*, Pathfinder Press, New York, 1971.
- Leon Trotsky *On Britain*, Monad press, New York, 1973.
- Leon Trotsky, *Problems of the British Revolution*, New Park Publications, London, 1972 edition.
- Leon Trotsky, *The Struggle Against Fascism in Germany*, Pelican, London, 1975 edition.
- Leon Trotsky, *Where is Britain Going?* Plough Press, London, 1960 edition.
- Leon Trotsky, *Writings on Britain, Volumes 1-3*, New Park Publications, London, 1974 editions.
- TUC, *The Mining Crisis and the National Strike*, 1926.
- TUC General Council, *Report of the Conference of Trade Union Executives*, 1927.
- Michael Woodhouse and Brian Pearce, *Essays on the History of Communism in Britain*, New Park, London, 1975.

The following journals were also read:

- British Gazette
- British Worker
- The Communist
- The Communist Review
- Daily Express
- Daily Herald
- Daily Mail
- Daily Telegraph
- Financial Times
- Forward
- Hansard
- International Press Correspondence
- Labour Monthly
- Lansbury's Labour Weekly
- Manchester Guardian
- Militant
- Militant International Review
- Newcastle Chronicle
- New York Times
- The Observer
- Offensiv
- Plebs
- the socialist
- Socialist Review
- Sunday Worker
- The Times
- Weekly Dispatch
- Workers' Weekly
- Morning Post

the socialist

weekly paper of the Socialist Party

Get your copy of **the socialist** delivered regularly by subscribing. There is a special introductory offer of 5 issues for only £5.00.

subscription rates:
- 12 issues: £7.50
- 6 months: £15.00
- 1 year: £30.00

You can telephone for either a standing order form or to pay by credit card on: **020 8988 8777**

the address to contact about subscriptions is: **Socialist Party - Subscriptions, PO Box 24697, London E11 1YD**

socialist books

All of the books listed below are available from Socialist Books. To order further copies of this publication or any from either the list or the many other publications published by Socialist Books contact us at:

Socialist Books, PO Box 24697, London E11 1YD
telephone: 020 8988 8789 or email: socialistbooks@socialistparty.org.uk
or online at the socialist books **website: www.socialistbooks.co.uk**

recent titles available from socialist books

● **A Socialist World is Possible:**
The History of the CWI
by Peter Taaffe
Published August 2004. 96 pages paperback
An account and celebration of the activity and contribution of the Committee for a Workers International (CWI) on the 30 Anniversary of its founding, showing how the role and influence of the organisation has developed and change -, in some regions of the world quite dramatically - from its humble origins.
Price £5.00

● **A Civil War without Guns:**
20 Years On: the lessons of the 1984-85 Miners' Strike
by Ken Smith
Published May 2004. 128 pages paperback
A balance sheet of this important struggle, the possibilities at the time, the actual results and the lessons to be learned that can assist the future struggles of trade unionists.
Price £5.00

● **Empire Defeated - Vietnam War:**
The lessons for today
by Peter Taaffe
Published February 2004. 128 pages paperback
A history of the Vietnam War drawing out the lessons to be learnt from this conflict, especially in the aftermath of the Iraq war.
Price £6.00

other titles available from socialist books

- **Pamphlet: Join the Campaign for a New Workers' Party**
by The Socialist Party
Published February 2006. 36 pages paperback
A brief explanation of why the Socialist Party has initiated the Campaign for a New Workers' Party.
Price £1.00

- **Socialism in the 21st Century:**
The Way Forward for Anti-Capitalism
by Hannah Sell.
Published August 2002. New Updated Edition February 2006. 96 pages paperback
An essential read for all anti-capitalists, trade union activists and socialists.
Price £5.00

- **Che Guevara: Symbol of Struggle**
by Tony Saunois.
Published September 2005. 96 pages paperback
An appraisal of the life and role of Che Guevara as a revolutionary.
Price £5.00

- **Cuba: Socialism and Democracy:**
Debates on the Revolution and Cuba Today
by Peter Taaffe.
Published 2000. 128 pages paperback
Defence of the Socialist Party's analysis of the Cuban revolution.
Price £5.00

- **The Rise of Militant: Militant's 30 years**
by Peter Taaffe.
Published 1995. 570 pages paperback
Story of Militant, forerunner of the Socialist Party (English and Welsh section of the CWI), from its birth.
Price £10.99

- **Liverpool - A City that Dared to Fight**
by Tony Mulhearn and Peter Taaffe.
Published 1988, 500 pages paperback
Militant led Liverpool city council's battle against the Thatcher government 1983-1997.
Price £7.95

the socialist party

join us

I would like to find out more about / join the Socialist Party ❏

Name

Address

Postcode

Tel No   Email

Trade Union (if applicable)

If you are interested in finding out more about the Socialist Party or our publications simply fill in this form and return to:
Socialist Party, PO Box 24697, London E11 1YD
email: join@socialistparty.org.uk tel: 020 8988 8767
website: **www.socialistparty.org.uk**

the committee for a workers international

The Socialist Party is the England and Wales section of the Committee for a Workers' International (CWI/CIT). The CWI has affiliated parties and organisations in more than 35 countries on all continents. The way to contact our comrades differs from country to country. Some you can contact directly (see next page). For others, it is easier to do it via the CWI offices in London. E-mail to the International Office of the CWI: cwi@ worldsoc.co.uk or contact us at PO Box 3688, London, E11 1YE, UK. Telephone: ++ 44 (0)20 8988 8760. Fax: ++ 44 (0)20 8988 8793. Our website is: **www.socialistworld.net**

Contacting the Committee for a Workers' International

The Socialist Party is the English/Welsh section of the Committee for a Workers' International which has affiliated parties and organisations in more than 35 countries on all continents. The way to contact our comrades differs from country to country. Some you can contact directly.

For others, it is easier to do it via the CWI offices in London... e-mail to the International Office of the CWI: inter@dircon.co.uk or contact us at PO Box 3688, London, E11 1YE, UK. Telephone: + 44 (0)20 8988 8760. Fax: + 44 (0)20 8988 8793. Our website is on: www.socialistworld.net

If you want to know more about us in... Cyprus, Finland, Kashmir, or anywhere else...then contact the CWI international offices above.

Australia: Socialist Party.
PO Box 1015, Collingwood, Victoria 3066.
phone: + 61 3 9639 9111;
e-mail: info@socialistpartyaustralia.org
Austria: Sozialistische Linkspartie.
Kaiserstrasse 14/11, 1070 Wien.
phone: + 43 1 524 6310;
fax: + 43 1 81749551464; e-mail: slp@slp.at
Belgium: LSP/MA. PO Box10011,
1190 Vorst 3; phone: + 322 3456181;
e-mail: lspmas@skynet.be
Brazil: Socialismo Revolucionario.
Caixa Postal 02009, CEP 01060-970,
Sao Paulo S.P. phone: + 55 11 339 5584;
e-mail: sr-cio@uol.com.br
Canada: Socialist Alternative.
e-mail: socialist@canada.com
Chile: Socialismo Revolutionario,
Celso C Campos, Casilla 50310,
Correo Central, Santiago.
phone: + 56 2 622 9004;
e-mail: jandresverra@hotmail.com

CIS: 125167 Moscow a\Ya 37, Moscow.
e-mail: pabgem@online.ru
Czech Republic: Socialistická
Alternativa -Budoucnost.
ul. V háji 4 170 00 Praha 7-Holešovice.
e-mail: budoucnost@email.cz
England & Wales: Socialist Party.
PO Box 24697, London, E11 1YD.
phone: + 44 (0)20 8988 8777;
fax: + 44 (0)20 8988 8787;
e-mail: campaigns@socialistparty.org
France: Gauche Revolutionnaire -
Les amis de L'Egalite. Centre 166,
82 rue Jeanne d'Arc, 76000 Rouen.
e-mail: grcontact@hotmail.org
Germany: Sozialistische Alternative.
Litten Straße. 106/107, 10179 Berlin.
phone: + 49 302 47 23 802;
e-mail: info@sav-online.de

Greece: Xekinima.
8 Gortynos Street, PO Box 11254 Athens.
phone/fax: + 30 1 210 2283018;
e-mail: xekinima@hotmail.com
India: Dudiyora Horaata.
PO Box 1828, Bangalore 560018.
e-mail: newsocialist@dataone.in
Ireland North: Socialist Party.
15, Lombard Street, Belfast BT1 1RB.
phone: + 44 (0)2890 232962;
fax: + 44 (0)2890 311778;
e-mail: socialist@belfastsp.freeserve.co.uk
Ireland South: Socialist Party.
PO Box 3434, Dublin 8.
phone/fax: + 353 1 677 25 92;
e-mail: info@socialistparty.net
Israel/Palestine: Maavak Sozialisti.
e-mail: feedback@maavak.org.il
Italy: Lotta per il Socialismo.
e-mail: lottaperilsoc@hotmail.com
Japan: Kokusai Rentai,
Kanayamache Biru 3F Kita-ku,
Temma 2-1-17 Osaka-shi 530-0043.
e-mail: kokusairentai@hotmail.com
Netherlands: Offensief.
PO Box 11561, 1001 GN Amsterdam.
e-mail: info@offensief.nl
New Zealand:
e-mail: socialist_alternative@hotmail.com
Nigeria: Democratic Socialist Movement.
PO Box 2225, Agege, Lagos.
tel: +234 1492 5671;
e-mail: dsmcentre@hotmail.com

Pakistan: Socialist Movement Pakistan.
tel: +92 333 433 1755
e-mail: revolutionary1917@yahoo.com
Poland: Grupa Na Rzecz
Partii Robotniczej.
e-mail: ebsgpr@wp.pl
Portugal: Alternativa Socialista.
Apartado 27018, 1201-950, Lisboa.
e-mail: alternativasocialista@gmail.com
Scotland: International Socialists. PO Box
6773, Dundee, DD1 1YL.
phone: + 44 1382 833 759;
email: cwi@blueyonder.co.uk
South Africa: Democratic Socialist
Movement. PO Box 596, Newton, 2113,
Johannesburg. phone: + 27 11 342 2220;
e-mail: democraticsocialist@mweb.co.za
Sri Lanka: United Socialist Party.
44/10 Pichchamalwatta Nawala Road
Narahenpita Colombo 5.
phone: + 94 1 1451 0289;
e-mail: usp@sltnet.lk
Sweden: Rattvisepartiet Socialisterna.
PO Box 73; 123 03 Farsta.
phone: + 46 8 605 9400;
fax: + 46 8 556 252 52;
e-mail: rs@socialisterna.org
USA: Socialist Alternative.
PO Box 45343, Seatlle, W4, 98145.
e-mail: info@socialistalternative.org

Index